Givenchy in the Great War

Givenchy in the Great War

A Village on the Front Line 1914–1918

Phil Tomaselli

Pen & Sword
MILITARY

First published in Great Britain in 2016 by
Pen & Sword Military
an imprint of
Pen & Sword Books Ltd
47 Church Street
Barnsley
South Yorkshire
S70 2AS

ISBN 978 1 47382 550 5

Typeset in Ehrhardt by
Mac Style Ltd, Bridlington, East Yorkshire
Printed and bound in the UK by CPI Group (UK) Ltd,
Croydon, CRO 4YY

Pen & Sword Books Ltd incorporates the imprints of Pen & Sword
Archaeology, Atlas, Aviation, Battleground, Discovery, Family
History, History, Maritime, Military, Naval, Politics, Railways, Select,
Transport, True Crime, and Fiction, Frontline Books, Leo Cooper,
Praetorian Press, Seaforth Publishing and Wharncliffe.

For a complete list of Pen & Sword titles please contact
PEN & SWORD BOOKS LIMITED
47 Church Street, Barnsley, South Yorkshire, S70 2AS, England
E-mail: enquiries@pen-and-sword.co.uk
Website: www.pen-and-sword.co.uk

Contents

The Cross

(On the grave of an unknown British soldier, Givenchy, 1915)

The cross is twined with gossamer, –
The cross some hand has shaped with care,
And by his grave the grasses stir
But he is silent sleeping there.

The guns speak loud: he hears them not;
The night goes by: he does not know;
A lone white cross stands on the spot,
And tells of one who sleeps below.

The brooding night is hushed and still,
The crooning breeze draws quiet breath,
A star-shell flares upon the hill
And lights the lowly house of death.

Unknown, a soldier slumbers there,
While mournful mists come dropping low,
But oh! a weary maiden's prayer,
And oh! a mother's tears of woe.

Ghosts of Givenchy

(to the tune of 'I want to go to Bye-bye' from *The Boy*)

There's never a chance of a sleep all the night
In the Craters.
You get 'bumped' with gas shells till at length
You put on Respirators.
And when it's all over and the sun starts to shine
The sanitary men sprinkle chloride of lime.

Chorus:
I want a gas-proof dug-out
When the shells begin to fall.
For the way they splash you
With mustard and gas you
Is a feeling not pleasant at all.
I want a gas-proof dug out
When the Huns begin to throw.
Strike the gong. Make a noise.
Rouse the rest of the boys.
And send for the gas N.C.O

Acknowledgements

Any book like this cannot be said to be the work of one person alone and a number of people have helped me in collecting the information required to produce this history. It was my wife Francine who introduced me to the sector and the village many years ago. Her grandfather, George Pepper, fought there with 55th Division in 1918 and, old soldier that he was, he rarely talked about the war, though La Bassée Canal was one of the few places he did mention. Together Fran and I have walked the village on numerous occasions, seeking out the old trench lines from maps, noting the buildings rebuilt on the foundations of those demolished and, most years, going back on 9 April to lay a wreath on 55th Division's monument. Much of the research into the fighting in 1940 is also down to her.

Chris Baker, former chairman of the Western Front Association and the man behind The Long Long Trail website, also has an interest in Givenchy, through a shared fascination with the 1918 Lys offensive, when the village defences stood firm. Both he and his website have been invaluable.

In Givenchy itself, M. le Maire, Jacques Herbaut, whose English is considerably better than my French, and his deputy, Ms Marie-Paul Lefebvre, provided information from the village records, arranged access to the church and gave me a copy of late local historian Jean-Claude Boulanger's history of the fighting in the area in 1914. Special thanks are due to Tracy Bernard, the village's English-born resident, who translated for us all and arranged our meeting. Sebastian Laudan kindly provided information from German sources. Peter Crane used his expertise to make some of the older photographs usable. Andrew Thornton kindly allowed me to use his photograph of the Gurkhas in the trenches. Paul Golding suggested a couple of sources I really ought to have known about. Thanks, as ever, are due to the staff of The National Archives at Kew, who have offered advice and assistance, and the staff of Swindon Libraries, who have located copies of rare books for me.

Preface

Why study Givenchy?

My interest in Givenchy goes back to my wife's grandfather's service in the area in 1918, but the area is worthy of study in its own right. Though the commune is about a mile and a half square, the village itself takes up only a fraction of this and was once prominent in the British press as scene of some of the fiercest fighting of the First World War. Reports of mine explosions, artillery duels and heroic defence against German assaults were reported regularly in the press.

The village sits on relatively high ground (about 12 metres higher than the land on the British side of the lines), so was one of the few places in the Bethune–Festubert sector where proper trenches could be dug and where deep dug-outs, as a protection against shelling, could be created. In the war visibility was normally restricted to the view you could get through an embrasure in a trench parapet, or through a trench periscope gingerly raised above the sandbags (and liable to be sniped at as soon as it emerged), so any height at all was an advantage, including the few feet raised as the lip of a crater from a mine explosion. Much of the small-scale fighting done on a regular basis at Givenchy was over these small but precious elevations; when visiting the battlefields it is important to remember that anyone standing up in the open was liable to be killed within seconds. The best way of seeing the battlefield as experienced by the ordinary soldier is to crouch in a drainage ditch and try peeking, rapidly, over the top.

As the front line dropped off the slight escarpment caused by the Givenchy spur, the water table was frequently only a few inches below the surface and, all too often, the line consisted of small emplacements, sufficient to hold a section, sitting like islands in what was virtually a swamp. If the Germans could capture the piece of high ground on which the village stood, they would have line of sight across the British lines to Bethune and its precious coalfield, the last major one in French hands and source of most of its fuel. It would also allow the Germans to dominate this sector of the front. This made it a major strategic objective in the April 1918 German offensive and, even throughout the relatively quiet years of 1916 and 1917, a highly desirable tactical one.

The village was levelled as flat as any on the Somme or around Ypres, and the defenders fought from deep dug-outs and battered trenches among the ruins. Eleven Victoria Crosses were won there, yet Givenchy is strangely neglected by the thousands of visitors who flock to the Western Front every year and tend to visit the same sites on the Somme and Ypres battlefields. It is a shame; in 1914, 1915 and again in 1918 there were battles fought around Givenchy as fierce as any anywhere else on the British front, and the village garrison was always prone to sudden attack. At least one Victoria Cross was won there in each year of the war. Givenchy fell briefly to the Germans only a couple of times in 1914, was recaptured both times and was the scene of fierce fighting both above and below ground, as tunnelling operations took place on a large scale. As the village was destroyed by shellfire (most buildings were gone by the summer of 1915), the network of trenches became a complex defence that included self-contained garrison areas known as 'keeps', linked by tunnels that allowed rapid movement of men underground. The position was too important to be abandoned by the British, even though it stood in a kind of salient, or to be ignored by the Germans, who might yet capture it by a sudden surprise attack. A network of defensive and offensive tunnels ran under the front-line trenches out into no man's land and towards the German lines. So many mines were blown between and under the front lines that by 1917 a 'crater field' that was virtually impossible to cross ran as a kind of additional protective belt around the north-east of the village. Small patrols and trench raids were launched into it, and there was a constant struggle to seize small elevated sections of ground, frequently thrown up by a recent mine detonation, from which a light machine gun could be fired at the enemy.

By 1918, as one divisional history records, 'it is no exaggeration to say that the Givenchy sector was the best and most scientifically defended portion of the whole British front'. British, Indian and French troops fought side by side there in 1914, famous men came and fought there and scarcely a British

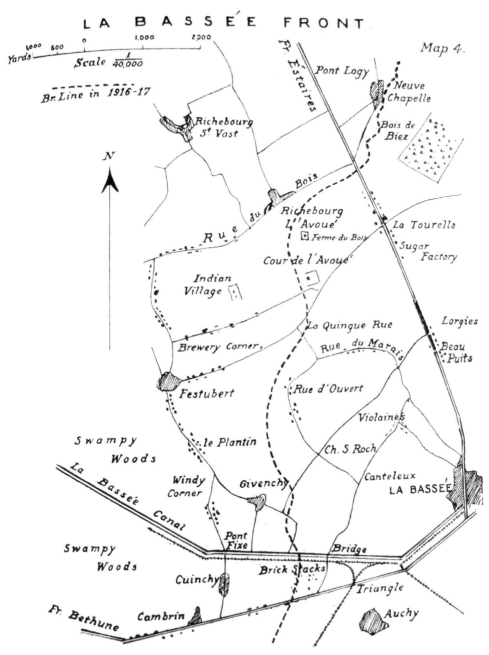

LA BASSÉE FRONT

Map 4.

Yards

Scale 1/40,000

Br. Line in 1916-17

N

Fr. Estaires

Pont Logy

Neuve Chapelle

Richebourg St Vast

Bois de Biez

Bois

Richebourg L'Avoué

La Tourelle

Ferme du Bois

Sugar Factory

Cour de l'Avoué

Rue du

Indian Village

La Quinque Rue

Lorgies

Brewery Corner

Rue du Marais

Beau Puits

Festubert

Rue d'Ouvert

Violaines

le Plantin

Swampy Woods

Ch. S. Roch

Windy Corner

Givenchy

Canteleux

LA BASSÉE

La Bassée Canal

Pont Fixe

Swampy Woods

Bridge

Cuinchy

Brick Stacks

Triangle

Fr. Bethune

Cambrin

Auchy

Givenchy's place in the immediate front. Neuve Chapelle, scene of the March 1915 battle, is top right. The ground around Indian village was captured during the Battle of Festubert in May 1915. Gorre is just off the map to the left and Bethune some miles distant beyond that.

regiment didn't send men there at one time or another. Yet it has been passed over by history. Hopefully this book will do something to redress the balance and encourage further study of the men and their fight, while commemorating the bravery on both sides.

Chapter 1

1914

The Givenchy sector was in front of the village of that name. It had a dry but sticky trench system running northwards to 'The Warren' where the ground fell sharply; thence the line ran west of north to Festubert since a small gain in June. Here, too, the Germans had the advantage of elevation. Nomansland was more than 300 yards wide on the right: at The Warren a rectangular projection in the German system narrowed it to 100 yards, and mine-craters nearly filled the space, reducing the distance between the opposed bombing posts to 25 yards. Craters along much of the front were mostly German-blown; they were of great tactical value in defence. Nowhere on the Western Front was mining as active as here. Yet, for all the underground devilry that comes at once to the mind of those who knew Givenchy, there was a strange charm about the northern shoulder of its gentle rise; the elements were a broken shrine, the broken fabrics of a church and of some cottages, each mean in itself, and a few maimed elms.

The War the Infantry Knew by Captain J.C. Dunn

On 1 August 1914, having carefully avoided mobilization of her forces in the face of mounting evidence that war was inevitable and, indeed, having pulled her frontier troops back from the German border to avoid provocation, the French government felt compelled to order a general mobilization to begin at midnight. The first posters confirming this were on the streets of Paris in the afternoon. The telegraph wires hummed and, in the little village of Givenchy-lès-la-Bassée, Monsieur Buisine, the mayor (*maire*) opened the safe of the Mairie and took out the proclamations held there for such an emergency and plastered them to the communal noticeboard. All Frenchmen were liable for service in the army, beginning with three years' full-time service starting when they were 19, followed by eleven years in the Reserve

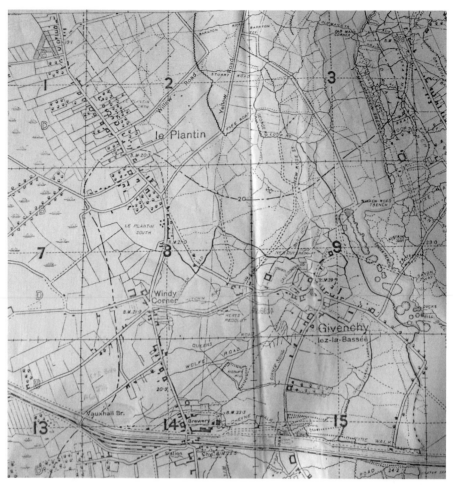

Givenchy and immediate environs. Windy Corner is clearly marked; Pont Fixe crosses the canal where the distillery is incorrectly marked as a brewery.

and then fourteen years in the Territorial Army and Reserve. Every man in the village, unless exempted for health reasons, between the ages of 19 and 47, was suddenly called away. A steady procession of young (and not so young) men began to walk down the slight hill to the Pont Fixe, the bridge over the canal south of the village, to catch the train to their regimental depot to rejoin the colours.

The men left behind not only their wives, families and sweethearts, but a typical small French community on the edge of the Bethune coalfield consisting of a dozen or so small farms and a scattering of cottages inhabited by agricultural workers and men employed in the coal mines. A few men were also employed on the La Bassée canal that ran south of the village and linked France's inland waterway network, via La Bassée and Bethune, with the coast at Dunkirk. The commune covered an area of less than 2.5 square miles, with most of the houses and cottages grouped around the Mairie, which stood where the school now stands, and the Church of St Martin, built in 1513 with a tall, square tower that could be seen for miles because the village stood on a rise of a dozen or so metres above the local countryside. The harvest still had to be finished and every remaining able-bodied man, woman and child worked until it was complete. The fields east of the village were soon covered in traditional French haystacks.

The early fighting passed by to the east as the German advance swept through Belgium. Then, instead of driving on through to the French coast,

Contemporary German sketch of the village in October 1914, from a regimental history. Note the haystacks, the firing of which caused problems for the Manchesters on 21 December. (*With thanks to Sebastian Laudan*)

the German army turned south and passed southwards about 50 miles to the east, driving the British Expeditionary Force before it. The main French offensives were taking place far to the south and the German aim was to swing south, take the French armies in the flank, and trap them south-east of Paris. The first of Givenchy's fatal casualties occurred on 9 September when 25-year-old Aubert Desmaretz was killed at Maurupt de Marthois on the Marne fighting with the 72nd Infantry Regiment, followed by 34-year-old Gilbert Herbaut, 100th Infantry Regiment, who died of wounds on 30 September, again on the Marne, and then by 22-year-old Pierre Bauduin, 37th Infantry Regiment, who was killed at Foncquivillers on 8 October. The village had already suffered, but the war would come a lot closer to home.

The Battle of La Bassée

At the beginning of October, the sound of gunfire could be heard to the south of the La Bassée Canal, off in the distance around Arras, where German troops were advancing on the town in an attempt to outflank French forces. This was part of the so called 'Race to the Sea', which, in reality, was a series of attempted outflanking movements as the opposing forces tried to wrest an advantage after the Battle of the Aisne, further south, had ended in stalemate. This was still a war of movement, although as the armies clashed they were forced to dig in due to the strength of their opponents' firepower. By 6 October the situation around Arras had stabilized and the Germans tried another outflanking attack, with I and II Cavalry Corps advancing between Lens and Lille, but they found themselves facing French troops of XXI Corps advancing eastwards from Bethune. In fierce fighting the Germans advanced north-west towards the town of La Bassée. In the meantime the British II Corps, consisting of 3rd and 5th Divisions, was moving secretly from the Aisne towards Bethune. Passing columns of French refugees from the fall of Lille, they arrived at Bethune on the 11th. The divisional history recorded:

Rumours came that the French were being hard pressed round Arras, that the German Cavalry were trying to get round our Northern flank, and that Lille was surrounded by the enemy, but was still holding out with a few French Territorial Battalions in it. Hence the hurry; but no one seemed to know anything definite except that the Division would soon be fighting again'.

That night the 5th Division billeted in Bethune, and, during the evening, details of the situation were received. The French army was being outflanked; it had been driven out of the important rail junction at Vermelles, though the Germans had not yet captured it, and also, it was believed, out of Givenchy.

On the 12th the advancing Germans captured Vermelles, south of the La Bassée Canal, which ran east–west between La Bassée and Bethune. German troops were also over the canal in the small but important town of La Bassée, and while many pressed north, reconnoitring patrols moved west and the civilian population fled before them. Opposing them, following discussions with the French, II Corps, with the 5th Division on the right and the 3rd on the left, was ordered to advance north of the Bethune-La Bassée Canal and to swing round gradually to capture La Bassée, pivoting the right on the canal. They were to cooperate closely with the French 58th Division, which was moving up to the vicinity of Noux les Mines, south of the canal, with the intention of recapturing Vermelles, driving the Germans east and advancing on Lille.

5th Division's line was a long one to hold and advance, and it was made longer when troops of 13th Brigade were sent south of the canal to assist the French in their attack on Vermelles. Immediately north of the canal was 15th Brigade. The 1st Dorsets were instructed to seize and hold Pont Fixe, the permanent bridge over the canal on the Festubert–Cuinchy road near Givenchy, then advance along the northern bank; north of them were the 1st Bedfords, who were detailed to seize and hold Givenchy – 'a straggling village on a slight rise, with a conspicuous church tower' – then to advance towards La Bassée. North of them again were the 1st Cheshires, who would hold Festubert, and north of them 14th Brigade held the line, in touch with 7th Brigade of 3rd Division north of Richbourg L'Avoué.

The 1st Bedfords were ordered to advance and occupy Givenchy, and they advanced through Gorre to the edge of the village. On their right the Dorsets moved along the canal towards Cuinchy, and on their left the Norfolks proceeded towards Festubert. D Company, the Bedfords, advanced into Givenchy early in the afternoon, coming under distant fire from La Bassée and Festubert, which hit a number of men in the open. Fortunately, because of the distance, most of the bullets were spent and resulted mainly in bruising. Though the village was thought to be occupied by the Germans, the only occupants turned out to be a group of French soldiers sharing a bottle of wine with a few Dorsets who had become detached from their unit, which was advancing closer to the canal bank slightly further south. The men occupied a rough trench (in fact a series of close foxholes separated from each other by thin walls of earth) to the east of the village and dug in under increasing shellfire.

South of Givenchy and on the Bedfords' right, the 1st Dorsets moved south to the canal and eastwards along the towpath towards Pont Fixe. A and D companies took up positions either side of the bridge and placed a

Another contemporary German sketch showing the tiny slit trenches from which the whole trench system began. (*With thanks to Sebastian Laudan*)

machine gun on the first floor of an unfinished factory (actually a distillery) at the north end of the bridge, opening fire on German troops debouching from the brickfields near Cuinchy on the south side of the canal. At about 4pm the Dorsets were ordered to advance towards La Bassée with French infantry on the right and the 1st Bedfords on their left. A company advanced along the south bank of the canal under cover of the high bank and surprised the Germans in Cuinchy, opening fire on them and inflicting severe losses. In the meantime, D Company began to advance towards a small farm about 200 yards to the east of Pont Fixe along the north bank, but came under sniper crossfire from Germans on the high bank on the south side. Major Reginald Trevor Roper, a 42-year-old staff-trained officer, was killed at about 4.30pm. The attack, however, made excellent progress and B and C companies dug in on a rise above the farm while A and D companies withdrew to Pont Fixe. As well as Major Roper eleven men were killed, thirty wounded and two missing.

528. La Grande Guerre 1914-15. - Les restes de l'Église de GIVENCHY (P.-de-C.)
Visé Paris 528.   ◊ PHOT-EXPRESS ◊

IMP. BAUDINIÈRE, NANTERRE

Givenchy church and damaged houses, October 1914.

Two platoons of the Bedfords had been sent out to support them. Caught in the open by shellfire and unable to hear orders, a few men pressed on while the others were still trying to work out what was going on. Some of these men managed to get back during the night, their comrades having been shot down by artillery fire and snipers. The Bedfords' casualties for the day were only one man killed and sixteen wounded. Two men, privates Albert Bentley and Ben Piggott, were later awarded the Distinguished Conduct Medal (DCM) for staying with wounded comrades under heavy fire, having helped to dress the wounds of three men who could not be moved.

Next day, the 13th, the Germans commenced a heavy bombardment at 6am, which they kept up all day. To counter the German artillery and support the attack being launched south of the village and along the canal by the 1st Dorsets, two guns of 11 Battery RFA moved up through Givenchy and took up position in the little hollows immediately south of the village. Two more guns went out to support the Bedfords, but were not required and withdrew

British soldier (probably Bedfordshire Regiment) guarding the entrance to the village, 1914.

to cover the road to Bethune. The Bedfords' war diary records 'About midday the cannonade became terrific. Practically every house damaged and neighbourhood of church continually shelled. Our own trenches, in continuation with the Dorsets, unable to hold on in the afternoon.' The 1st Battalion and two companies of the 2nd Battalion of the German 114th Infantry Regiment, supported by two machine-gun sections, advanced from La Bassée. The two companies of 2nd Battalion advanced to the south of the village, while 1st Battalion attacked towards the north and centre. Coming under heavy fire from the Bedfords, the commanding officer, General von Trotta, called down more artillery fire from the 30th Artillery Regiment. They were also supported by fire from 76th Artillery Regiment south of the canal, which enfiladed the Dorsets to the south of the village and forced them to withdraw. The French historian reports that the British made astute use of haystacks, bushes and trees as cover, but the Germans threw in their reserve. At 3.45pm the barrage ceased and the Germans made a final charge against the shallow trenches. According to the war diary 'Smoke of shells and dust of falling houses made it impossible to see what was going on to flanks. Enemy attacked front and flanks and battalion retired about 300 yards to rear of village.' Brigadier General Count Gleichen had already given permission for a withdrawal and some of the wounded, who had been sheltering in the village school, had already been taken out. The men fell back through the village in small groups. The Germans took about fifty prisoners in the village itself, most of them wounded. They also captured the two guns of 11 Battery, whose crews had found themselves under close rifle fire from both flanks. Captain Ambrose Grayson was killed and command devolved upon Lieutenant Boscawen, who instructed the men to remove the breech blocks, which they did, and the crews slipped away in the confusion. Half a dozen other ranks were wounded, but got away; three other ranks were reported missing.

In the meantime, at 5.30am the Dorsets continued their attack of the previous day, with B and C companies in the firing line, A and D in support and the machine gun in a house on the north bank near Pont Fixe. The advance was made slowly to allow the units on either flank to get into line. At 7.20am the line was 200 yards east of the track that ran down from Givenchy, but movement had been checked, not by opposition, which was slight, but by the need to conform with the units to the right and left. The situation remained the same until after 9am, as the village of Cuinchy on the south side of the canal had still not been cleared. At 11.20am the Germans began a heavy artillery bombardment from the north-east, and at noon a machine gun opened up at close range from the right, near the canal bank, enfilading B Company, which was forced to withdraw. Lieutenant John Reginald Turner, a Bournemouth solicitor and officer in the 3rd (Reserve) Battalion, who had volunteered for foreign service and arrived in France in August, was killed, as was 18-year-old 2nd Lieutenant Thomas Sydney Smith. At 1.45pm a group of German lancers were seen advancing from the east end of Givenchy. They were at first assumed to be French, so C Company, whose rear they threatened, did not open fire. Shortly afterward, a battalion of infantry were seen about 900 yards to the left flank of C Company, who opened fire. The Germans were from the 7th Company of 1st Battalion, the 114th Infantry Regiment, supported by a section of the 4th Company, all under the command of Lieutenant Haberichter, an energetic and intelligent officer who made what the French historian described as 'an audacious flank attack', although the British records say they advanced with their hands up, which was taken as a surrender, so some Dorsets left the trench and moved towards them, but the Germans suddenly rushed them and enfiladed the trench. The divisional historian wrote:

> The Dorsets, who had advanced a bit and dug themselves in, were violently attacked at the Pont Fixe on the Canal, fire being opened on them from their left flank, which was now uncovered, and also from the railway embankment on the South. An act of treachery on the part of the Germans was responsible for many men being killed; a party of some twenty of the enemy advanced holding up their hands, and, as the Dorsets advanced to take their surrender, these twenty suddenly fell flat down, and a fusillade was opened on our men from a flank.

The Dorsets' B Company was virtually annihilated by fire from the right as the whole line began to fall back on the reserve trenches. Major Saunders was sent back to organise the reserve company and inform the artillery commander of the situation. The whole position had now become untenable and the commanding officer, Lieutenant Colonel Louis Jean Bols and the adjutant, Lieutenant James Maxwell Pitt, remained in the trench till the last while the men fell back. Pitt was killed and Bols was severely wounded and taken prisoner. The Germans advised him to wait for an ambulance and, having waited till dusk, he slipped away and regained the British lines. He survived the war, ending up with a KCB, KCMG and DSO as Chief of Staff to General Allenby in Palestine.

A Company skilfully covered the retreat of their comrades and the battalion fell back on Pont Fixe and established a line in the buildings there, with two companies of the Devons on their left. Two attacks on this line were made overnight, but repulsed successfully. Casualties were fifty-one killed, fifty-two wounded and twenty-one missing. The Germans claimed to have taken 150 prisoners, but this total probably included the Bedfords and men from other units.

At dawn on the 14th A Company held the refinery building at Pont Fixe, with the Devons on their left. The remains of B, C and D companies were

British troops breakfast in the trenches at Givenchy, 1914 (probably the Norfolk Regiment).

formed into a composite company under Captain Henry Beveridge and placed in reserve half a mile west of Pont Fixe along the canal. A Company held out all day in the distillery under heavy shelling, having been told by the brigade that 'Pont Fixe must not be given up. I know I can rely on you to stick to it with the help of the Devons'. There were orders to attack in the late afternoon to support an attack by 13th Brigade south of the canal, but this was prevented when the Germans launched their own attack. A final German attack on the distillery was repulsed at 8.30pm. After spending part of the next day under German shellfire, A Company were finally relieved by the Devons at 7.20pm on the 15th and the battalion went into billets at Loisne.

The new line adopted by the Bedfords ran along the road from Festubert to Pont Fixe at the point soon to be called Windy Corner. The Norfolks, who had also been pushed back earlier, took up positions on the left, with the Dorsets on the right. Both guns from 11th Battery RFA had been lost, as well as seven officers and 140 men. Over the next two days they held the line of shallow trenches under sniper fire from the higher ground around Givenchy. To the south of the village the Dorsets launched an attack to try and recover the two 11th Battery guns lost to the Germans the previous day, but despite a heavy bombardment they made no progress and the guns were taken back to La Bassée by the Germans during the night of the 14th. As a result of the raid there was heavy firing on both flanks during the night and a moment of panic and confusion caused a sudden retreat, but the men rallied and returned to their trench. On the night of the 15th the enemy were reported to be evacuating Givenchy (they had been ordered to withdraw at 10pm because the village formed a dangerous salient in the German line), and next morning, the 16th, after a short artillery barrage, a small group of scouts led by 2nd Lieutenant Leonard Rendell, a 23-year-old officer from Taunton, crept into the village to reconnoitre. Apart from a few snipers (one of whom mortally wounded Rendell), they found the village empty and in the late afternoon A and D companies, the Bedfords, moved in, mopped up the few Germans remaining and 'recovered a number of wounded officers and men, most of whom had been given rough 1st aid by enemy'. Private Brazier wrote home to his family: 'The Germans were very kind to the wounded; they dressed their wounds and gave them wine to drink. We had to leave these behind because they were down in the cellars in people's houses'. Private Pigg wrote that 'He [a wounded soldier] told us the German officer made the men go out and milk the cows for milk for our wounded men'.

The former inhabitants of Givenchy, who had fled before the German patrols out of La Bassée a few days earlier, but had not gone far, made an attempt to move back, thinking the liberation was permanent. They were allowed to gather up what belongings they could find that had not been irreparably damaged or looted, and were then escorted from the scene. Many of the men were employed in the nearby Bethune coalfield and were reluctant to move far unless absolutely necessary, and the French government was keen to keep them working in what was one of France's few remaining coalfields. Many had relatives nearby and moved in with them; others moved to Bethune and found accommodation there.

On 16 October 1st Battalion, the Devonshire Regiment, which had been in divisional reserve for the last few days, was assembled and received orders

LA GUERRE DANS LE NORD
162 GIVENCHY-lez-LA BASSÉE – L'Eglise - The church

Givenchy church from the north, late 1914.

for a night advance in the direction of the bridge across the La Bassée Canal south of Canteleux and entrenched on the rising ground east of Givenchy.

At 5.30am the battalion began to advance in conjunction with the Bedfords on their left and the French on the other side of the canal. B and D companies formed the firing line and supports. German fire was heavy, but the advance was pressed until after 2pm, when it had to be halted due to lack of support. Three men had been killed and two officers and sixteen men wounded.

On the 17th the Bedfords were engaged in digging trenches and erecting sandbag barricades in the village as cover against shelling, but other parts of the brigade continued to advance on La Bassée according to the plan. To the north the Cheshires captured Violaines and the Norfolks took Canteleux. The remaining guns of 11th Battery RFA moved up to a position just north of the village to support a proposed advance by the Bedfords, and shelled the German positions on the north bank of the canal towards La Bassée. Though the Bedfords pushed their line of posts forward towards La Bassée, they could advance no further because the Germans still held the south bank of the canal, despite ferocious French attacks towards Vermelles and the important railway triangle junction there. German artillery south of the canal had a clear view and could sweep the ground the British needed to advance over with shrapnel.

On the 18th the battalion stood ready to support a French attack along the canal towards La Bassée. The 6th Battalion of the 295th Infantry Regiment crossed the canal and passed through the trenches south of the village, supported by French artillery, and under heavy fire from German artillery and machine guns managed to advance 750 yards before they were forced to a standstill. Count Gleichen sent a congratulatory message to General Joubert: 'Please convey my very best congratulations to General Joubert and to Lieutenant Colonel Perron commanding the detachment on the gallantry and success with which their troops have executed a very difficult and dangerous attack'. Of the 800 men who had taken part in the attack seventeen were killed and 137 wounded. The Devons, acting in support, resumed the advance and dug in on a line north and south of Canteleux with their right flank bent back in a south-easterly direction. They lost two men killed and seven wounded. On the 19th the battalion improved its position and the southern part of the line was straightened after dark in conjunction with the French battalion on their right.

Because they were unable to advance across the ground in front of them, the Bedfords remained in the village and effectively became the brigade reserve battalion. Private Arthur Basham gave a brief description of life: 'In the midst of a shell shattered village with pigs, cows and a dog or two all wandering disconsolately about streets heaped with the debris of cottage homes, here and there a house afire, we are sitting on the edge of bomb proof shelters.' Because the battalion was acting as a reserve, on 19 October B Company was sent to support the Cheshires at Violaines, who were attempting to advance on La Bassée. That same day the French sent a battery of artillery from 3rd Group to assist on the Givenchy front, which positioned itself 200 metres west of the village and provided welcome support. German artillery seemed remarkably accurate and eventually a group of Germans in civilian clothing, equipped with a field telephone, was located behind the lines. Their fate is not recorded.

On the 20th the British artillery began heavy bombardment at dawn. The Germans responded at 9am with a cannonade on the left of the Devons' position and on the Norfolks, and launched an attack on the Cheshire Regiment. The Devons were busy placing the houses in Canteleaux in a defensive state and Lieutenant Colonel Gerald Gloster was wounded, so command passed to Major Edward George Williams. Captain Henry Chichester was killed, as were three other ranks and an officer. Ten men were wounded. Some British shells fell on the Devons' position during the afternoon, but the night passed quietly. On the 21st the trenches were heavily shelled and two other ranks were killed, nine wounded and one died of wounds.

After a couple of relatively quiet days, on 22 October things heated up. For two days the Cheshires and B Company of the Bedfords had been fighting in Violaines, holding on against German day and night attacks. At 4am B Company was sent out to dig a new defensive trench near Rue de Marais, when three battalions of the German 112th Infantry Regiment, which had marched up through La Bassée overnight, burst out of the mist and took them by surprise. There was fierce hand-to-hand fighting; the British troops had no time to grab their rifles and fought with pickaxes and shovels. Eventually some kind of defensive line was organised around Rue de Marais and the 1st Bedfords were ordered out of Givenchy to march to Chapelle St Roche to act in support, which they did under heavy artillery fire. Counter-attacks against Violaines came to nothing and eventually B Company rejoined the main battalion. By midnight, orders had come in to take the battalion back into the front line and they moved to create a new one 1,500 yards east of Festubert where, for the next few days, they held a long section of the line. They did not return to Givenchy, and at midnight the Devons were ordered to withdraw to the Givenchy line and conform with the French troops on the northern canal bank and the Norfolks on the left. The withdrawal was carried out without incident and a line north of Givenchy was entrenched.

On the 23rd C and B companies of the 1st Devons were entrenched covering the village, with A and D companies in support in Givenchy itself, though they were later ordered up into close support. The Germans were seen advancing but did not press home their attack, though they continued a heavy shellfire. A party of reinforcements that was coming up was caught by the artillery barrage and Corporal Warwick was wounded. Lieutenant Ralph Escott Hancock immediately left his trench and dashed back 60 yards over open ground, picked him up and carried him to cover at the corner of a haystack before returning to his trench. He was awarded the Distinguished Service Order (DSO) posthumously, as he was killed a few days later at Festubert while trying to reinforce another company in difficulties.

The main German attacks on the 24th were made on the battalions flanking the Devons, but the battalion still lost Lieutenant Denys Ainslie and fifteen men killed and twenty-nine wounded during the day. One of the casualties was Corporal John Alexander Harris. Captain Percy R. Worrall wrote to Harris's family, and the letter was published in the *Wells Journal* on 27 November 1914:

At Givenchy, in France, not far from Bethune, on Saturday, October 24th, we were holding a line of entrenchments, and at intervals were attacked by Germans, who kept coming to close quarters, especially on our right. Our artillery, in their endeavour to hit them, unfortunately put some shells into our own line, killing an officer and five men. Seeing from where I was that this must be stopped, I sent a man back with a message. He, poor fellow, was killed, a second was hit, and a third, and then I went myself and got back, Deo Gratia, as I had to take command of my company. About half an hour after I was back I suddenly saw your brave son when it was too late to stop him as he was some way behind the trench, crawling to the wounded with a water bottle. In doing so he was hit, and met what has proved to be his death. He was hit through the back and I had every hope that he would recover, but God decreed otherwise.

On the same day, having received orders that Givenchy village was to be defended by the French, C Company and part of A Company handed over their positions to French troops during the evening. Two companies of the 70th Infantry Regiment took up position in the trenches north-east of the village, with two more companies in reserve at the crossroads 800 yards west of Givenchy church on the Festubert–Pont Fixe road. 295 Infantry Regiment held the trenches down to the canal.

80th Battery RFA placed four guns at Le Plantin, with an observation post in a house on the canal close to the French trenches and connected to the battery by 2,400 yards of telephone wire. From there Major Charles Rudkin directed the fire against German positions all day. A small section of men was placed in the trenches to assist in the event of a night attack. The battery itself came under fire, though there were no casualties and driver Walter J. Gates was awarded the DCM 'For gallantry and coolness in the engagement at Givenchy on 24th October 1914, when the teams were under heavy fire, and also for conveying a message into the trenches when they were under heavy fire'.

On the 25th the Devons continued to hold part of the Givenchy defences north of the village with one platoon of A Company and the whole of B Company in the firing line. Sergeant H. Webb, a veteran of the Boer War with twenty years' service, saw all his officers killed or wounded. He maintained the defence of his trenches for two to three hours, despite the fact that his right flank was exposed and daylight was rapidly failing. He was awarded the DCM (*London Gazette*, 11 November 1914), but was badly wounded by shrapnel at Festubert on 30 October. He was taken to hospital in Calais and transferred to hospital in Cosham, but died there not long afterwards.

Major Rudkin was still in his observation post on the canal and was able to direct his guns against the developing attack with devastating effect, despite heavy German fire, which on more than one occasion caused him and his staff to take cover in the French trenches. He later wrote:

> About 2pm I observed parties of Germans assembling behind some buildings in Canteleux. This was outside my area but I switched Battery onto them, 12 degrees from my line. About 2.30pm numbers of Germans began to double in batches of about 50 each along a path or road towards a newly made trench about 150 yards from the French trenches. It was easy to get the battery on at once, as I had (the) range absolutely. I fired gun fire rapidly, varying my ranges from 3,000 to 3,200 yards. The enemy was advancing straight into the line of fire of my guns in sections of fours. Those who did not fall under fire turned left handed into the trench which was enfiladed by the fire of the battery. I do not think very many of the Germans who took part in the attack survived – I was about 700 yards from the trench and could see them throwing bodies on to the top of the bank. 2 men stood up on the bank and held up their hands up but were hit. About this time, 2.55pm, my house got (a) shell through it and was knocked about and the telephone wire was cut… The Battery went on firing and I sent the BSM back to explain the situation and to try and get more telephone wire. I and the rest of my staff took cover in the trenches for a bit as we were getting heavy rifle fire from S side of canal. Later we ran back to the factories at Pont Fixe to our horses and rejoined the battery.

Rudkin estimated German losses at between 400 and 600.

Although the Devons held their part of the line, the Germans had success elsewhere. 1st and 2nd battalions of the 114th Infantry Regiment, despite taking heavy casualties, got into the French defences. The 1st Battalion reached the northern edge of the village and part of 4th Company even managed to get close to the church. The commander of 2nd Battalion sent back an urgent request for reinforcements in order to consolidate the gains, but was told none were available. Virtually surrounded and subject to superior British fire, the remnants of the attacking force held out until the evening when they withdrew to their starting point.

Lieutenant C.F.W. Lang of the Devons made a good reconnaissance in the evening to report on the situation of the enemy. Considering the ferocity of the fighting – and probably an indicator of how much of it had been carried out by the French – British casualties were remarkably light. Captain Barton Hope Besly, Lieutenant Edward Owen Quicke and five other ranks had been killed, with fourteen other ranks wounded. Three died of wounds and one man was missing. This was Private Hogan, who rejoined the battalion two days later.

On 26 October, after a quiet day, the Devons were relieved by a battalion of the French 285th Infantry Regiment. The defence of Givenchy as a whole had now been entrusted to the French, though all French forces north of the canal were generously placed under the command of the British.

On 29 October the whole section of front between the La Bassée Canal and a point near Fromelles, north of Neuve Chapelle, began to be taken over by the Indian Corps. Givenchy itself remained in the hands of the French, at least for the time being, with the Indian Corps taking over the line more or less where the trenches dropped off the 'high' ground, ending up in the lower and wetter trenches. Divisions from the Indian Army had been sent to France in October and had already seen considerable action at Ypres and Messines. They had lost heavily, especially in officers, and were not in any condition for more serious fighting, although they were to see plenty over the next couple of months, in wet, cold and muddy conditions. On the whole they acquitted themselves well, but they lost Givenchy to the Germans in fierce fighting in December.

Fortunately for the exhausted French troops holding Givenchy village and the north bank of the canal, the main German assaults shifted further north, around Festubert and beyond, as the Germans set about testing the newly arrived Indians. Both sides commenced digging in. There was constant artillery fire and a danger from snipers; on 30 October two NCOs of 285th Infantry Regiment were killed by snipers concealed in houses behind German lines who fired at anyone raising their head above the parapet. On 31 October, when cases of dysentery were reported among 285th Regiment, they were relieved by a battalion of 295th Regiment, which continued to try

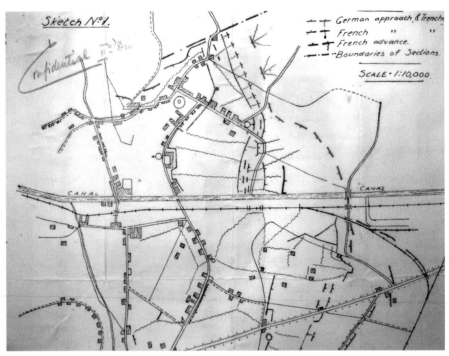

French positions east of the village, November 1914. They have pushed their saps well forward into no man's land nearer the canal.

and push forward saps and trenches towards the enemy where they could. Taking advantage of seasonal fog, which can be remarkably thick in spring and autumn, the 6th Battalion of the 295th Infantry pushed reconnaissance patrols forward. They discovered that the Germans had abandoned some of their advanced positions, which were subsequently occupied by French troops. Apart from artillery bombardments and patrolling, most of November passed reasonably peacefully and the troops were mainly occupied in reinforcing their existing trenches and digging communications trenches. Some of the older trenches were abandoned and a new line was established 200 metres closer to the enemy. Saps were pushed forward between 25 and 60 yards closer to the enemy. On 18 November an impromptu truce was agreed between 285th Infantry Regiment and the troops opposite, which allowed both sides to recover bodies from no man's land. A sudden French artillery barrage forced both sides to dash for their respective trenches. In the confusion an NCO and private of the German 3rd Battalion, 170th Infantry Regiment, ran the wrong way and were made prisoners. On the 19th the Germans began bombarding the trenches with a new weapon, a trench mortar that sent projectiles a metre in diameter that contained metallic fragments. On the 21st it was reported that the Germans had been digging saps forward from their trench by night, and it was feared they were about to link up the ends of the saps by digging a trench between them, thus pushing their front line forward. To interfere with this the French, under Captain Alleau, began digging three mine tunnels out under no man's land at the closest points between the lines. This is the earliest mention of mining operations in Givenchy, which would later become, for a while, synonymous with underground warfare. Alleau also warned of the dangers of sudden

Monument to 58th French Infantry Division, troops from which held Givenchy in November 1914 and whose artillery gave valuable support. It is situated just off the D941 between Cambrin and Auchy-les-Mines.

German attacks being launched from saps and on 23 November the German 112th Infantry Regiment did just that, launching a series of attacks along the Festubert front from saps that had been pushed, in places, to within a few feet of the Indian trenches. The 9th Bhopal Light Infantry, in the trenches opposite Festubert, were quickly bombed out of their trench. Over 600 yards of the front line was captured. Fortunately, half a battalion of 2nd Black Watch and some men of 58th Rifles still held the section immediately adjacent to the French and they continued to hold out throughout the day, though most of the 58th were forced to withdraw. When the inevitable Indian counterattacks were launched, the French were able to offer supporting fire from the high ground, and the fire of 58th Division's artillery from south of the canal was invaluable as the Indians managed to get back into their old front line and spend the night clearing it. The troops of Givenchy garrison faced no direct attack, but were subject to a heavy fire throughout the day.

On 8 December, against the opinion of Lieutenant General Willcocks, who wanted to take the time afforded by the arrival of recent reinforcements to rest some of his troops, the Indian Corps took over the line through Givenchy itself and down beyond the canal to the La Bassée–Bethune road. Givenchy itself was taken over without incident and apparently unnoticed by the Germans, during the course of the 10th.

On 12th December Lieutenant General Willcocks attended a meeting at which he heard that the Commander in Chief of the BEF, Field Marshal Sir John French, was planning an offensive in the Messines area in support of French operations further south, and that local offensives should be launched all along the British front to help prevent German troops being moved as reinforcements.

To this end, it was decided to capture two German saps opposite the trenches of the 15th Sikhs in the neighbourhood of Givenchy, and then to extend the operation by securing a portion of the German main trenches. Sapping, or the digging of deep trenches forward from the front line, posed a special danger as the Germans, with their much more efficient bombs (grenades), could bombard the British front line with them with virtual impunity. If, however, the end of the sap could be captured, it provided a covered route into the German main trench without having to cover too much open ground.

At 5.20am on 16 December, the 129th Baluchis, with 57th Rifles in support, moved up to the HQ of the 15th Sikhs at the crossroads west of Givenchy (later known as Windy Corner) and entered the communication trench leading up to the firing line that ran round the village. They were to attack out of the village at 6.30am. The Connaught Rangers were at Pont Fixe ready to exploit any opportunities, and a battalion of the French 142nd Territorial Regiment was close by in reserve. 129th Baluchis were to attack out of the fire trenches, followed by 57th Rifles, and when they had cleared the narrow trench the Connaught Rangers were to follow them up it. The trench was too narrow to allow all three units to go forward together. The Baluchis were ordered to seize the two German saps opposite the 15th Sikhs, then storm the German fire trench and begin working right and left up it, with 57th Rifles coming up behind to help and the Connaught Rangers pushing through if possible. Major Potter's company was to assault the left sap and Major Buist's company the right.

At 6.30am, each company attacked on a narrow front of about 40 yards in front of each sap, advancing by platoon, and the attack was reasonably successful. Both sap heads were captured and an advance was made down each sap to within a few yards of the main trench. Digging parties immediately started pushing a communication trench forward towards each sap to facilitate the movement of the support troops forward. On the left, the leading men of the first platoon had hesitated to enter the German sap and, seeing this, Major Potter rushed forward, led them into it personally and took command for the rest of the day. Major Hannyngton, who had gone into the firing line to observe, reported later:

I saw the 4th platoon of Major Potter's move forward and then I looked over our own trench at the point from which the attack started. I saw 15 men lying as if dead on the ground round the sap head but beyond that I could see nothing – the men who had gone forward except the dead and wounded being in the sap. The enemy had brought a very heavy fire on the 25 yards separating our trench from their sap head and I saw at once that I could not reinforce Major Potter until the communication trench was cut thro'. At this point one or two of the men lying at the sap head began to dive into the sap or try to run back towards our trench. Not one of the latter got back.

On the right, led by Captain Browning and Jemadar Dadin, the men got into the sap and Havildar Wazin Khan drove the Germans down the trench with bombs. Sepoy Ghazam Shah was with him and threw thirty-five bombs into the German trenches. They got close to the German trench before German counterattacks gradually drove them back.

There followed a mix-up in communication. Hannyngton received a note from Major Buist, which he interpreted as meaning Buist's attack had failed and that it was useless for Potter to press his attack on his own. After much effort a message tied to a weight was thrown into the sap to this effect. Only an hour or so later did Hannyngton realise his error; Buist's men had almost reached the German main trench too. It had also become obvious that the rate of progress of the communication trench was woefully slow. The plan called for it to get through in four or five hours, but it was clear that the trench to the left sap would not be finished until after dark, and the one to the right, being much longer, might take two days. Hannyngton wrote:

> As time passed, matters became worse – we could not reinforce and the enemy began pushing the men in the saps towards the sap heads. The left sap with Major Potter held its own well (the Sepoys were delighted that the Germans had miscalculated the fuse lengths of their bombs so that it was usually possible to pick them up and hurl them back) but the right sap having its British Officer (Captain Browning) and its Nat(ive) Officer wounded began to give way until eventually the remainder was collected in the sap head where it defended itself until dark.

A party of 15th Sikhs had accompanied each attack and they were, in the meantime, working furiously to dig trenches back from the sap heads to the main trench. The 21st Company Sappers and Miners and working parties of the 34th Pioneers were engaged in the same process to join up with them from the Indian side. By 6pm the communication trench was sufficiently developed to allow Potter and the men in the left sap to get out and be replaced by men of 15th Sikhs.

After consulting with brigade HQ and the colonel of 15th Sikhs, the order was given to evacuate the right sap after dark. Unfortunately, before a connection could be made the men remaining in the sap head made an attempt to cross the fifteen yards of open ground that still separated them from the advancing British trench. Even though the distance was short, devastating German fire killed or wounded every man as he ran. The Germans rushed the sap head and began to fire down into the communication trench, which had to be abandoned. Though there had been great heroism, both attacks had failed to reach the main German trench. The attack at Messines, though it gained a little ground, was also a failure.

On 17 December further orders came from Field Marshal Sir John French for local offensives to be launched all along the British front in support of a French attack near Arras. Though this was queried by Lieutenant General Willcocks, it was decided to go ahead with two attacks, one by the Meerut Division opposite Festubert and one by the Lahore Division opposite and to the north-east of Givenchy.

Detailed planning for the attack at Givenchy seems to have been scanty, especially after a plan for the Lahore Division to attack out of Givenchy on a front of 1,000 yards was restricted by higher authority to an attack on a front of just 300 yards. The 59th Scinde Rifles marched from Bouvray at 2am on 19 December and arrived at the HQ of 129th Baluchis at 4am. Their orders were to attack 150 yards of German trench on the left of the Baluchis' position, and 200 yards or so of trench had been evacuated to accommodate them. None of their officers or men had seen the ground over which they were to fight at all, not even in daylight.

The 59th Scind Rifles' war diary gives as clear a picture of events as one could wish:

The CO and Adjutant returned at 9pm and gave out orders after explaining the situation. Most of us had not had an hour's sleep and marched at 2am and arrived at the headquarters of the 129th Baluchis at 4am and after a hasty discussion were led on to the support trenches by Major Barrington.

Our plan of attack was for 129th Baluchis to evacuate 200 yards of trench with the support trench too immediately in rear. Nos 1 and

4 coys were to crowd into the firing line trench and make the attack, supported by nos 2 and 3 coys in the support trench. The signal for the attack was four minutes rapid fire by the artillery and the men were to issue directly out of the trenches directly it was over. Hardly had nos 1 and 4 got into the firing line trench when the signal was given. There had been no time to confer with the OC attacking party on the right of the Sirhind Brigade who were supposed to keep in touch with us. Never having seen the trenches before there was of necessity a great deal of crowding in them and they wound in and out to such an extent that once out of them, unless one had seen them before, it was very hard to tell even the direction of the enemy. The trenches were very deep and to get out of them after it had rained all day was no easy matter. Captain Anderson and Lieutenant Atkinson with B coy and a sprinkling of A Coy got out and started off. Capt Scale and Lieut Bruce got out on the right with 1 Coy, the latter seemed to have great difficulty in getting out of the trenches and everyone practically lost all idea of direction the moment they issued from the trenches.

A platoon under Jemadar Maughul Singh went out first and captured the offshoot of (F) of the right German sap, he held it all day capturing a German officer and was only relieved at dawn on the 20th when the sappers had dug through to the sap head. There is no doubt that this party did very well indeed and were well led. Another platoon started off under Captain Scale and got up to within 30 yards of the enemy trench when it appears they were repulsed after suffering pretty severely. Capt Scale was wounded twice in the ankle and crawled back 150 yards. When he got in he was wonderfully cheerful thereby setting a fine example to his men. Meanwhile Lieut Bruce, who was supposed to go straight to his front started off with a platoon and Jemadar Maggar Singh. No one knows, nor can anyone tell, but somehow he reached a portion of the German trench at the point H with a very few Sikhs. To carry on the narrative it will be best to enter here a statement made by Havildar Dost Mahomed, 4 Coy. Lieut Bruce must have run into this party and gone on with them:

'I and my platoon reached the German trenches, Lieut Bruce was the first man in the trenches. The enemy said they would surrender and handed up rifles but men who put their heads over the trenches were killed, the writer Mohamed Hussain was killed in this way; eventually we got into the trench. Lieut Bruce told me to fortify and hold the left. Lieut Bruce was wounded in the neck and later killed. Our men held on all day and killed many Germans, our bolts jammed and we could not fire much. Lots of Germans were piled up in the trenches on both sides and they seemed to be all round us. The Germans soon brought up a bomb gun into action. I told our men to go but they refused for they said the Sahib had told them to stay. Finally when I went all others were dead – killed by bombs. I and another wounded man started off up a sap, there was a British officer there who told us the Germans held this sap. We went out into the open and taking a wrong turning found ourselves in front of a hostile trench. We waited until bursting of shells showed us our line and we crawled up to our firing line which fired on us. I shouted out that I was a man from India and a sergeant said 'Come on'. I went in and then went back to bring the other wounded man in. The sergeant said I ought not to go back.'

To follow on the narrative I will put in hear [sic] a copy of the reports sent in by Captain B.B. Anderson who commanded the left section of the attack with No 4 Coy:

'Shortly after arrival in the trenches occupied by 129th Baluchis the artillery bombardment commenced, the noise and the congestion in the trench made communication of orders difficult. As soon as the bombardment ceased I advanced. It took a long time to get the men out of the trenches without prepared exits and as the fire on our right seemed to indicate that the attack there had begun I advanced with the men who had got out. I could not find the sap head so I advanced towards the enemy's fire. We advanced about 250 yards before we came to the enemy's trench where we found men of the Highland Light Infantry, 4th Gurkhas and Germans mixed up. I had great difficulty stopping my men going in at them with the bayonet. We moved off to the right and I walked up to a trench asking the occupants who they were. They replied HLI and Gurkhas. I said 'Don't shoot, we're

59th'. They said something about 59th and opened fire. I saw by their bayonets that they were Germans so we went at them but they were too close in the trench for us to get in so we shot at them from outside, they disappeared and we got in. We were then closely mixed up with the other attacking regiments. Then a support of some regiment came up and I went forward to them and tried to stop them, they fired at me and charged but with difficulty I persuaded them not to bayonet us. We occupied the German trench which I thought was the sap head and I gave orders to move along to the left to find the communication trench. The squash was terrible and our men kept pulling Germans out of shelters and making them prisoners which made matters worse. I ordered prisoners to be handed over to British troops. A line of men to our left front advanced on us, we took it for a German counter-attack and opened fire, it turned out to be some British troops. The confusion was extraordinary and everyone who moved outside the trench was shot at or bayoneted by some of our people. Nearly every British officer I met held a pistol to my head and threatened to shoot.

Shortly afterwards I was hit on the pistol I carry on my belt by a bullet fired at very close range and I was rather knocked out. I felt very weak and after a bit I asked a British officer to help me out of the trench. Some men of the Highland Light Infantry helped me back to the 4th Gurkha lines. I found I was not wounded and went back to the sap head which I thought was the one we had taken and nearly half of my company then were, I did not realise till some time later that we had gone into the German main trench. I was told Capt Lee had gone forward up a communication trench. Capt Gilchrist went forward too and shortly came back and asked for support which I sent up. Later I heard both were hit and the people in front hard pressed. I went up the communication trench and found Lieut Scobie who was making most plucky efforts to remove Capt Lee who was dead and Capt Gilchrist who was still alive. They were in a bit of German communication trench from the sap to their main trench. The parapet was not bullet-proof and they were fired on from three sides. Hav. Abdul Wahab with some men was pluckily holding the head of the communication trench very close to the Germans. Lieut Kisch, RB, was there too, selecting a plan for a sandbag barricade. He showed me the place he considered best, which I told him to prepare. I told Lieut Scobie to get back Capt Gilchrist who I saw was still alive and to leave Capt Lee, who I saw was dead, and other bodies, I thought it best to risk no further lives. Capt Gilchrist was got behind the barricade with great difficulty and died soon after. One wounded man who was being helped back, got back later by himself. Lieut Scobie by holding on to a most dangerous and difficult point and by his personal example enabled us to get back a wounded officer and did his utmost to bring back a dead officer but the narrowness of the trench made it impossible. We held the advanced sap and up till about 10pm, the fire was heavy and we lost some men.

Lieutenant Atkinson was with me up to the time when we got to the German main trench. I last saw him lying outside it and thought he was firing into it. I spoke to him and I believe that he must have been hit at that minute as he lay down against the trench in the position in which I afterwards saw him through field glasses. I looked for him outside the trench after we had got in and could not find him. Before I left the trench it was reported to me that he was on my right.

I think about 25 of my men reached the German trench. Three got back last night and reported that very few had been wounded. The Germans were then advancing on them and an officer of the 4th Gurkhas had given the order to get out if they could. I saw many acts of individual gallantry after I got into the German trench. Several men went out and pulled in wounded men under fire but I could not recognise them in the dark.

After daylight there was continual fire going on from both sides with rifle and artillery. No 1 Coy had a great many wounded lying in their trenches and owing to the narrowness there it was frightfully difficult to get them away. Throughout the day the Sappers and Miners did splendid work in both saps.

It was a miserable day, raining hard at times and we had a wretched time of it, the men had no food or blankets and there was no head cover in the trenches where men could rest. We hoped to be relieved at 4pm having done something for 129th Baluchis we expected something from them but they did nothing for us and were most diffident in forwarding messages, their conduct towards us was distinctly strange to say the least of it. After the worst day the regiment has ever had we were relieved by 10pm and got back to billets at 11.35pm'.

Total casualties were four British officers killed and one wounded; four Indian officers wounded and missing; twenty-nine other ranks wounded and fifty-seven missing. The author of the war diary concluded that 'Most of the other ranks missing must be dead'. In an unusual and possibly risky attempt to highlight the horrors and folly of the day, the diarist added: 'These lives were sacrificed to gain nothing tangible, it was (a) pure waste of the best material and all who knew what we were in for it [sic] prophesied it, let's hope the Generals, who stay so far behind now realise what folly these local attacks are.'

Captain John Dymock Scale recovered from his wounds and, as a Russian speaker, was posted to the British Intelligence Mission in Petrograd. The body of Captain Gilchrist was buried next day when the battalion was back in billets at Beuvry.

It was only after the war, when some of the other ranks returned after four years as prisoners of war, that Lieutenant Bruce's heroism on 19 December was recognised and he was awarded a posthumous Victoria Cross. It was gazetted on 2 September 1919, and the citation read:

For most conspicuous bravery and devotion to duty. On the 19th December, 1914, near Givenchy, during a night attack, Lt. Bruce was in command of a small party which captured one of the enemy's trenches. In spite of being severely wounded in the neck, he walked up and down the trench, encouraging his men to hold on against several counter-attacks for some hours until killed. The fire from rifles and bombs was very heavy all day, and it was due to the skilful disposition made, and the example and encouragement shown by Lt. Bruce that his men were able to hold out until dusk, when the trench was finally captured by the enemy.

Lieutenant William Bruce was 25 years old. Born in Edinburgh, he was the son of an Indian army colonel and grandson of the Laird of Symbister. He had been educated at Cliff House School in Hampshire, then at Victoria College, St Helier, Jersey, and at Sandhurst, where he was commissioned as a second lieutenant in January 1910. After a year with 1st Northumberland Fusiliers he joined the 59th Scinde Rifles (Frontier Force) and became a lieutenant in April 1912. He was actually home on leave when war broke out and, hurrying to rejoin his regiment, he met up with them in Egypt en route to France.

On the left of 59th Rifles an assault had been made by a composite battalion of 4th Gurkha Rifles and 1st Battalion Highland Light Infantry, two companies of each. The attack, which went in against the front of the 56th Westphalian Regiment, was carried out in four lines and was initially successful. A sap some 90 yards away was captured, the main German line was attacked successfully, and about 200 yards of the enemy's main trench was captured. Several prisoners were taken and nine rifles were brought back to the Gurkha lines. The war diarist noted 'It was very difficult to distinguish friend from foe in the German trench. The enemy called out "Don't fire, we are HLI and 15th Gurkhas" to the 59th and then shot down some of their men'.

The diary continues:

It was very difficult to ascertain the actual fire trench of the enemy, as their line consisted of a labyrinth of trenches and communication trenches. Being enfiladed and unsupported on both flanks and bombed from the front by the German reserve companies which moved up on both flanks, the line was compelled to retire into the communication trench leading to the advanced sap. Here some men of C Coy were sent back to our lines as there was not sufficient room to contain the force. A & B Coys remained under Major Nicolas and Capt Cramer Roberts. Capt [David] Inglis was shot through the head after he had gallantly led the attack which took the enemy's fire trench. The Subadar Major Sher Singh Rana and the Jemadar Adjt Lachman Thapa were also killed here. Around dawn a group of Gurkhas crawled forward and were able to get into another German trench where they fought hand to hand with the Germans using their kukris. After dawn, about 6.30am a heavy fire was kept up and the party in the sap was heavily enfiladed and suffered severely. Communication was impossible and Capt Cramer Roberts gallantly volunteered to cross to our line to bring information. He ran about 120 yards under a heavy fire and was hit in three places by the enemy's machine-gun fire falling on our trench where he was helped over by Corporal Ward and some men of the HLI. The remainder of the party including some wounded returned to our lines shortly after dusk. Some of our men who had never seen a German before entirely failed to recognise them as an enemy and were sitting by them when an HLI Sergeant came up and they were taken prisoner. The enemy made use of several words of Hindustani. Casualties approximately 1 B.O. killed, 1 B.O. wounded, 2 G.O's killed, Rank and File 13 killed, 14 wounded, 28 missing.

Captain Charles North Dalrymple Inglis (brother of David Inglis), who was attached to 8th Gurkhas, briefly described the fighting in a letter dated 21 January 1915:

The story roughly is that on the 18th we received orders to attack, with two companies HLI and two companies 4th Gurkhas, a portion of the German trenches at 5.30am the following morning. We didn't receive our orders until 8pm, and we had to do a night march over ground we didn't know. We started at 3am the following morning and got up all right, though we lost a few men from gun-fire which they got onto us just as we were getting into position. At 5.30am our guns opened a heavy fire for four minutes on their lines, and at 5.34 our line advanced. We took two gaps and two lines of German trench practically without loss, and captured a good many prisoners. We could have got further and taken a village as well if we had been supported. A brigade who were supposed to be operating on our right failed; in fact the regiment on our extreme right lost 5 officers taking one sap. Sappers and miners who were to cut communications on our extreme left had their British officer killed and failed to do it. Our first line was thus left isolated, and lost heavily with bombs and machine guns and finally the Germans got into their trench again, and, we hope, took some of the survivors prisoners. The officers there were Pringle and Anderson; the remainder withdrew into a sap and got back in the dark.

The loss and recapture of Givenchy

During the night of 19/20th there was a good deal of rain, making the condition of the shallow trenches even worse, with over a foot of mud in the bottom and parapets collapsing. 3 and 4 companies of the Gurkhas held the front line trench. On their right were a half company of the Highland Light Infantry and on their right again the machine-gun section of 1/4 Garwhal Rifles under Captain Phayre, plus the machine-gun section of 125th Napier Rifles slightly to the rear. At 8am Captain Wylie relieved Captain Phayre. Between 9 and 9.30 the Germans blew up the Gurkha trenches using mines, then advanced *en masse*. Fire from all serviceable rifles caused the Germans considerable loss. The rifles were badly clogged with mud, in spite of all efforts to keep them clean, and the explosions caused by the mines did not improve matters.

A rare photograph of Gurkha troops huddled in their shallow trench just north of Givenchy in December 1914. The trench was demolished by mine explosions on 20 December. (*With thanks to Andrew Thornton*)

A lance corporal of 1st Battalion, the Seaforth Highlanders, whose position was on the left of those obliterated, described the sudden and totally unexpected detonation of what turned out to be ten small mines the Germans had placed under the Gurkha line:

> About 8am last Monday a German aeroplane overhead gave the signal, and the poor old 'Glory Hole' was blown up bodily. It appears the Germans had undermined it. Talk of explosions! The earth shook. I had to hang on to keep from falling. My dugout was doing a tango. Lumps of clay were falling on and all around me. This lasted for about a minute, and you can believe it was not conducive to keeping a really steady nerve when I tell you that each explosion came nearer and nearer to me. Starting about 90 yards away the last one was no more than 20 distant. The Germans were 'hoching' loudly, the HLI wounded screaming, and it was a cheerful corner indeed. I was momentarily expecting our trench to get blown up in a similar manner, and I can assure you the prospect did not look good to me.

The ten mines were only small, each about 110lb of explosive, and had been pushed forward from saps the Germans had driven close to the Gurkha trenches using tunnels created by augers. The effect was devastating, not only in terms of material damage (parapets collapsed, and bodies and other debris were flung 20 feet into the air), but also to morale.

The Gurkhas' war diary continues:

> In spite of stout resistance the enemy gained several portions of our trench when hand to hand fighting ensued. Bombs were used by both sides. Difficulty in lighting our pattern of bombs was experienced. Captain Randall was killed while aiding a bombing party after he had killed two Germans with his revolver.
>
> At this period we lost heavily, but although heavily outnumbered a large number of the enemy were accounted for. Owing to the rifles being clogged with mud, and the enfilade fire, a retirement was ordered down the communication trench and through Givenchy. At [blank] am Major Travers with some of No IV Coy retired through

Givenchy which was being heavily shelled at the time. At this time Capt Wylie was still in position with his machine guns. It appeared from Festubert that this portion of the line was also mined about this time but it is impossible to ascertain the true facts as none of that party returned and Capt Wylie was also missing. No men of E Coy who were with Capt Yates returned either, and that officer, with his two Subadars, Prem Sing Thapa and Pirthi Sing Rana also Jemadar Nain Sing Gurung were also missing.

The remaining Gurkhas fell back on the reserve trenches some 500 yards behind, close to Festubert, but they were full of water owing to the marshy condition of the country. The men were forced to lie in the water and later suffered severely from rheumatism. Their feet swelled up and once they took off their boots they could not get them on again. It was their first experience of 'trench foot'. Heavy artillery fire and local counterattacks blunted the German attacks near Festubert, but in Givenchy itself things were not going well.

Captain Charles North Dalrymple described the events in another letter:

The following morning the Germans retaliated by blowing in our front trench in six places, and, following this up with a shower of bombs, rushed the trench. Practically not a man got back – only two small parties on the extreme flanks. Our second line stood firm, though the Indian right fell back. Luckily we had the Seaforths on our left, but the Indian regiment beyond them also fell back. We held the line for another 36 hours before being relieved, the Germans luckily failing to realise our weakness. Had they made a serious attack they must have broken through, as we had no reserves behind us.

A staff officer who went forward to Pont Fixe arrived about 12.30pm to find the place under heavy bombardment.

Very shortly parties of Indian troops were seen coming from the direction of Givenchy Cross Roads, and then withdrawing westwards behind the houses on the west of the road. As these became more numerous, I went down the bank of the canal towards which they seemed to be moving, to find out what had occurred. I found half a battalion of 15th Sikhs digging in, near the 81st battery RFA, which was in action on the north of the canal. A detachment of 15th Lancers were near the same place; also 3 companies of the French Territorial battalion (142nd) halted under cover. OC 15th Sikhs informed me that he had withdrawn to that place from a position near Givenchy Cross Roads, on seeing troops retiring from the defensive line. I then saw the OC 129th Baluchis arrive with some of his men who were evidently in disorder. He crossed the canal and told me that his men had been driven from their trenches and he had not been able to rally them. The arrival of a second battalion of the 142nd French Territorials at the Pontoon Bridge was also reported to me at about 1.25pm. I ordered OC 15th Sikhs to cover the battery and reconnoitre

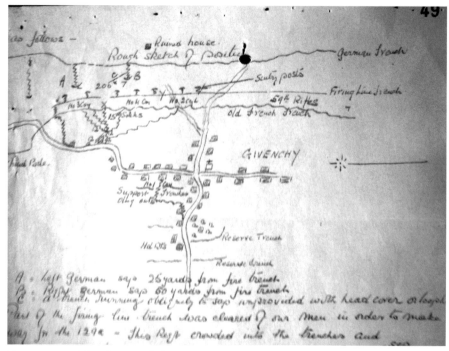

Contemporary sketch map of the Indian positions, from which they were forced on 20 December 1914.

towards Givenchy, with a view to clearing up the situation as far as possible.

The Germans had begun bombarding Givenchy heavily at about 9am. Major Potter, who was holding the left portion of the trenches, reported that the Germans 'had seemed a bit jumpy in the night, but he did not think that they meditated an attack'. On a brief tour of inspection the Commanding Officer of 129th Baluchis, Lieutenant Colonel William Southey, was told that Major Hannyngton, not knowing he was coming, had gone to try and find him and set off to locate him.

When close to the village of Givenchy the enemy's bombardment started and their high explosive shells plastered every inch of the road in the village and searched the ground all round us. Lt Griffin and I finding we could not get on took shelter in some dug outs in the communication trench. We could see from a sandbag barricade on the road that an attack was being made on the Sirhind Brigade and we could see some of the trenches in that section being vacated.

Southey eventually met up with Hannyngton and took him to battalion headquarters to discuss repositioning his line and to request reinforcements. When the Germans launched their assault on the village the two senior officers were thus out of the firing line and a good distance behind it. News came in from Major Potter that he had been forced to abandon the sap so hard won a couple of days earlier. He also asked for ammunition. The telephone wire had been cut by shells and everything had to be carried by runner. There was heavy firing between 10.30am and noon, but then it seemed to go quiet. It is possible that the arrival of Major Travers and the remnants of his Gurkha company spooked the Baluchis (though Major Buist later claimed they panicked when their rifles became clogged with mud as the Germans got close to their trench) because, at about 1pm, an orderly reported that troops seemed to be abandoning the village. When Colonel Southey and Hannyngton ran out to stop them 'They said the whole section had retired and that no one was left in the firing line. The first lot of men coming down were Sikhs and Gurkhas, then some of our men, then some cavalry'. The cavalry were presumably men of 15th Lancers who had come up earlier as reinforcements and must barely have had time to get into position.

Southey endeavoured to get the troops into some kind of defensive position, but the Sikhs 'as fast as they were put in on one side, went off on the other', and he decided to fall back to occupy some trenches close to the crossroads. Here he met the CO of 81st Battery, who had come forward to investigate, 'who told me a lot of stragglers of all corps had been collected at the Canal Bank by his Battery, so I decided to proceed there. When mustering the Regiment I found there were 5 British Officers, 4 Indian Officers, 210 other ranks present, 60 men without rifles'.

Majors Buist and Potter were absent, as were Captain Davies and Lieutenant Lewis. Of the Indian officers Subadar Major Malakhan, Subadar Amir Khan and Jemadar Id Muitammad were missing. Subadars Ahmed Din Jem and Karim Khan were known to have been killed. Major Buist and Lieutenant Lewis rejoined shortly afterwards, having come back by a different route.

> From them I learned that the attack was most sudden and attach their reports. I cannot understand how such little resistance was made, but the men were worn out after the attack carried out on 16th Dec they have had consistent work of the most harassing nature, with no sleep to speak of; during the night of the 19th/20th it poured with rain, the parapet was constantly dropping away, and the men were trying to repair it all night. Their rifles were clogged with mud and only 1 in 3 or 4 would fire. They were heavily bombed by the enemy's mortars and while I was in the trenches one bomb killed an Indian Officer and 1 man was wounded. This undoubtedly shattered their nerves, all through the night casualties were occurring and I fear completed their demoralization.

A havildar from Major Potter's company rejoined the regiment overnight. Major Potter and his men, he said, resisted for some time and killed many Germans. They were forced to go, finally, as Germans had surrounded them on all sides; as far as he knew they had captured Major Potter (he was in fact killed), Sub Major Mala Khan, Subadar Amir Khan and about fifty men. The havildar himself jumped out of the trench into the open and lay down among some dead bodies. Close to him was an officer in charge of the machine guns on the left of the line, who had been badly wounded, who died while the havildar was there. As soon as it got dark the havildar crawled away and escaped. He spent the morning looking for the regiment and came in during the afternoon.

Lieutenant Hugh Victor Lewis (who went on to become a major general in the Second World War) left his account of the action:

At about 9am on the 20th Major Hannyngton and I having spotted the position where we thought the enemy had bomb guns and machine guns, went to Givanchy [sic] to make further observations from the gunner observation station and to inform the gunner officers. While in the top story of the observation house the bombardment of the village began. We came out of the house and found trenches to get into, they were our support trenches. The bombardment was very hot. While taking cover we saw the Germans entering the trenches of the Sirhind Brigade on our left, so started back at once for the trenches. We met Col Southey who took back Major Hannyngton to HQ and I went on alone to the trenches. On arrival at the support trenches I saw Capt Davis sitting there and asked him the situation. He said 'The right sap has been evacuated but they should be alright now as I have sent up some bombers'. I said it was a very dangerous place and there should be a British Officer there. I told him I would go there myself. When I arrived I found Mir Badshan standing at the entrance throwing bombs. I crept up the sap until I could see the German hats and bayonets over the next bend. Satisfied that the Germans held the sap I ordered Mir Badshan to build up a barricade about 15 yards out to cover the straight sap we had dug out to the German sap. Having seen this started I went to my machine gun (I am a machine gun officer) and removed screens so as to enable immediate fire to be opened across the left of our position to cover the sap.

Sep Fatch Saidar did very good work clearing the earth in front of the parapet exposing himself to very close range fire. Having perfected the position I went back to see how the barricade in the sap was going on. Jem Mirbad Shah tells me it was completed but I never saw it as before we arrived there we heard the MG fire. I ran back to them. The men in the trenches were calm and did not know what was happening. The loopholes were practically useless. I suppose 9 out of 10 were blocked by the very heavy rifle fire preceding the attack. The trenches were too deep and concave to fire over the top. Three out of four rifles were jammed.

When I arrived at the machine gun position (it was in a sap) I saw the enemy advancing across my front. I took the gun myself. During a temporary stoppage I heard the enemy's cheering and looking up saw them advancing about 15 yards off into my sap head. I knew of no retirement so as my gun position was not made to fire to the front I went back into the main trench. On my arrival there were only 4 or 5 of my regiment, while the next man on my right was a German. Two machine gunners who survived 3 PMs, one Mahsud and myself then retired down the one trench for the first 50 yards quickly. All the men with me behaved admirably, stopping whenever I told them to fire at the enemy. I told them to fire at the Germans standing about in groups on the parapets, and often without being told. We retired in front of the enemy, keeping about 30 to 40 yards off. The Germans came straight over the firing trenches and supports, but for each line the numbers diminished. We held a ditch and hedge W of Givenchy for about 5 minutes and the enemy did not come any further across the open, but worked their way into Givenchy round my left. I had now been joined by some 5 or 6 more men, who also behaved well. When the Germans got on our left flank we retired to the village some 30 yards behind where we met Major Buist. We then retired E across the open plain towards Pont Fixe. On arrival at the Festubert–Pont Fixe road we held the trenches. We were joined by Jem Dadin, 2 havildars and sepoys who came back having finished their ammunition. There we stayed until we heard the regiment was on the canal when we rejoined. Only two machine gunners of that section came away with me. I don't know what happened to the others. Two at least were killed. Sep Fatheh Haidar and Hav Ramin Ali, Sep Sattar Khan and a Mahsud whose name I cannot yet discover were conspicuous by their coolness.

As regards the numbers of the German attack, the first mass to advance was so thick that daylight was only here and there visible between them. I should put them down at two men per yard. More followed. The firing line trench apparently would not hold them as men stood on the parapet waiting for others to climb out. Those who climbed out went straight for the support trenches. It would have required a large number of rifles, with free use of them, to stop the advance.

With the village itself now in their hands, the Germans began to outflank the 57th Rifles who were holding the trenches down to the canal. They got into the trenches on the left and at about 11am entered some houses in the rear of the left company, which had already lost Captain Shepherd. He had been mortally wounded and the command had been taken by Captain Mahon. Fearing that they would be cut off, Captain Mahon ordered a retreat down the trench, which was conducted very coolly, with one or two riflemen holding each traverse while their comrades fell back. Lieutenant Deedes remained behind and managed to get Captain Shepherd's body away. Captain Jardine, who had been holding the right of the line with seventy men, barricaded the trench and Captain Mahon managed to get into an old communication trench facing north. Between them they halted the German advance. Later in the day a company of the French 142nd Regiment came up to reinforce them. They lent what little support they could to the Manchesters as they recaptured the village and attempted to push forward to the north in the early evening. They spent most of the night huddled in the cold and wet in anticipation of a night attack.

The situation in the afternoon looked perilous, but help was on its way. The 1st Manchesters, one of the regular British battalions that always served with an Indian division, were in billets in Bethune on 20 December, but had been 'standing to' on a regular basis for two days as the situation at the front line six miles to the east changed. At 11.15am on the 20th they finally received an order to march to Gorre and report to the commander of the Sirhind Brigade. En route they passed numbers of Indian troops, many of them wounded, making their way to the rear; they were also ordered to move instead to Pont Fixe, where they were ordered to counterattack the enemy trenches east of Givenchy. They were supported on their left by three companies of the French 142nd Territorial Regiment (the remainder of the regiment, which had been attached to the Lahore Division as part of its reserve, was guarding the Pont Fixe) led by Capitaine Salle, and by an artillery bombardment from French guns south of the canal. They were advised that Givenchy was unoccupied. No. 1 Company under Captain Tillard, on the left, and No. 2 Company, under Lieutenant Mair, were ordered to advance and seize the village, with Major Hitchins in command of the whole operation. Once they had established themselves in the village, No. 3 Company under Captain Creagh was to move up on the right and they were to scout toward the German trenches beyond.

The war diary says:

> This counter-attack started at 3.10pm, the village being unexpectedly found to be held by the enemy and this delayed the attack on the trenches until the following morning as by the time the communication

The 1st Battalion, the Manchester Regiment, recapture the village, 20 December 1914.

trenches on the far side of the village had been reached after the village had been cleared of the enemy it was too dark to distinguish the country and locate the direction of the enemy trenches. Twelve prisoners were taken while the village was being cleared of the enemy.

In fact the village was only lightly held, and No.1 Company, fighting house by house, made it to the orchard and the old trench line on the left, where they found Captain O.W.E. Bannerman (Indian army) of the 15th Lancers, who had been wounded earlier in the fighting and taken prisoner. He had been abandoned as the Germans fell back. In the centre, No. 2 Company advanced through the centre of the village, but encountered some Germans who, possibly as a trick but just as likely because of the cold, had put on British khaki caps and overcoats. The supposed 'ruse' was detected but it did almost lead to tragedy – two Royal Field Artillery officers and a sergeant had been observing from a house in the village when the Germans moved in and had hidden in the cellar. When they emerged they were spotted, but fortunately not fired on, before they could identify themselves. With the village now in the Manchesters' hands, No. 3 Company moved up on the right and they advanced into the old support trench. No.1 Company, at the orchard, was well to the left and somewhat ahead of the other two.

In the support trench they came under heavy fire from the Germans in the old front line trench. No. 1 Company provided covering fire, while 2 and 3 companies attempted to crawl forward. It was now 6pm and dusk had fallen, but the Germans had set fire to a couple of haystacks on the edge of the village and used the light to pick off the men as they crawled forward. It was impossible to help the wounded and the advance became bogged down, with the men having to fall back to the support trenches.

The troops of the 142nd Regiment had, meantime, made it into some of the trenches north of the village previously occupied by the 129th Baluchis, though Capitaine Salle was seriously wounded as they did so. Capitaine Ribes took command and they dug in and prepared to conform with the Manchesters when they resumed their attack.

Overnight an attempt was made to contact the 57th Scinde Rifles on the slope down to the canal, but this was not a success. The 1/4th Suffolk Regiment moved up in support, but due to heavy enemy fire and the crowded nature of the trenches it was impossible for them to move up to Givenchy itself, though one company did skirt the village and get in touch with No. 1 Company, while some men of No. 4 Company under Captain Rose worked forward and linked up with No. 3 Company on the right. Contact was maintained with the troops of 142nd Regiment and they, in turn, linked up with some dismounted cavalry from the Indian 7th Dragoon Guards, who had managed to advance from Festubert as part of an early morning attack, which had generally foundered in the mud and heavy rain. Orders also arrived to say that the attack was to be resumed on the trenches still held by the Germans.

Next morning, as the Manchesters' war diary records:

The attack was timed for 6.30am and was met by heavy maxim and rifle fire. Two burning haystacks showed up our men and, after an hour's fighting, it was found impossible to reach the enemy's trenches. The previous night the line had been advanced to try and reach the enemy's trenches and had met a very heavy fire and sustained severe casualties.

Captain Leo Creagh was killed and Major Henry Ernest Hitchins and Captain Alfred Barnes Rose were injured.

One act of humanity was recorded. A German medical officer came out of their trenches and dressed the wounds of an injured German soldier in the open, then moved on to dress two wounded British men nearby. He wasn't fired on. British stretcher-bearers also carried several wounded Germans to the local dressing stations.

In front of No. 1 Company, in the trenches at the orchard, lay a small farmhouse (this probably later became known as the 'White House'), towards which the Germans had previously dug a sap. They managed to run a short tunnel (most likely a bore) from the sap to the farmhouse, and in the late morning blew a charge that demolished part of the defences and scattered the defenders. Three companies of infantry debouched from the trenches and stormed the British trench. After some fierce fighting the troops fell back towards their comrades in the village itself.

The war diary continues:

At about 11am the village and trenches were shelled severely by heavy guns and shrapnel for 45 minutes. Then a heavy attack was made by the enemy. All was going well until the French retired on our L(eft) leaving our flank there in a dangerous position.

The French troops, as a territorial regiment, were older than average, having already done their three years' national service in the regular army and eleven years in the regular reserve, so most were in their mid to late thirties. They were forced to retire into the village, but continued to hold out near the church, even though Capitaine Ribes had been wounded and Capitaine Adde had taken command. Their presence was missed by the Manchesters, who clearly felt themselves abandoned, but they were still there, holding the large farm known later as 'French Farm', and then 'Stench Farm', when the counterattack was launched later in the day.

The Manchesters' war diary goes on:

French Farm as it is today. Though missed by the British troops nearby, it was captured by French troops of 142 Territorial Regiment on 20 December and held throughout the battle.

The enemy worked round and the L[eft] was forced to retire through the village and on to the road with the enemy attacking strongly on the R[ight] and centre and it was considered advisable to retire the L[eft] and part of the supports and take up a position in rear to cover the retirement of the centre and right. These held on so tenaciously that on receipt of a message to this effect another advance was made and the original line was reoccupied, driving back the enemy on the L[eft]. This was accomplished about 2pm.

Counterattacks were mounted and by 3pm the old support line east of the village was still being held. The Germans began working round the right flank, however, and the diary continues:

At 3.20pm a sharp attack was delivered by the enemy and a considerable number of the enemy appeared on the R[ight] flank and rear. There was no position from which to deal with this and as a maxim appeared and accurate shrapnel opened from the R[ight] dispositions were again made to retire. The centre and right held on for some time while a second position was taken up and a hand to hand fight took place there and on the road in rear of them before they retired. Half way back to Pont Fixe a party of Scots Guards were met holding a small trench N of the road. We went into reserve on arrival at Pont Fixe.

In the course of the fighting retreat Lance Corporal (acting sergeant) Cecil Humphries won the DCM for going back and bringing in the body of a company commander. After being wounded later, Humphries, who was a New Zealander, was commissioned into the Highland Light Infantry and killed in August 1918 as an acting lieutenant colonel in the Duke of Cornwall's Light Infantry, attached to the 1st Battalion of the Norfolk Regiment. In addition to his DCM he had been awarded the DSO and the Military Cross and bar. Two other lance corporals and two company sergeant majors also won the DCM at Givenchy on the same day: Lance Corporal Charles Gavin for carrying messages under heavy fire, Lance Corporal Michael Flannery for continuing to conduct operations after his officers were killed, Company Sergeant Major Herbert Harland for conspicuous gallantry and presence of mind during the night attack and for gallant conduct next day and Company Sergeant Major Herbert Heywood for displaying great resource and presence of mind at a critical time when in command of two platoons and for leading his men into Givenchy under heavy fire.

The casualties were recorded as two officers killed and three wounded, with sixty-four other ranks killed, 123 wounded and ninety-three missing, half of whom were known to have been wounded. The vast majority of the dead are recorded on the Le Touret memorial to the missing; their bodies were never identified. The French battalion's casualties are given as eighty-nine killed and fifty-nine wounded.

The Manchesters' epic fight at the village was soon being used for recruiting purposes. The *Rochdale Observer* ran an advert, which included the headline 'Think of the Manchesters. They captured Givenchy and held their positions in a thirty hour struggle against overwhelming odds. Don't you want to be with them?'

Lieutenant General Watkis, commander of the Lahore Division, said:

… Yours was the battalion detailed to carry out the attack on Givenchy. It was a magnificent piece of work … In my reports to higher authorities, I could only use the term 'Gallant Manchesters' … When you were called to go back in, by God men, you went back in … You are a very brave set of men.

At daybreak on 21 December a patrol of the 57th Rifles under Subadar Arsla Khan confirmed that the Germans were still in their old left section trenches, and even managed to shoot a couple of them at their barricades. Attempts to establish contact with the Manchesters failed. Lieutenant Fasken brought up the men of 9th Infantry ,who had been with the local reserve, and about thirty rifles of the Punjabi–Mohamedan Company, who were also with the local reserve, also came up and were sent into the old communication trench facing north. There were now no effective rifles in the reserve and the few men still available were constantly being called upon to carry stores and ammunition along the trench, which 'was long, very narrow and tortuous and knee deep in liquid mud'. At about 3pm the Manchesters were forced to evacuate the village and the Germans again began to work round the battalion's flank and left rear, and were only held back with difficulty. The men in the old communication trench were reinforced by Subadar Arsla Khan and 20 Afridis and together they repulsed three German attacks. Fortunately, at about 4pm the counterattack by the Cameron Highlanders that retook the village relieved the pressure and contact was made with the men of 1st Brigade. Overnight the Scots Guards occupied a line to the north and the line was stabilised.

Givenchy was now back in German hands, but it was too important to be allowed to stay that way for long. The party of Scots Guards met by the Manchesters were part of 1st (Guards) Brigade who, along with 3 Brigade, had been ordered to Bethune the previous day and then marched to Pont Fixe that morning. The 1st Brigade was ordered to recapture Givenchy village itself and 3rd Brigade to advance from Festubert and regain the ground to the north.

1st Cameron Highlanders, part of 1st Brigade, arrived at Pont Fixe at 2.40 and received orders from the brigadier to attack Givenchy village. At about 3pm A Company advanced, followed by B. They discovered the village was only lightly held by the Germans, so proceeded to occupy most of it. They found a company of French infantry from 142nd Regiment still holding a large farm north of the church and there were, they said, a few Munsters holding out in some of the houses (though this seems unlikely and one wonders if they were actually Manchesters). A Company took up position in a trench to the north of the French-held farm and B Company to the south, while C Company remained in reserve near Pont Fixe. During the evening half of C Company was used to prolong B Company's line to the right. Slightly later D Company, with a company of the London Scottish, extended the line even further. The battalion lost two officers wounded and three missing, with six other ranks known to have been killed, sixty-four wounded and 132 missing over the course of two days' fighting, the majority on the 22nd.

The Scots Guards in the Great War (John Murray, 1965) gives the clearest explanation of the confused fighting south of Givenchy on 21 December.

The objective of the 1st Brigade in the attack on this day (21st Dec '14) was the capture of the trenches about the Rue d'Ouvert (to the east of the village), which had been lost the day before. The Scots Guards were on the right of the brigade, just north of the canal as far as Givenchy. … It was nearly dark at 4.15pm when the battalion was ready for the attack in position west of Givenchy. No opposition was met until Givenchy was reached. Here there was an unfortunate accident, due to the darkness and the fact that the ground was quite strange to the troops engaged. The right of the Cameron Highlanders lost direction and they and the Scots Guards narrowly escaped attacking one another and are believed to have actually exchanged shots before the mistake was discovered. The losses that day were not serious – Lt H.G.E. (Hillyar Edgar George) Hill-Trevor who had only joined the battalion on the 18th November at Borre, and of course was in his first and last action, was killed with two men. Twenty-three men were wounded or missing.

Unfortunately neither Hill-Trevor's surviving War Office personal file (WO 339/11127), nor the battalion war diary (WO 95/1263) gives any detail of the manner of his death. The war diary merely records 'Objective – to drive Germans east and establish ourselves in the old trenches at Rue D'Ouvert… Heavy shelling across Canal. Attack began at 4.15 pm and took up position W of Givenchy. Killed Lt H.G. Hill Trevor'. After the war his family erected a monument to him in the village, on the site of a former shrine opposite Orchard Farm, and it stands there to this day.

The Coldstream Guards followed the Camerons into Pont Fixe and were ordered to attack Rue d'Ouvert, cooperating, if possible, with 3 Brigade on their left. With the Camerons on their right they advanced at 3pm with 2 and 3 companies in the front, 4 Company behind and 1 Company in reserve. A few shells were fired at them as they crossed the Pont Fixe, but as they spread out to advance across the open country they were subjected to heavy enfilading rifle and machine-gun fire. Fortunately a heavy hailstorm came down, right in the faces of the German defenders, and they crossed without serious casualties, only one man killed and a handful wounded. Nos 2, 3 and 4 companies managed to occupy some old French trenches on the reverse slope of the Givenchy spur about 300 yards west of the trenches that had been lost by the Indian troops on the 19th, which were now occupied by

The monument to Hillyar Edgar George Hill-Trevor, Scots Guards, killed on 21 December.

the Germans. Colonel Ponsonby established his HQ in the most westerly house in the village and 1 Company took up positions nearby. A patrol under Second Lieutenant Mills went further into the village and reported it clear of Germans as far as the church. Overnight an attempt was made to straighten the line and get in touch with the Gloucesters on the left and the Camerons on the right, but a proper touch could not be made.

The light casualties suffered by the three battalions seem to confirm that there was little resistance in Givenchy itself, but there was a lot harder going further north. 1st South Wales Borderers at Festubert advanced in the darkness of the late afternoon and reached the original support trenches at 5.25pm, linking up with a few men of the Highland Light Infantry who had remained there. The rest of the support line was unoccupied by either side and it spread itself as far as it could, but it had suffered losses in the advance, partly from enemy fire and partly from the boggy nature of the ground, which had broken up the companies. The Germans were in a trench about

150 yards ahead of them and they were unable to make contact with the Gloucesters on their right.

The 1st Gloucesters, advancing south of Festubert, managed to gain about 500 yards before darkness fell, but they had lost six officers wounded and one missing, sixteen other ranks killed, eighty-six wounded and ninety-four missing, most of them to fire from the high ground around Givenchy. They could not make contact with any units on their right either.

The 2nd Munster Fusiliers were ordered to fill the gap between the right of 3rd Brigade (the Gloucesters) and the left of 1st Brigade, so after a reconnaissance C and D companies under Major Thomson moved to fill the gap, occupying the road to Givenchy from the Festubert–Pont Fixe road, while A and B companies under the CO moved to support them, taking up a position east of the Festubert–Pont Fixe road. At 10.30pm, in total darkness, the battalion was ordered to advance over boggy ground to recapture the trenches north of Givenchy and to try and link up 1st and 3rd Brigades. Two companies (C and D) did so, but came under accurate rifle fire and were forced to dig in some 300 yards east of the main road.

The action over the two days is difficult to differentiate. The battalion war diary is not clear and does not mention the advance on the 21st at all;

The Givenchy ridge from near Festubert. The slightly elevated ground at the end of the track is where the mines exploded; the Munsters counterattacked across the ground on the right. In the centre of the picture, between the trees, is French Farm.

the 3rd Brigade war diary does mention the advance on the 21st but says little about it. The Commonwealth War Graves Commission website says that fifty-eight men were killed on the 21st and only six on the 22nd, which does not seem right when compared to surviving accounts. The map in the battalion history seems to show the advance taking place about 1,000 yards too far north.

At 7am on the 22nd the battalion was ordered to advance, with C and D companies now in support. There was, at first, little opposition and the battalion seems to have skirted Givenchy and advanced around 900 yards from the Windy Corner road junction. Heavy rifle and machine-gun fire was met with, casualties were heavy and the companies got badly split up, though they had almost certainly regained the trenches originally occupied by the Lahore Division beyond the crest of the ridge. By midday the battalion was held up and under heavy shellfire so took what cover it could, unsupported on either flank.

A further attempt to advance was made and the senior major in the battalion, Edmund Peel Thomson, a Boer War veteran and occasional cricketer with the MCC, was killed leading the charge. Major Francis Innes Day, aged forty-three, had seen active service in Nigeria, Uganda and South Africa. A letter from a brother officer described how:

He was rallying his men for a second attack when he was shot in the face and legs. A Private Wills, who was just behind him, turned him over, and called some men to carry him away, but he said 'Go on lads! Don't waste your time on me! Here, Wills! Take this revolver and give it to my wife. Tell her I died happy!

Captain Hugh Conor Henry O'Brien, aged thirty-four, who had also seen action in the Boer War, was reported as leading his men in the charge shouting 'Now, Munsters! This is your chance to get back a bit of your own!' before being hit in the left side as he knelt to take temporary cover. It may have been O'Brien who was reported by the Germans as shouting 'Surrender! We outnumber you three to one, and the Prussians are beaten all along the line', before he and the men with him were shot down. While O'Brien's wound was being dressed by a brother officer a shrapnel shell burst above them and both were killed. Lieutenant James Francis O'Brien was killed by a shot through the head leading his men and Major Ryan wrote to his parents that 'a Corporal and all the men said that nothing could have been more gallant than the way that he led them.' Second Lieutenant Roger Assheton Young, whose twentieth birthday had been the day before, was killed. He had only been commissioned into the regiment in August. Lieutenant Colonel Arthur Milton Bent, coming up behind his men in order to find out what was happening, had his entire side laid open by the explosion of a shell, so his intestines were clearly visible. He pitched forward and landed on the body of a dead German, which prevented him slipping into a pool of water and drowning. Miraculously, after lying out for eighteen hours, he was recovered alive and suffering from frostbite; the cold, paradoxically, had probably saved his life by reducing the bleeding. He subsequently contracted pneumonia but survived that too, dying eventually in 1940 at the age of seventy.

With no support on either flank the battalion dug in and held out. No messages could be got back and it was only at dusk that Major Ryan, who had been left behind to transmit messages to brigade HQ, succeeded in making contact and discovered that the battalion was way in advance of the units on its flanks, had suffered heavy casualties and was vulnerable to counterattack. With the permission of brigade HQ, those men that could withdrew overnight. It was not until 5am on the 23rd that the first company was assembled at Windy Corner. Altogether the battalion had lost seven officers killed and four wounded, and about sixty other ranks killed and 150 wounded. Almost all the dead are commemorated on the Le Touret memorial to the missing.

The Coldstream Guards were also told to resume the attack. On the 22nd three companies (2, 3 and 4) in the forward trenches attacked the German trench along the road leading from Givenchy to Chapelle St Roche at 5.45am. The attack went ahead in the face of intense rifle and machine-gun fire. It was not a good day for former pupils of Eton College. Second Lieutenant Bevil Douglas Tollemache's platoon was one of the first to leave the trenches and he reportedly encouraged his men, saying 'Come on men! Keep your spirits up! We will shift them out of it!', but he was hit just before they reached the German trench and lay wounded in a fold in the ground as his men poured past him and managed to capture it. Without support, they were counterattacked and driven out by German bombers. The three companies lost 50 per cent of their strength. Sergeant Briggs, who was also wounded, tried to bring back Lieutenant Tollemache, but was told 'You must leave me Sergeant Briggs or you will be captured', so reluctantly abandoned him. Though some men said they were sure he must have been taken prisoner, his body was later found, although his grave was subsequently lost in later fighting. Another Old Etonian, Second Lieutenant Luke Frederick Reynold Coleridge, was also hit and was seen by Private Whitehouse to roll himself into cover. He was last observed supporting himself on one elbow, looking around. Unlike Tollemache, his body was not recovered and his family refused to acknowledge his death. It was believed that he'd told Captain Geoffrey Stewart that he was 'done for', but as Stewart himself was killed shortly afterwards, having gone out alone on reconnaissance, the War Office decided not to tell his family this. As late as December 1918 his family was asking the War Office to investigate reports of secret German prisoner of war camps where officers were being held incommunicado. A third Old Etonian, Second Lieutenant Edward Archibald Beauchamp, was shot through the chest and sent back badly wounded to 4 Clearing Hospital at Lillers, where he died of his wounds. The fourth Old Etonian, Second Lieutenant John Henry McNeile, was luckier – he was reported wounded and missing, but months later word came via the Red Cross that he was a prisoner of war in Germany. When he got back to Britain in November 1918 he was obliged to explain his capture to the War Office and said:

After crossing a sunk [sic] road, I had just come to a deep trench when I was hit through the hip and fell into it. Very shortly afterwards Captain Campbell, the senior Coldstream officer present, came down the trench in which I was lying and told me the battalion was holding the main line of trench and told me to stay where I was with some other wounded. He said nothing about having to retire himself. The next thing I remember was hearing a lot of noise and eight of our men coming running down my trench. They told me Captain Campbell had at last been obliged to retire and that the Germans had already cut us off from him. At that moment about 100 Germans left the(ir) trench and advanced towards us. The trench we were in ended abruptly in the middle of a field of roots and we retired to it, hoping that a counter attack or artillery fire might save us. We only had one serviceable rifle, and that eventually became gummed with grit, but the Germans lay down about 10 yards in front of our trench and started to bomb us, to which we could make no reply. I do not know how long this lasted, but eventually some of the Germans crawled up till they could enfilade us at short range, so we surrendered.

The survivors of the attacking companies fell back on 1 Company to the north of the church, where battalion HQ had also moved overnight. The battalion's machine guns, which had gone forward with the leading companies the previous day, were dug in at the corner of the orchard, 100 yards north of French Farm, but there was very little firing all day and the trenches were gradually consolidated with the help of companies from the London Scottish and the Camerons. At 9pm they were relieved by the Black Watch and went to billets south of the canal.

Captain Geoffrey Stewart, who went out alone on a reconnaissance, was killed on his way back, as were nine other ranks. Second Lieutenant Edward Archibald Beauchamp and one other rank died of wounds. 129 other ranks were wounded. Four officers were known to be wounded and missing, with fifty-seven other ranks missing, all of whom seem to have been killed or died of wounds.

1st Camerons were also ordered to press forward. At about 9am on the 22nd 'an advance was ordered by someone on the left of our line'. A and B companies proceeded to attack the German trenches in front of them, covered by heavy fire from C and D. They got to within 25 yards of the German line but were shot down 'and then were all wounded, killed or taken prisoner'. A note in the war diary says 'A large number of dead could be seen in front of the German trenches'. They were relieved by the Royal Berkshires in the evening.

Rather than being ordered to advance, 57th Rifles actually found themselves under attack. In the morning some seventy Germans made a determined attack on the left flank, on a section of trench held by the men Subadar Arsla Khan had brought up the day before. He immediately led a counter-charge with the bayonet, but the Germans fled, with rifle fire from the Afridis accounting for at least thirty of them, including two officers. The Germans did manage to get a machine gun into the communication trench only 40 yards from the company of the 142nd Regiment, but fortunately it did little harm. A company of 59th Rifles came up during the morning and was sent to the right of the line next to the canal to allow Major Williams to send back the sick men he'd been forced to keep in the line through lack of reserves. Though not strongly attacked, the men in this section had suffered badly thanks to the condition of the trench, which was over ankle-deep in mud. The battalion was relieved overnight by the South Staffords, but not before the Afridis, on the left, accounted for three men of a German patrol who came too close to their trench.

The firing died down gradually and both sides took stock. The British had had an almighty scare and lost ground, but none of it of any great significance. They still held Givenchy, which the Germans seemed to have given up with remarkably little resistance considering the effort they had put into taking it. The incidents with the mines had seriously scared the troops, and there were constant reports of enemy activity that could be heard underground. 1915 was to see an intensification of mine warfare in Givenchy, as it became probably the most mined section of the line.

Anglo-French cooperation had proved itself once again. The assistance offered by the French Territorials, even if it was not immediately acknowledged by the men on the ground, was appreciated by senior officers. Though only quoted as 'A British General commanding one of the British armies', we can conclude that it must surely have been Willcocks who said:

> I wish especially to draw attention to the fine conduct of the French Territorial Regiment which were detailed as supports for the Indian Corps by the General commanding the French Army on the occasion of the German attack in the neighbourhood of Givenchy on December 20th and 21st, and in the operations which followed in order to re-establish our lines there. Two battalions took an active part both by making a counter-attack and by helping to hold the village of Givenchy. Their conduct was admirable from every point of view and their resistance to the enemy under heavy fire remarkable.

Chapter 2

1915

1915 has been called 'The Loss of Innocence', and it was a hard year. Casualty lists lengthened and hopes of a rapid end to the war ebbed away. The Germans turned their attention away from the Western Front and committed themselves to the destruction of the Russian army in Poland, leaving major operations in France and Belgium more or less in abeyance. This left the field open to the French, the dominant partners among the allies on land, to launch their own offensives to liberate their country, which the British were expected to support. The First Battle of Champagne, fought between December 1914 and March 1915, petered out with a few gains after heavy casualties. The fighting around Givenchy in December 1914 had been part of the British contribution to the early stages. The Battle of Neuve Chapelle (10 to 13 March) was a belated contribution and the first wholly British offensive of the war. In May the Germans attacked at Ypres using poison gas for the first time on a major scale. Though it led to a breakthrough, there were insufficient reserves to exploit it (they were in Poland fighting the Russians), and fierce counterattacks bought time for the British troops around the city to shorten their line and dig in once again. Also in May the French launched the Second Battle of Artois to try and capture Vimy Ridge, leading to the disastrous British supporting attack at Aubers Ridge (11,000 casualties on one day with no ground gained) and the rather more successful Battle of Festubert, which began a fortnight later, lasted eleven days, and gained some important ground. Vimy Ridge was not captured until 1917. In September three offensives were launched, again with limited success: the Second Battle of Champagne, the Third Battle of Artois and the all-British attack, the Battle of Loos.

If nothing else, these battles did prevent the Germans moving too many reinforcements to the Eastern Front where, following a surprise offensive by Von Mackensen's 11th Army, which punched a hole in the Russian line on the Galician front, a general advance began that saw Warsaw captured, the fall of Brest Litovsk and the pushing back of the Russian armies, exhausted and horribly short of ammunition, nearly 250 miles.

Elsewhere, Italy was bribed into entering the war on the side of the allies in May and began a long series of poorly conducted operations against the Austro-Hungarians that did little but pile up casualties over the next three years. A joint Anglo-French fleet tried to force the Dardanelles in March and failed when it sailed into a minefield and lost several ships sunk or damaged. The failure led to the landing of allied troops at Gallipoli on 25 April and the start of a hellish campaign that ended with the withdrawal of the last men in January 1916.

The appalling casualties (they were to get worse) led to worries that not enough men were volunteering to keep the ranks full. The introduction of conscription was being seriously discussed. News had filtered out about munitions shortages, leading to the creation of a Ministry of Munitions under a coalition government, still led by Mr Asquith.

1915 also saw the fiercest fighting over Givenchy until the April 1918 German offensive. At the start of the year it was still recognisable as a village; much of the church was still standing, and the Royal Engineers had constructed a lookout in the remains of the tower. Other houses, though damaged, still provided some cover. Mining operations to counter the German subterranean threat began in January, with two tunnels dug north of the village in response to possible German tunnelling near the White House. This work became increasingly sophisticated in February with the arrival of dedicated tunnellers, and by the end of the year no man's land was a mass of craters caused by underground detonations. A complex network of offensive and defensive tunnels underlay the whole area. British offensive operations at Neuve Chapelle and Festubert to the north and Loos to the south involved subsidiary operations at Givenchy to assist or provide diversions, but it was the Germans who struck first, on 25 January, launching a serious attack to capture the position (known as the First Action of Givenchy).

On 14 January the 3rd Brigade officially took over the Givenchy defences, stretching from a point on the canal about 1,000 yards east of Pont Fixe up the slope and round the east and northern sides of the village, a distance of 2,600 yards. The 2nd Royal Munster Fusiliers held the canal bank and lower

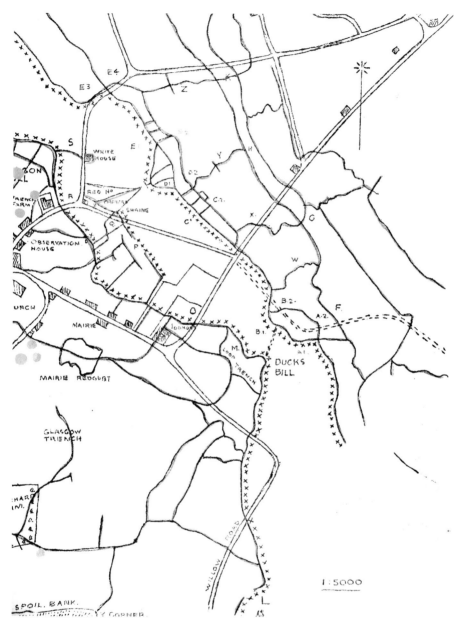

Sketch map of British and German positions in early 1915, showing such landmarks as White House, The Shrine and Duck's Bill.

slope, with the 1st Gloucesters south and east of the village itself, the 2nd Welch east and north-east and, most northerly, the South Wales Borderers. The Royal Welsh Fusiliers were in reserve.

1st Gloucesters had relieved the Camerons in the southern part of the village on 12 January, with three companies always in the front line and one in reserve near Pont Fixe. Companies relieved one another at intervals of 48 hours. Battalion records include statements like 'Snowed all day, conditions getting bad' (18 January); 'a severe thaw set in, condition in trenches very bad, water causing parapet to collapse' (19 January). On the 21st 'A Company relieved B in trenches… Great difficulty experienced in keeping the trench fit to occupy on account of continual collapse of parapet owing to water.' On the right, the condition of the trench was so bad that a dozen saps were driven forward with the intention of linking them up and creating a trench further forward.

On the 13th the 2nd Munsters marched from Bethune during the afternoon and took over some trenches near the canal from the Scots Guards. C and D companies were in the front line, with A Company in reserve at the redoubt and B Company in the distillery. The next few days were quiet, the companies taking their turns in the line, though the condition of the trenches, due to rain and snow, was described as 'deplorable'. 26 Company Royal Engineers sent Captain Lewis and six sappers up to supervise the draining and scooping of water out of them. No sooner had they been drained, however, than fresh rainfall refilled them, and there was a constant battle to keep them even reasonably dry. The troops were harassed by German snipers, who caused some casualties. On the 23rd the commanding officer, temporary lieutenant colonel Major George Julian Ryan, was hit by a sniper as he returned from visiting his men in the trenches and died ten minutes later. Two men of B Company were also killed by snipers and another man was reported as suffering from frostbite.

On 14 January 2nd Battalion the Welsh Regiment relieved the Queen's and part of the Gloucesters in the trenches north-east of Givenchy, occupying 400 yards of trench with the South Wales Borderers on the left and the Gloucesters on the right. The war diarist noted that in the rear of the trenches there were seventy men in a redoubt, and that a total of 390 men were required in and around the village so the rest of the battalion was in billets near Pont Fixe. Their spell in the village was quiet, with few incidents apart from the Germans using a mortar they had brought up into their trench to drop a few bombs on the morning of the 17th. The men were mainly employed in improving the trenches and making bombs. A new scheme for sniping was developed, with a dozen good shots assigned to battalion HQ, who deployed them into buildings around the village to counter German snipers. On the evening of the 17th Second Lieutenant James went out alone to The Shrine, got close up and heard German voices – three German snipers were returning to their trench. He lay still and was undetected and the information he provided caused the battalion rifle grenadiers to fire several bombs into that part of the trench. The next night, the 18th, after a heavy fall of snow in the morning, Private Church crept out to the same spot and reported the trench was now empty.

Further heavy snow, then heavy rain, damaged the trenches and parapets. On the 20th the regimental goat (presumably in the Pont Fixe billets) died of heart failure. Also, presumably at Pont Fixe, the war diary records 'Coy S M Hayes was killed [the word was crossed out and replaced with the word shot] by drunken soldier (Pte Price C Coy)'. CSM Hughie Hayes, 5019, died of wounds next day. Though there seems to be little surviving documentation of the crime, the writer Robert Graves heard the story of the killing when he was attached to the regiment later and wrote that two soldiers had supposedly approached the battalion adjutant saying 'We've come to report, sir, that we are very sorry but we've shot our company sergeant major'. They claimed it was an accident, but when asked if they thought he was a spy, responded 'No sir, we mistook him for our platoon sergeant'. The men were Lance Corporal William Price, 12942, and Private Richard Morgan, 11967, both of C company, the same as their victim. They were arrested immediately and Private Morgan wrote to his wife not long afterwards: 'My mate shot a Sergeant Major and the sergeant that had it in for me swore that I encouraged him to do it and that we are to be held over a general court martiall [sic].' It seems likely that both men felt they had been victimised by their unnamed platoon sergeant and, under the influence of drink, had fired on the wrong man in the dark. Price, who had served in the regiment in the 1890s, had certainly had a few discipline problems previously, having been convicted for being drunk at his post, using insubordinate language and striking his superior officer in 1892, and using insubordinate language in 1899. Price, it seems clear, fired the fatal shot, but Morgan, under military law, was just as guilty unless he could prove that he'd actively tried to discourage the act. Both men were tried by field general court martial at Lillers on 6 February and found guilty. They were shot by firing squad on 15 February and lie in Bethune town cemetery, along with their victim.

On 22 January Private John Alridge went out into no man's land at 9.30pm and recovered some small books from the bodies of some of the dead who lay out there. He also reconnoitred The Shrine and reported the trench there still empty.

The new sniping scheme proved its worth on 23 January. Some German snipers were successfully sniped from French Farm and no German snipers fired for the whole morning. On the 24th German artillery was in action during the night and at about 9am some big shells fell in the Village Trench support. At 3pm four shells fell near the Keep, one of which was close enough to cut the telephone line to brigade. Two men were killed and two wounded during the day.

Also on 14 January the 1st Battalion South Wales Borderers, who had been at Gorre and providing company-sized reliefs to the battalions in the line (the weather had been atrocious and many trenches flooded), were ordered to relieve the Black Watch in the line north-east of Givenchy. A and B companies (total strength 360 men), with 100 men of the Royal Welsh Fusiliers and a machine gun, were in the front line trench, with C and D companies in the support trenches. Though there was heavy firing during the relief (which was completed by 10pm), things quietened down overnight with only some sniping taking place.

During the next couple of days work was carried out improving the defences, thickening parapets and deepening communication trenches. At 4pm on the 16th C and D companies went forward and relieved A and B companies, who went back into billets. On the morning of the 17th Lieutenant James MacNaught-Davis was killed and his body taken back to be buried at Cuinchy. There was a lively exchange of bombs in the right section. On the 18th it rained and there was heavy snow. The trenches began to flood and for the next couple of days, as the bad weather continued, troops were kept busy bailing the trenches and trying to keep them defensible.

The weather improved on the 22nd, with frost in the mornings that helped solidify the ground. The situation was quiet, with both sides working on repairs. On the 24th the trenches were shelled with shrapnel and three men were slightly wounded. The shelling continued all day, with heavy rifle fire overnight.

On the 24th the Germans shelled the lock gates near Pont Fixe; 136 8in howitzer shells fell in the vicinity. One gate was damaged, but there was still no serious leakage of water. There were no casualties but so many shells fell in the canal that the men were able to haul out and cook scores of fish that had been killed.

Early on the 25th a German deserter came in saying that a large-scale attack was imminent. The Kaiser's birthday was to be on the 27th and it was said that he had been inspecting troops in the area recently and that the capture of Givenchy on the 25th was to set the stage for a major breakthrough two days later, as a birthday present for Kaiser Wilhelm. Whether this is true or not, to many men it was known as the Kaiser's Birthday Attack. Another hint at possible trouble came from the CO of the 2nd Welsh, who suggested that the Germans had carried out reliefs during the night, it having been noted that sniper fire was coming from different directions.

A heavy German bombardment began at 7.25am on the 25th, directed at the fire trenches, the village itself and the Pont Fixe bridges and canal ranging back as far as Bethune, Beuvry and Gorre. There was a very violent bombardment of the East, Village and Scottish trenches, French Farm and of the Givenchy village generally – the guns employed were field guns, 15cm and 21cm howitzers. The Germans also began to bomb the nearest British trenches heavily, using trench mortars. Timings for events hereafter become confused, but the brigade war diary seems the most consistent, so times have been adjusted in line with it. At 8.20am a rocket was fired from the German lines, immediately followed by an infantry assault directed against the trenches north and east of the village and against the barricades across the roads. In the first few minutes the Germans attacked near The Orchard and down the road. A good number were killed and some retreated, but some came on and were only halted 50 or so yards from the front line trench. A few managed to take cover in a communication trench, but most were killed. Several gaps were blown in the right of the parapet of the Scottish Trench, manned by the

South Wales Borderers, but Captain Lord de Frayne immediately ordered the parapets on each side of these gaps to be thickly manned. The attack was mainly directed against the salient of the Scottish Trench and French Farm; neither trench was penetrated by the Germans who, although they made several attempts to reach the trenches, were each time repulsed with great loss. Sergeant William Wilcox, 8836, had his machine gun overturned and was buried by shell fire, but succeeded in remounting the gun unaided and keeping it in action until the parapet was demolished by the enemy. The whole of his section was killed or wounded. Acting Corporal Evan J. Williams, 11337, handled his platoon with great courage and coolness after his officer and sergeant were wounded, and by his skilful direction of fire succeeded in keeping the enemy away from vulnerable parts of the line. Both men were awarded the DCM. Captain Hugh Maxwell Broome Salmond was awarded the DSO because, though wounded, he brought up men from the local reserves under heavy fire on two occasions, and remained with his company in action throughout the day.

Also at 8.20am the infantry attack against the left half of the East Trench began, covered by machine-gun fire sweeping the Gloucester Regiment's parapet. Six German companies attacked in the vicinity of French Farm and Village Trench. The Germans climbed over their parapet, but immediately inclined to their right, forced in that direction by the Gloucesters' rifle fire. Having gained the road running at right angles to the trench, the Germans attempted to advance down it but were mowed down in such numbers that the attack broke up; some retired, while others tried to reach the orchard in front of Village Trench. At 9.45 brigade HQ received a message reporting:

> The Orchard was full of Germans... It afterwards appeared evident that this body of the enemy consisted of men who had been driven back from the trenches and were taking cover among the trees while awaiting a favourable opportunity to regain their own trenches or to resume the attack if reinforcements arrived.

More Germans entered the old communication trench, but were prevented from advancing by the throwing of bombs. About 150 yards in, the centre of the Village Trench had been blown in and between 120 and 150 Germans penetrated into the village at this point, capturing the Royal Welch Fusiliers' machine gun and about 150 yards of trench. Second Lieutenant Frederick Joseph Dibdin and one platoon of 2nd Welsh on the right of the Village Trench next to the Gloucester Regiment held their trench the whole time. The officer in command of this portion, Second Lieutenant Albert Richard Peck, who had been with the battalion for less than three weeks, was buried in the trench. The survivors retired, some into the Keep, and others collected by Lieutenant Leycester, who had come up from the right of the trench and took up a position between French Farm and the church. Two platoons of the 1st Black Watch, who had been blown out of their dugouts and cellars by the bombardment, fell back to the rear of the Keep.

In the Gloucesters' section of the trench, captains Harold Richmond and William George of D Company were killed and a battalion machine gun was put out of action, when it and its crew were buried in a shell explosion. A runner reached Second Lieutenant Hodges, who had assumed command, and said that the Germans had broken through on the left. Hodges immediately reinforced his left flank to prevent the Germans getting into that part of the front line. Private Hotchkins, who commanded that section of the trench, had his men line both sides of the trench, facing front and rear, as their predecessors had done at Alexandria in 1801 to earn the regiment the privilege of wearing a regimental badge on the front and back of their headdress. At 9.05am brigade HQ were advised that the Germans had broken through the South Wales Borderers and were advancing on the Keep. By this time, the OC 26th Brigade RFA had made his way to brigade HQ and was able to direct the fire of his batteries onto the German trenches and the parts of no man's land over which the Germans were advancing.

The 2nd Welsh were also driven back in their portion of the Village Trench, and at least sixty of the enemy had already entered the village to the rear. At 9.35 brigade HQ received a report from the Welsh that some of them were holding the crossroads near the church, and that a platoon of the Black Watch was holding near the curé's house. French Farm was also holding out. About forty Germans were reckoned to have got as far as the church, and had begun working their way round the rear of the right flank trenches, around the Keep. The South Wales Borderers received a message that the General's Trench (to the rear of French Farm) had been blown in, and the Scottish Trench damaged in places. Half of B Company was ordered up to Wagon Hill to support C Company, and a platoon of D Company moved up into the main trench. Their war diary makes it clear that there was heavy fighting: '9 am the other half of B Company went up the road to counter-attack the Germans. No 5 platoon and 1 Coy of Black Watch with 1 Coy of Welsh.'

The entire local reserve, based near Pont Fixe and Windy Corner, had, without waiting for orders, moved up to the threatened points. Two platoons of the Black Watch under Captain Green, and one platoon of the Welsh Regiment under Lieutenant James, had arrived at the road to the north of the Keep, where they were joined by the two platoons of the Black Watch under Lieutenant Edwards. Captain Green then moved his company to the south of the Keep, and at the crucial moment two platoons of the Black Watch counterattacked into the village. There was fierce hand-to-hand fighting and Acting Serjeant William Swan took three other men into a

Serjeant William Swan captures five Germans and wins the DCM on 25 January 1915.

house that the enemy had seized and surprised and captured five Germans. He was awarded the DCM.

Lieutenant James also counterattacked the Germans, who were still holding the Church and the northern edge of the village. He moved his party of the Welsh Regiment and two platoons of the Black Watch by both sides of the Church and drove the Germans out of the houses and cleared the village. In the work of clearing the houses there was a considerable amount of close fighting by small detachments, and the party became scattered. On reaching the northern edge of the village, Second Lieutenant James found himself with only fifteen men. Nonetheless, he charged down the communication trench into the Village Trench, which was occupied by about forty Germans, all of whom were killed or taken prisoner. The Royal Welsh Fusiliers' machine gun was recaptured. Lieutenant James was awarded the Military Cross. Corporal William Thomas, 6406, who was with him in the charge, was awarded the DCM. Lieutenant Robert Leycester (2nd Welsh) gathered up his men once they'd been driven out of the Village Trench and quickly established a new line and helped to clear the houses in front of the church. He later led another charge against the Village Line and recaptured part of it, winning the Military Cross in the process.

In the meantime, back in the Gloucesters' front line, Second Lieutenant H.G. de L. Bush, who was on attachment from 3rd Battalion, succeeded in digging out the Vickers gun and its crew and getting them firing again. The Germans were cleared out of the village and B Company of the Gloucesters came up from the local reserve to reinforce the men in the front line. Second Lieutenant Hodges was awarded the Military Cross for holding his position when his senior officers were both killed, as was Second Lieutenant Bush for getting the machine gun back into action. The Germans had their own brave deeds, one of which was very much appreciated by the British. According to a report in the *Birmingham Post* (13 February 1915):

one of our officers had been partially buried by the parapet of a trench, which had been blown in on the top of him. A German officer who saw him, regardless of the fact that he himself was out in the open under a hail of bullets, stopped to dig him out, and gave him brandy from his flask. To the great regret of those of our men who witnessed this deed of gallantry and self-sacrifice, and deeply appreciated it, the German was killed by a stray bullet.

2nd Welsh picked up three more DCMs: Private L. Rogers, 1946, located eight Germans in a house and, after obtaining the assistance of two men from the Highland Light Infantry, captured four of them and wounded the remainder; Company Sergeant Major W. Weeks, 8384, took up reserve supplies of ammunition under very heavy fire and Private G. Church, 8377, under very heavy shellfire, went forward to open communications with the Gloucestershire Regiment.

By 11.15am all the trenches were back in British hands and the Germans had resumed shelling. The parapet was repaired and the trench strongly reoccupied by the Welsh Regiment, Royal Welsh Fusiliers and the Black Watch, one platoon being sent up from the Keep. Shortly after 12.40, thirty-six German prisoners reached battalion HQ. Reports came in over the next half an hour confirming that the Gloucesters and South Wales Borderers were in their own old front lines. The OC 26th (Field) Company, Royal Engineers, was sent forward to consult with the battalion commanders about repairing the trenches and parapets.

During the action the German supports had been prevented from coming out of their trenches to assist their firing line by the fire of the 26th Field Artillery Brigade and the 30th (Howitzer) RFA, which swept the ground along the front of the German trenches, preventing the enemy from bringing up reinforcements or moving across no man's land to assist their comrades.

On the extreme right of the line the Royal Munster Fusiliers had been able to take little part in the action; they were shelled and fired at in their trenches, but no advance was made against their front. Conversely, the advance of the Germans along the south bank of the canal, which had been prefaced by the explosion of a series of mines dug under the British front line, as it progressed beyond the rear of the Canal Trench, rendered it untenable. Considerable execution was done by the machine guns and company in this trench until the Germans reached a point where they could enfilade the trench. The company and machine guns then retired and took up a position about 300 yards in rear of the Canal Trench, facing south along the canal. Though they had played only a small role in the action, Second Lieutenant Colin Herbert Carrigan was awarded the Military Cross for gallantry and resource in handling his machine guns effectively against the advancing enemy. Having been compelled to retire, he extricated his guns under heavy fire and brought them into action again 300 yards to the rear. South of the canal further German attacks in strength had threatened to break the line, but counter-attacks by 1st Cameron Highlanders, 2nd King's Royal Rifle Corps and 1st Black Watch had eventually stabilised the situation. At 6.45pm the Royal Munster Fusiliers were able to reoccupy the Canal Trench.

There were occasional bursts of fire after dark, but by 8pm all battalions reported the situation was quiet. At 8.20pm a Very light, fired from British lines, revealed a large number of Germans in the Orchard, apparently waiting till all fire had ceased to get back to their trenches. A heavy fire was brought to bear on them, and the war diarist recorded: 'it is doubtful whether any got away'.

Casualties had not been light, though considering the ferocity of the fighting they might be considered so. The South Wales Borderers had two officers wounded (Captain Hugh Maxwell Broome Salmond and Second Lieutenant Douglas Guille Nisbet), twenty-one other ranks killed, thirty wounded and eight missing. The Gloucester Regiment had three officers killed (captains Harold Richmond and William George, and Lieutenant William Robert Norman Leslie, who was killed by a shell near Pont Fixe) and one wounded (Captain William P.S. Foord), nine other ranks killed and twenty-seven wounded. The Welsh Regiment had Second Lieutenant Francis Henry Hawkesworth (attached from 3rd Battalion, Border Regiment) killed and lieutenants Peck (who had been dug out alive) and James Alexander Gordon Leask wounded, eighteen other ranks killed and thirty-eight wounded. The Royal Munster Fusiliers had two other ranks killed and seventeen wounded, while the Royal Welsh Fusiliers had Lieutenant Geronwy Robert Griffith (adjutant) and Second Lieutenant John Arthur Hughes wounded (died of wounds next day), ten other ranks killed and twenty-four wounded.

Seventy-two Germans (two of them officers) were taken prisoner, belonging to 56th Regiment and 7th Pioneers. Over 100 German bodies were counted in front of the trenches and thirty-five were discovered in the village. Total German losses, in terms of killed, wounded and prisoners, were estimated at 500.

A Press Association correspondent wrote a dramatic account of the action that appeared in numerous newspapers:

> On Monday morning dense masses of the enemy emerged from their trenches and charged down upon our position. Rifle and machine gun fire was opened upon them from our trenches and from houses in the village. Heavy loss was inflicted upon them. They were repulsed again and again, but each time, reinforced by their supports, they returned to the charge. For nearly three hours the issue hung in the balance. Then the weight of overwhelming numbers began to tell in favour of the enemy. Our fire could no longer stay them. They came right up to our trenches, throwing hand grenades with considerable effect as they came. Then, with a final rush with the bayonet, the trenches were won. Our men retired in good order upon the village and the second line of trenches. The enemy, flushed with their success, pressed forward with the object of capturing Givenchy. The 56th Prussian Infantry and body of the 7th Pioneers actually penetrated the village streets. A furious fusillade was opened upon them from the houses. They broke and fled. It was now one o'clock in the afternoon [all the war diaries suggest the bulk of the fighting was over well before noon] and the British counter-attack began to develop. The units directed to retake the lost trenches, aided by a French force on their right, did it manfully and well, charging often knee deep in water and mud. By nightfall the lost position had been regained.

Next day, 26 January, 2nd Welsh expected another German attack and were surprised when this did not occur. Apart from an occasional artillery shell the next couple of days were quiet, but on 30 January at about 4pm the Germans began bombing the trenches around French Farm from behind the Orchard, killing two men and wounding three. British artillery soon responded and the bombing stopped. After a few more quiet days the 2nd Welsh were relieved by a battalion of the King's (Liverpool) Regiment on 3 February. They had been in Givenchy for twenty days.

On 3 February 1915 (though the war diary says 1914), 6th Infantry Brigade took over the Givenchy sector from 3rd Infantry Brigade 'Without incident'.

Givenchy from the low ground – Red House and French (Stench) Farm on the right, the sunken road (centre) and the crater field left. The site of White House was just behind the trees.

2nd South Staffordshire Regiment took over from the north bank of the canal to a point east of the village and 1,250 yards north of the canal (Sub Section B1). Two companies were in the front line trenches and two companies in reserve north of Pont Fixe. The trenches east and north of Givenchy were taken over by 1st King's Liverpool Regiment, including French Farm (Sub Section B2). They had three companies in the line and one in reserve around the Keep. 1st Battalion King's Royal Rifle Corps took over Sub Section B1, which ran from just outside French Farm to near Le Plantin, where they connected with 5th Brigade. One company was in Scottish Trench, one back in echelon and two in reserve near Windy Corner. 1st Battalion the Berkshire Regiment were in reserve with three companies at Le Preol and one between Pont Fixe and Windy Corner. The war diarist noted:

> The 3rd Brigade that had been attacked the week before and successfully cleared the enemy who had temporarily got into the village, had their tails up and had done a fine bit of counterattacking. The Kings and South Staffs hold the same line we held at Christmas.

The first ten days of occupation were fine and occasionally bright and also reasonably quiet, though German guns were clearly ranging on the church and the front line trenches, raising some concern that there might be another attack. The premature explosion of a bomb caused some casualties among the 1 KLRs on 5 February. South of the canal the 4th (Guards) Brigade launched a successful attack against the Cuinchy brickstacks on the 6th to shorten their front line, which was supported by machine-gun fire against the embankment from two machine guns in trenches along the northern bank. On the 7th a German counterattack at Cuinchy was driven off, but the Givenchy sector remained quiet apart from a little shelling. On the 8th the KRRC successfully sniped a German with a new telescopic sight rifle and on the 9th two wire hawsers were stretched tight across the canal to prevent the Germans floating mines against the lock gates.

Patrols regularly visited the White House and Orchard by night, and KRRC did a good job repairing old trenches and digging two new communications trenches between Windy Corner and Givenchy Road. On 12 February daylight visits were made to White House, the Red House and Orchard Shrine, and posts were established at each. Communication trenches began to be dug towards them and it was discovered that the German main trench formed a salient at the north-west corner of the Orchard. On the 13th it was noted that a good deal of work had been done over the previous few days, improving communications and strengthening defences. Houses had been loopholed and barbed wire erected round them, and work had been completed on a defensive work just south of the ruined Mairie (to be known thereafter as Mairie Keep).

On 14 February the war diary records a visit by Major Norton Griffiths MP, to examine the two mines that were being worked on at the junctions of the B1 and B2 subsections where the Germans were only 80 yards away. Whether these were continuations of work begun by the French in November is unknown. The two mines were close together and the Staffs supplied men to one and the Berkshires to the other. The East Anglian Field Company, Royal Engineers, supervised their construction. Work on them was continuous, with three teams of one NCO and six other ranks each working an eight-hour shift. In addition to the mines exploded under the Gurkhas and the one exploded under the Manchesters at Givenchy in December, there had been a series of explosions under the trenches at Cuinchy, south of the canal, on 25 January, followed by a German advance which had captured two lines of trenches from the Guards Brigade. It was clear that the Germans were mining in an organised fashion along the front and nervous soldiers reported all kinds of unusual sounds, which were taken as a sign of such activity. Counter-mining, in which tunnels were dug out under no man's land so that listening posts could be established, and from which counter-mines (usually referred to as 'camouflets') could be exploded to collapse enemy passages, began on an *ad hoc* basis.

It had rapidly become obvious that a serious solution to the German mining operations must be found, and Major John Norton Griffiths was appointed by the War Office to consult GHQ in France about the number of men and type of organisation that would be required. Norton Griffiths was the kind of slightly eccentric but highly focussed man that thrived in such circumstances. He had been Conservative MP for Wednesbury since 1910, and before that had served as a trooper in the Life Guards for 199 days in 1888 (aged eighteen) before buying himself out for £18. He served in the South African Police during the Matabele Rebellion of 1896, and also in the Boer War, before becoming a mining engineer specialising in tunnelling and the digging of sewers. As an imperialist he had formed, on the outbreak of war, a regiment of volunteer cavalry, which he presented, fully formed, to the War Office. They were christened the 2nd King Edward's Horse, much to the chagrin of the already established unit of the same name.

Even before the first use of German mines, Norton Griffiths had spotted an opportunity for mining, and asked the War Office for permission to start collecting a body of men who were experts in the field with a view to beginning operations in France. In fact, work on the first British mine had already begun near Festubert, where Indian sappers and miners had dug a shallow tunnel some 70 feet long towards the German lines as part of a planned attack. It had to be abandoned when the trench it had started from was flattened by trench mortar fire, but the success of the German mines on 20 December galvanised the War Office and GHQ in France, which issued orders for mining operations to proceed. The mines begun at Givenchy were to be continued, although, as in most places, they were too shallow to be really effective and the Royal Engineers supervising them were massively overstretched.

Norton Griffiths' suggestion was, at first, looked on with a certain amount of suspicion. Experienced soldiers were not sure how well amateur soldiers, however good at digging, could work in battle conditions. However, a series of detonations at Cuinchy on 25 January forced their hand. Orders were sent out to recruit former miners from troops already in France and Norton Griffiths was belatedly sent to France to investigate the possibilities. He reported to the engineer in chief in France on 13 February 1915 and next day travelled to Bethune, then on to Givenchy to inspect the trenches and the mine that had been started at the Orchard. After a close inspection Norton Griffiths and his experts declared that the ground was suitable for his proposed method of digging, known as 'clay kicking', which involved men lying at an angle to the tunnel face on a wooden frame and 'kicking' the clay ahead of them out with a special type of spade. Awkward as it sounds, an experienced man could dig forward at quite a pace. Norton Griffiths had employed the method digging sewers and could obtain volunteers from his workforce. After further discussions about the exact form his organisation would take, he hurried back to London. He wired ahead, and on his arrival found twenty volunteers waiting for him. Two failed the medical, but the rest were rushed to the Royal Engineers' depot at Chatham to be given uniforms, kit and rifles. On Thursday 17 February 1915 the men were digging sewers in Manchester; by Monday 21 February they were working underground at Givenchy. They were joined by twelve former miners drawn from regular army units and the whole group was posted to 11th Field Company Royal Engineers under Captain Preedy, who had just started work in the village. It was the start of an underground campaign that made Givenchy a major focus of the subterranean war and shaped the nature of the ground, which became horribly scarred with craters.

In the absence of any other means of dealing with German mines in the short term, drastic remedies had to be tried. On 20 February 2nd Battalion South Staffordshire Regiment was in the front line and it was thought the Germans might be tunnelling from their trench opposite. Volunteers were taken up from A and C companies under Second Lieutenant Leonard Terry Despicht, a Territorial Force officer with the 4th Bedfordshires, who was on attachment, and Second Lieutenant Jack St Claire Gainey Harris, who had been a sergeant in the Buffs before being commissioned into the South Staffs the previous November. Despicht led a party of fifteen South Staffs men and five men of 9th Highland Light Infantry, and Harris took twenty men from the South Staffs. After a 20-minute bombardment both storming parties dashed from their lines at 5.20pm and set off for the German trench. Despitch was almost buried by a German shell and after being extricated he was immediately shot, but he behaved 'extraordinarily well', crawling to the enemy's parapet, cheering on the men and continuing to direct operations. Second Lieutenant Charles Humphrey Humphreys, 1st East Anglian Field Company Royal Engineers, led a party of Royal Engineers who were to check for mine shafts and demolish them if necessary. He was wounded by shrapnel in the first few yards of the advance, but continued with his men into the German trench and assisted in driving them out with bombs. Harris was wounded close to the German parapet and toppled into the trench. No evidence of mining activity was found, so the storming parties demolished what they could and withdrew. Harris was too badly wounded to be moved and told the men who went to help him to leave him behind, which they reluctantly did. Attempts to discover his fate via the Red Cross appear to have come to nothing, though Corporal Hunt of the battalion did tell his parents something of the action and their son's gallant conduct. His body was, unusually, recovered at some point, as he is buried at Cabaret Rouge British Cemetery. Other casualties were one man killed and four wounded. Humphreys and Despicht were both awarded the Military Cross.

During February 6th Brigade was joined by a fresh Territorial Force battalion, 1/5th King's Liverpools. A young officer of that battalion wrote a brief letter that was published in the *Liverpool Daily Post* on 11 March 1915:

Today I had my first task of being under fire. The rifle fire (lots of stray bullets whizzed near me) does not worry one, but the shrapnel is not at all pleasant. I was in a communication trench today when we were shelled, and two of them came within forty yards. One does not, however, feel as funky as you would imagine. There is one place where the stray unaimed rifle fire shoots past all the time. This is called Windy Corner.

Whether one is hit or not seems to absolutely be a matter of luck, unless one puts one's head up in the trenches, because otherwise the only things are stray bullets (the result of unaimed rifle fire) and shrapnel. The shrapnel you can hear coming through the air and if the whizzing sound suddenly stops immediately over your head, you fall down absolutely flat on the ground; that is one's safest place.

A funny thing happened today. I was standing with our senior subaltern, and happened to say I would like to see a shell drop in the canal, by which I was standing. A minute after, we heard the whizz of a shrapnel shell, and not a hundred yards from us a shrapnel shell dropped bang into the canal.

March 1915 saw Norton Griffiths' first (albeit brief) report on mining operations at Givenchy, which followed an equally brief report on workings at Cuinchy, where it was stressed that operations were purely defensive, but that good progress was being made. It read:

Work at Givenchy, protective work of a similar nature, has been stopped on the morning of my visit, the 12th of March 1915, on account of a general attack. Much energy and good progress has been made by Captain Preedy and the officers under his command.

As a much later report on mining operations throughout the whole war says:

1915 maybe looked upon as the experimental period during which the British miner made such progress… in the branches of this science that he was enabled finally to vanquish his enemy and reduce him to absolute impotence.

The operation referred to by Norton Griffiths was part of 'the first large scale organised attack undertaken by the British Army during the war' (The Long Long Trail website) at Neuve Chapelle, some three and a half miles north-east of Givenchy. General Rawlinson's IV Corps and General Willcock's Indian Corps were to assault the village and, it was hoped, break through onto the Aubers Ridge behind and beyond that the plain of Douai.

THE KING'S (LIVERPOOL REGIMENT).
The Bayonet Attack at Givenchy.

The attack of the 1st Battalion, the King's Liverpools, 10 March 1915, from a contemporary postcard.

To provide a diversion, 2nd Division's 6th Brigade was ordered to stage an attack at Givenchy, which it was hoped would prevent German troops moving north to reinforce the defence.

On the morning of 10 March the artillery opened fire at 7.30, and for ten minutes poured shells on to the 700 yards of trenches to be assaulted. At 7.40 the first bombardment ceased; at 7.50 the second bombardment began and continued until 8.05 when it became 'intense'. Five minutes later the range was lengthened to the second-line trenches and to both flanks.

As the guns lengthened their range (at 8.10) the three assaulting parties simultaneously rushed from their trenches towards the enemy's position. The South Staffords, forming the right column, had only 80 yards to cover, but no sooner had the troops left their trenches than they came under severe crossfire from machine guns, and men began to fall. A handful reached the hostile trenches, only to find that the wire entanglements had hardly been touched and there were no wide gaps through which a rapid attack could be made. Second Lieutenant Hewat and fifteen men attacked one of the machine guns – but according to the war diary, 'none of them returned'. 2nd Lt Wood, with twelve men, did succeed in getting into a German trench, but he and his party were bombed out again. He then formed another party and returned to the attack. Second Lieutenant Richardson next led a party of C Company forward, but a permanent lodgement could not be made, and eventually the attack ceased.

The centre column fared no better. Here the 1st King's assaulted in two columns, B Company (under Lieutenant Percy Snatt) moving forward over the 300 yards which divided them from the enemy's trenches under a perfect hail of bullets, and A Company (under 33-year-old Captain Frank Feneran) attacking a trench some 100 yards from their own trenches. The foremost man of B Company did not get farther than 150 yards, and by this time all the officers of the company had been killed or wounded. A Company got as far as the barbed wire, but the men of the leading section were all shot down and some actually fell across the wire. With the exception of Lieutenant Miller all the officers of this company were also were killed or wounded. Lieutenant Miller was slightly wounded.

The left column (1st King's Royal Rifles), which had also been divided up into two assaulting parties – right and left – was likewise unsuccessful. The right party:

advanced at the double over the intervening ground and soon came under a heavy fire from rifle and machine gun, losing many men; those remaining continued their advance, but when within thirty yards of the wire entanglement were almost annihilated by cross machine gun fire. Others threw themselves on the ground, as they could not get through the entanglement, which had nowhere been breached and which consisted of trestles and high wire entanglements. Only a very small number succeeded in reaching the wire, and none got into the enemy's trenches.

The left party was slightly more successful.

This party succeeded in crawling through [the wire] and established themselves in the enemy's front trench by blocking two places and a communication trench, and maintained possession, notwithstanding heavy fire and bomb throwing, till nearly 2pm, by which time only one sergeant and two men were unwounded, and they succeeded in crawling back to our line... There were 2 officers [Captain Grazebrook and Second Lieutenant Ward], 2 sergeants and 10 men in the party, and both officers were wounded early in the morning. Two supporting parties which were sent to assist the party were practically wiped out by fire – rifle and machine gun.

Second Lieutenant Lt H.H. Slater did good work saving two machine guns, which had been carried forward as far as the entanglements but could get no further. Private David Hyles was awarded the DCM for staying with a wounded officer until 2pm, when he was ordered to return to the British line.

Captain Charles Grazebrook was reported missing and great efforts were made to discover his fate. Survivors were closely questioned by the Red Cross and their reports are still in Grazebrook's file in The National Archives. Corporal Jeyes reported that he'd been left in the German trench, adding 'There were only a few who got up to those trenches at all and he was one and Lt Ward another. We got terribly cut up at the time, I was there in the charge.' Private J.W. Durrant (described as 'not very intelligent'), told how he'd been informed by Lance Corporal Hyles (or Eyles) that '(Hyles) had shot the German who knocked over Capt Grazebrook, and he bandaged Mr Grazebrook. There were only a few men in the trench and they then had to retire. Mr Grazebrook was unconscious when left'. Sergeant Cook reported:

He was wounded at Givenchy. He was in the attack on the German trenches about the same time as Neuve Chapelle. The wire had been cut. Capt Grazebrook, another officer, Sergeant Crooks and about 10 men got over the wire and reached the second line of German trenches. Capt Grazebrook was wounded I believe and carried into a German dug out by Crooks. The attack failed and they remained in the German lines. Crooks and three or four men made their way back to us the same night… We went out at dark to bring back the wounded lying between our lines and the Germans, but the Germans threw vitriol bombs at us. I do not know whether Capt Grazebrook was alive when Crooks left him.

Lance Corporal Curtis, who was hospitalised himself, said 'I was repairing parapets, and I saw the ground swept by German searchlights, and they were firing on the wounded with machine guns if they saw them moving. I don't think anyone could have lived who was left out.' Though a couple of men reported that Grazebrook had been killed earlier in the attack, it seems likely he died in the German trench. The search continued for months, despite the War Office having received confirmation of his death in the form of a letter from Lieutenant Ward, who had been wounded and captured, dated 1 April 1915. A copy was placed in the file of Second Lieutenant Alec Harron, who

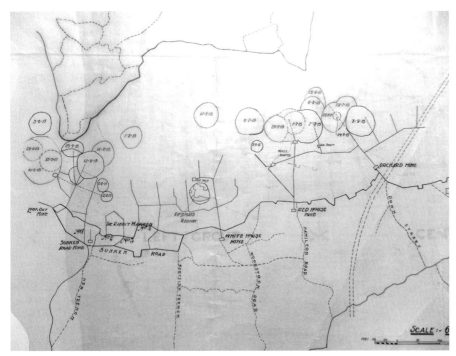

Map of the mine shafts, tunnels and craters, left sector, 1915, showing the main shafts and passages under no man's land.

was also killed, and in Grazebrook's file, but no one seems to have informed his family. Grazebrook's body was never recovered and he is commemorated on the Le Touret memorial to the missing.

In the afternoon a further attack was planned by the South Staffords, but it rapidly became clear that, despite a second barrage, the wire was not sufficiently cut. The artillery found it difficult ranging over the village and the lie of the ground made observation difficult. The attack was cancelled. Total casualties in the operation amounted to twenty-six officers and 582 other ranks killed, wounded and missing. Despite heavy casualties and the fact that no ground was gained, the attack was judged to have drawn off German troops from Neuve Chapelle at a critical time in the fighting there.

German mining operations continued to pose a threat to the troops in the front line, as this extract from *The Irish Guards in the Great War* shows:

On the night of the 22nd April the sector was held by the 15th County of London, the Irish Guards and the Post Office Rifles, the remainder of the Guards Brigade being in rest. To the normal strain of a watching front line in foul weather was added a fresh burden. A few days before, the enemy had blown a mine in an orchard about fifty yards short of our trenches. It did no damage at the time, but the R.E. Mining Officer, Lieutenant Barclay, in counter-mining towards the crater it had made, saw, through the wall of his mine, Germans engaged in turning the crater into an advanced-post. Trench-mortars were fired at once to discourage them. Then came reports of underground workings heard in other directions and, notably, close to the parapet of a trench near the White House. This was on the evening of the 24th. Hardly had orders been given to clear the White House trench, when the ground at the junction of Lieutenant Barclay's counter-mine and the German crater went up and the Lieutenant was killed. At the same time an explosion occurred near the White House. Two privates of the Irish Guards (2845 J. Mansfield and 3975 M. Brine) volunteered to enter our mine and see what had happened. They recovered Lieutenant Barclay's body at great risk from the asphyxiating gases, and both men were recommended for the D.C.M. The explosion near the White House was, after inspection, put down as the work of a heavy shell, not a mine;

but listening parties reported more underground noises and another section of trench was evacuated accordingly. To prevent the Germans consolidating themselves further in the crater which connected with Lieutenant Barclay's mine, our 4.5 howitzers bombarded it on the 25th, and it was decided to blow our end of the mine as soon as possible to prevent the enemy working up it. This was difficult, for the galleries were full of foul gas – whether leaking from some adjacent coal-pit or laid on by the enemy was uncertain. The R.E. officer who went down to lay the charges was asphyxiated and several of his men were injured.

Not till the 29th of April were the difficulties overcome; by which time the enemy had driven a fresh shaft into it. After the explosion, a field battery (17th R.F.A.) and the 47th Howitzer Battery fired a salvo at the German trenches. 'There was a little rifle-fire, but soon all was quiet.' Mining, like aerial and bombing work, was still in its infancy, and the information supplied by the Intelligence was said to be belated and inadequate.

On one point, at least, this account is incorrect. At the Orchard mine an enemy gallery had been detected; conversations in German could be clearly heard. An immediate attack was planned and a barricade was built at the face. Behind it, at a distance of four feet, a second barricade was being constructed. A charge was to be detonated between the two, in the hope of destroying the German tunnel, but before the work could be completed the Germans fired a charge of their own. Lieutenant Allen Barclay and Lance Corporal Bishop, who were working on the second barricade, were killed instantly. Two Guardsmen bravely entered the mine and spent over an hour underground, but were unable to recover the bodies. Barclay's file records that he was buried below 17 feet of earth at a spot 60 yards north of The Shrine. There is even a map that shows the spot.

It was decided to resume the attack next morning and Lieutenant Torin, who had a lot of experience handling high explosives, was given the job, assisted by Lieutenant Boardall and Second Lieutenant Martin. At about noon, Private Bishop went down the mine, but was overcome by residual gas from the German explosion and had to be brought out by Sapper Smith and Private Hesson.

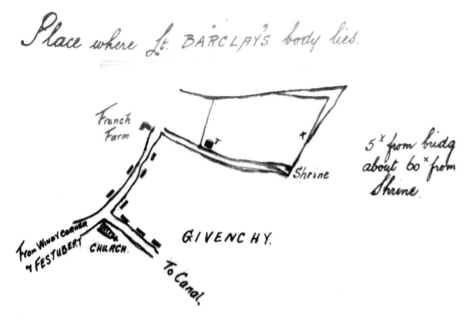

Contemporary sketch map showing where Lieutenant Barclay was buried in April 1915.

At 2pm the shift in the mine changed, but the new shift was not warned that there might be gas, probably because it was thought to be only present in small amounts and the air pump would keep it at bay. Unfortunately a bombardment of the German line opposite meant the forward saps were evacuated (according to the usual practice at the time) and the pump fan was stopped. Once the bombardment stopped Lieutenant Torin entered the mine to check what was happening, accompanied by Martin, Boardall and Sergeant Ford. There was no obvious sign of gas, but the party was soon overwhelmed, with the exception of Lieutenant Boardall who managed to scramble to the entrance and raise the alarm. Corporal Hutchinson went down and managed to rescue Second Lieutenant Martin before he, too, was overcome.

Lieutenant Whidbone of the Coldstream Guards organised a rescue party and eventually all the men were brought out. Torin was dead before he reached the surface. He is buried in the Guards Cemetery at Windy Corner, less than a mile from where he died.

A letter describing the rescue, written by one of the participants, Lance Corporal Leonard Arthur Dinwiddy, No.3 Company, 3rd Battalion, Coldstream Guards, appeared in *The Western Times* on 14 June 1915:

My latest adventure happened on a Sunday. The Engineers were driving a sap towards the German trench for the purpose of laying a mine. As they got near the German lines the enemy probably heard them, or got to know of our purpose, so they started sapping from their trench. They got to within striking distance of one of our sap heads, and proceeded to lay a mine for the purpose of destroying it. Our fellows did likewise, but the enemy were first, and blew in the head of our sap, killing an officer and a corporal of the R.E.'s. This happened on the Friday.

On the Sunday evening it was decided to blow up our sap to prevent the Germans coming forward. An officer, a sergeant, and then another officer went down for the purpose of getting the place ready. A little while afterwards one of the men at the top of the mine rushed out to say they were gassed, and shouted for men to get them out.

Being near, I was soon down, followed by my pal. I assisted a corporal of the R.E.'s with the first officer, and then my pal and myself went off up the mine for the other fellow (a sergeant). We got him down to the mine head or shaft, and handed him over to the corporal of the R.E.'s and one of our fellows on the ladder. We were told not to go up again, but there was the leading officer still up there, so we crawled back. The officer had a candle in his hand, and another burning beside him.

I said to 'Fairy' (my mate), 'He's dead. I believe.' Anyhow we turned him over and commenced to draw him back. 'Fairy' says to me, 'How are you feeling, lad?' 'Faint.' I said. 'So am I,' he answered. 'Never mind; keep going.' I told him. It seemed a long way, and then the corporal of the R.E.'s crawled up and said, 'Stick to it, lads.' I went off soon afterwards. I remembered no more till I came round again. Then I remember being carried down the trench and put on a wheeled stretcher. I was under the impression that I was dreaming or had suddenly gone mad. I was talking volubly all the way. They took me to the dressing station, where they gave me some medicine and took off my clothes. Wrapped in some blankets, I was put in a motor ambulance and taken to the hospital, where they put me to bed and gave me some oxygen to drive out the gas. A lot of the doctors asked me what was the effect of the gas. My mate was brought in as well. We were all serene in a couple of days, and went off to join our company in the trenches. Then they told me I was lucky to be alive, as having been furthest away from the shaft I was the last to be taken out. The last officer proved to be dead. 'Fairy' was wounded the same day we came back from hospital. A big German shell wrecked a piece of trench which my section held, killing the section commander and wounding three others, including 'Fairy.' Owing to the fact that my kit had been sent away to the stores I was with the sergeant-major, otherwise I should probably have been in trouble again, as I should have been with 'Fairy' and the others. However, Providence is kind to some.

Tell Ted he may now put 'Corporal' on my correspondence. I think we want a lot more men out here, as the Germans are using every means to put us 'out of mess.' We are now supplied with a pad, and a supply of solution is kept in the trenches to dip them in to counteract the gas. The Germans use every means in their power to kill us. Yesterday they blew up a mine which made the earth rock like a cradle. They use big bombs as well, which make a terrific noise when they burst, but we manage to dodge 'em as a rule. We have some fine ones now, and have a bomb duel occasionally.

Lance Corporal Dinwiddy was awarded the DCM for his actions. The citation for the award was published in *The London Gazette* on 3 June 1915:

For conspicuous gallantry on 25th and 26th April, 1915, at Givenchy, in assisting to rescue Officers and men from a deep mine full of poison gas. The courage and devotion to duty displayed were very pronounced, the risk of death through asphyxiation being very great.

On 27 April Private Hall of 1st Black Watch volunteered to enter the tunnel and twice went down into the gallery attached to a rope. On a third trip he succeeded in placing a charge and this was successfully detonated on the 29th.

Though the infantry of the regular army was organised on a county basis, some counties were considered too small to support a permanent county regiment. Hertfordshire was one, and it was represented instead by a battalion of the part-time Territorial Force. On 4 August 1914 they became full-time soldiers and were sent to Bury St Edmunds to guard against a German invasion. Though originally intended for home defence only, casualties to the BEF meant there was a desperate shortage of men who could be sent quickly to France, and the battalion volunteered for service overseas. They went to France on 6 November 1914 and came under the command of the 4th (Guards) Brigade in 2nd Division. A couple of companies had seen a few days in Givenchy at the end of January and early February serving alongside the Welsh Regiment, but on the evening of the 11th the battalion took over from the King's Royal Rifles, expecting at any moment a German counterattack to follow up their defeat of the 6th Brigade attack the day before. Two companies were in the firing line, with two in billets at Windy Corner, where Lieutenant Colonel Croft made his HQ in an undamaged building, writing 'We were very comfortable there, with many of the conveniences of civilisation close to hand.'

On their first day in the trenches the battalion had eight men slightly wounded, all shot in the head as the parapets were weak. They set about repairing and improving them. There was vigorous patrolling into no man's land by night, with Sergeant Barber of 1 Company reconnoitring the ground to the northwest and Sergeant Gregory of 4 Company bringing back important information on the enemy trenches to their front. On the night of the 13th Company Serjeant Major Raven went out alone to the German wire, where he found a corporal of the King's Royal Rifles lying wounded, having spent three days playing dead close to the enemy parapet. Picking the man up, Raven brought him back across heavily cratered ground in the pitch dark and under German fire. Though the war diary names him as Corporal Bearer (or Beaver), there seems to have been some confusion over the spelling. The next night two KRR men crawled back and were picked up by the Hertfordshire's listening patrols and guided back to the British line. Both men had played dead so successfully that the Germans had stripped them of food, valuables and equipment, but left them lying. On the 15th Colonel Croft was with Major Page observing the Germans through a periscope from Scottish Trench when a sniper hit the top of the device and a glass splinter gashed Page badly in the head.

Company Serjeant Major George Raven was awarded the Conspicuous Gallantry Medal on 3 June 1916 for his action. The citation read:

For Conspicuous gallantry at Givenchy on the night of 13th – 14th March 1915, in rescuing a corporal of the King's Royal Rifle Corps, who was lying wounded close to the enemy's breastwork, whilst exposed to heavy fire. Company Serjeant Major Raven has been noted on other occasions for his courageous ability.

The 2nd Battalion of the Grenadier Guards took over part of the village on 12 March and their history offers a description of the place as it was then.

The trenches, which were comparatively new, were shallow and the parapet not bullet proof. The village was a complete ruin, the farms were burnt, and the remains of wagons and farm implements were scattered on each side of the road. This part of the country had been taken and retaken several times, and many hundreds of British, Indian, French and German troops were buried here. The roads were full of shell-holes, bricks, tiles, cart-wheels and debris of every description.

The entrance to Givenchy, 1915.

The historian also noted that it was an area where the habits of the Germans opposite were known, so that it was usually possible to estimate how long shelling was likely to last.

Serving with the Grenadiers was Lieutenant Oliver Lyttleton (later Lord Chandos), who also left a pen portrait of his time there, which was fortunately quiet:

On 12th March we moved to another sector around Givenchy and our trenches were at the summit of a little knob or hill and ran through an orchard which had been much fought over. In this context the word orchard means a pock-marked pattern of shell holes, one touching the other, some tangled undergrowth, and the stumps of the tortured trees standing out like Calvarys against the sky.

I used to do a good deal of patrolling. I personally feel braver in the dark, and in those days could see better in the dark than most. I rather enjoyed these patrols, and the thwack of an occasional bullet was not alarming if you were crawling on your stomach. It was exciting, but the horrible part of it was that we had to thread our way through decomposed corpses that still littered the ground. The cats of the village had gone wild: they looked fat and sleek and did some patrolling of their own.

Trenches dug by the Brigade were narrow and deep, carefully sited for fields of fire, and with very thick traverses. We could only sit still, endure the shelling and keep a look out. I spent my time counting the shells that fell within sight of me – they were a mixture of 77mm and 5.9c – but I lost count at 1,000. Only one shell hit the parapet full, and that beyond the traverse next to me. It killed one man and we had to dig out three others; two men were nearly suffocated but untouched, the third was horribly wounded. I learnt that highly trained and disciplined troops cannot be shelled out of well dug trenches, and that the casualties from shellfire are very small compared with those inflicted by machine-guns in the open.

Though April 1915 was, supposedly, a quiet period in the Givenchy section of the line, 1st Herts still saw plenty of small-scale fighting and took a number of casualties.

A battery of four trench mortars and eight rifle grenade stands were now placed in my charge and were manned by our bombing section, which had recently been trained to fire these old fashioned weapons. Two or three times a day we fired our battery, and soon got going with our new playthings. At the second shot we got a direct hit on the German parapet at Duck's Bill and one also right in the enemy's trench, which blew a German into the air.

On the canal bank we also set to work and on the 12th we got two direct hits there, and after this we kept up our policy of 'frightfulness' and strict orders were given that for every enemy bomb fired, we were to fire two.

On April 15th we returned to B, and in the early hours of the 16th the enemy opened a fierce bombardment on our lines and to the south of the canal. Fortunately the bombardment was far more noisy than harmful, and did us very little damage, though a working party under Mr Borwick [Lieutenant Robert Geoffrey Borwick] had a narrow escape, four of them, including the officer, being knocked over by the concussion of a 'Fizz Bang' shell which fell right in the trench but fortunately wounded no one. The 'Fizz Bang', otherwise known as the 'Pip Squeak', is a very amazing gun, as it is brought up quite close to our lines and no one can hear it coming, the bang and explosion being almost simultaneous. On the 17th I made the personal acquaintance with this creature as I was passing down the communication trench known as Finchley Road. The man immediately behind me was hit in the arm and back, and the man in front of me had his coat torn by a bullet, so I considered myself lucky. On the 18th we had a bad day from shell fire. One shell fell in the middle of the right trench and wounded five men, one, Pte Jones, of the machine gun, mortally and Sergeant Arnold was very seriously wounded. Another high explosive shell over Pont Fixe mortally wounded Pte Croft of the Regimental Police.

Private Jones, aged twenty-two and from Berkhamsted, was taken away down the trench to the Casualty Clearing Station but died en route and was buried in Bethune Town Cemetery.

On the 20th 1st Hertfords took over the B3 section of trenches and discovered that the Coldstream Guards had done an excellent job of improving the communications trenches in the three weeks since their last tour there. They announced their arrival with a salvo of mortar bombs and by firing on an enemy working party that night. The Germans retaliated by shelling the Scottish Trench with 5in guns and Captain Longmore (Phillip Elton Longmore, an Oxford graduate), Lieutenant Borwick and ten men of 3 Company were buried alive and had to be dug out and sent to hospital suffering from shock.

> Mr Borwick's experience was a rather trying one, as he was in his dug out when a shell burst upon it and the exit was completely closed. He was, however, dug out like the others and complained chiefly of the fumes of the shell with which he had been closeted.

On the night of the 24th/25th the Germans exploded a mine close to the Irish Guards on the left of 1st Herts, burying a British mining officer (Second Lieutenant Barclay Allen, Royal Engineers) who was visiting part of the British mine complex at the time, but causing no other casualties. 'Mine bursting lately has become very frequent' wrote the regimental chronicler. 'They cause a kind of earthquake shock and make the houses rock. All the German mines lately have burst short, and we have exploded two or three in order to destroy other enemy mines.' That same evening they received news of the first use of poison gas by the Germans at Ypres and, as a most basic precaution, 'we all provided ourselves with tins and pails of water, with muzzles and rags for our noses and mouths, but we had yet to be convinced that both our lines can be asphyxiated.'

May 1915

May 1915 saw two important British offensives north of Givenchy, the Battle of Aubers Ridge and the Battle of Festubert, which were, to all intents and purposes, two stages of the same British operation. This, in turn, was part of a major Allied offensive designed to threaten the German communications (essentially railway) centre at Lille. While the British attacked in the north and captured the Aubers Ridge, the French 10th Army was to attack and seize Vimy Ridge to the south and then both armies were to advance on Lille itself.

The Aubers Ridge battle can be dealt with summarily. It was an enormous (for the period) and costly failure. Following Neuve Chapelle the Germans had reinforced the defences in the area and the two-pronged attack, at the north end of the ridge between Fromelles and Aubers and south of Neuve Chapelle, failed utterly. A short and intensive barrage did not dent the defences and although the troops advanced into no man's land only a very few got across. Those that did get into the German trenches were speedily killed or taken prisoner. No objectives were captured and there were over 11,000 casualties in the 24 hours following the start of the attack at 5.40am on 9 May. The British attack was halted, though the French had achieved some considerable success and were keen to press on.

The Battle of Festubert, which commenced on 15 May, was a further attempt to take the southern end of Aubers Ridge. Again it was to be a two-pronged assault, in the north around Neuve Chapelle and in the south out of Festubert eastwards. This time 2nd Division, which had barely been involved in the earlier battle, was moved north of Festubert and did much of the fighting; its place in the line was taken by the recently arrived 47th (2nd London Division). It was specifically mentioned in the plan that Givenchy was to be the right end of the line, but a fixed point; there was to be no advance from the village, at least in the first stages.

The battle began with a two-day bombardment that started on 13 May and the first infantry assaults were launched at 11.30am on the 15th. Troops of 2nd Division made good progress, but there were heavy casualties and virtually no advance further north. Further progress was made on the 16th and on the 17th the Germans began secretly abandoning some of their trenches and falling back 1,200 yards to another trench line. On the same day, because of the successes in the southern area, General Haig switched the direction of the attack away from the Aubers Ridge (due east) towards the town of La Bassée and the canal (south-east), with the first objectives being the capture of Violaines and Chapelle St Roch. These were close to Givenchy, which took on a new importance in the fighting. Over the next week the Canadians chipped away, often in appalling weather, at the German trenches north of Givenchy, and on 25 May 47th (2nd London) Division was ordered to assault the German line immediately north of Givenchy with the objective of Chapelle St Roch. The job was given to 142nd Brigade, consisting of 21st, 22nd, 23rd and 24th battalions.

At 5.30pm on 25 May, the 24th Battalion of the London Regiment (the Queen's) took over the Scottish Trench section of Givenchy in anticipation of an attack to start at 6.30pm. Though a message reached them that the 23rd Londons on their left were unlikely to be able to start at 6.30pm, it was decided to attack on schedule so as not to interfere with the artillery barrage. In the event 23rd Londons got themselves organised and at the scheduled time both units advanced, with A Company in the vanguard advancing on a platoon frontage. They quickly gained the German trench, though they lost three of five officers. One was 22-year-old Lieutenant Eric J. Garner-Smith, an accountant who had enlisted and been commissioned in September 1914. According to his commanding officer he was 'hit several times, once in the head, and his death must have been practically instantaneous. As he was falling, he shouted pointing to the enemy's trench: "That's the way".' His body was never recovered.

B Company and part of C Company crossed no man's land to join the men of A Company and they were joined shortly afterwards by the rest of C Company and, in error, the whole of D Company. Just before 7pm the commanding officer of B Company reported that they were unable to advance beyond the initial objective, but were digging in. Between 6.45pm and 9pm there were German counterattacks along the whole section being held and urgent requests for bombs (hand grenades) were received. During this period the battalion lost five officers killed and three wounded and 'a severe bomb fight' took place. Reinforcements were rushed up including a company of 22nd Battalion, a platoon of 20th Company and the bombers from the Divisional Cyclist Company. Lieutenant Denys Max Thomson Morland of 3rd London Field Company, Royal Engineers Territorial Force, who was accompanying the advance, discovered the entrance to a German mine and entered it alone, capturing eighteen German soldiers who'd taken refuge

Lieutenant Denys Max Thomson Morland, Royal Engineers, captures the German mine on 25 May 1915 and wins the Military Cross.

there. For this, and for displaying great energy and bravery throughout the night, he was awarded the Military Cross, as was Second Lieutenant Carlton Griffith Davies, who led the bombers and threw bombs up a trench himself, keeping the enemy's bombers at bay at a critical moment. According to his citation he also 'took a leading part in capturing 20 Germans in a mine'. Private John Allen was awarded the DCM for going back into no man's land on several occasions to take water and first aid to the wounded lying out under fire. Conscious of the shortage in the captured trench, he also removed ammunition from both dead and injured and took it back with him.

Captain Donald Whiteley Figg led repeated rushes with bombs into a German work, and when most of the bombers were killed continued the attack single-handed, enabling the dangerous flank he commanded to hold its own against constant assaults by the German bombers and riflemen.

By 1am attempts to press forward on the left were abandoned because the Germans, being on higher ground, were able to out-bomb the British troops. As the war diary says:

Private John Allen giving aid to wounded men in no man's land, 25 May 1915.

Captain Donald Figg wins the Military Cross for single-handedly continuing to bomb German positions on 25 May 1915 when the rest of his bombing party were incapacitated.

henceforward it was rather a question of holding the trench gained in face of heavy bomb attacks and sniping from the right flank.

The most noticeable feature of the operations was the retention of the captured trench by a few exhausted and in many cases wounded men after it had been subjected to a very heavy enfilade rifle fire. I should like to draw attention to the good work done by the bombers both of this battalion and of the Divisional Cyclist Company. The battalion bombers went into action 75 strong and came out numbering 17.

Among the bombers was Lance Corporal Leonard James Keyworth, a Lincoln man who'd been rejected by the Lincolnshire Regiment and had enlisted with the 24th Londons instead, on 16 September 1914. One of the surviving seventeen, he was awarded the Victoria Cross for his part in the action, the citation reading:

For most conspicuous bravery at Givenchy on the night of 25–26th May, 1915. After the assault on the German position by the 24th Battalion, London Regt, efforts were made by that Unit to follow up their success

Lance Corporal Leonard James Keyworth wins his VC for standing, fully exposed, on the German parapet, throwing bombs.

by a bomb attack, during the progress of which 58 men out of a total 75 became casualties. During this very fierce encounter Lance-Cpl Keyworth stood fully exposed for 2 hours on the top of the enemy's parapet, and threw about 150 bombs amongst the Germans, who were only a few yards away.

Keyworth wrote later to his sister and his letter appeared in the press:

We were told to mount the trenches and straight away commence our attack on the German trenches, which were about 250 yards away. The attack was made without any artillery covering fire. Our lads went at it with go and determination and were very soon successful. I was with the bombing party and came through without a scratch. I went along a ridge on my stomach and threw bombs into the German trench, my distance being about fifteen yards. Men were shot down by my side. I continued and came out safe.

He described the action in another newspaper article on 17 July:

I had plenty of bombs; I was fed with them by various men from behind. I didn't think of the slaughter that was going on. There was no shelter. There was just a tiny parapet made of sandbags. I got over that, and on I went throwing bomb after bomb – I suppose for about two hours. I did not realise that I was fully exposed, but I was conscious that I was being continually sniped at and that, in some miraculous way, the bullets passed me and struck down other poor fellows. A bit of shell did brush my ear; I was blinded with dirt; and a shot hit the metal case of a little mirror I carried in my pocket. When I was throwing bombs the few fellows left about kept on shouting for me to lie down. Now and then an effort would be made to bring sandbags up to serve as a protection; every man who tried to do it was either killed or wounded. There seemed little or no escape for anybody except me. To get the VC is fine, but every man who took part in that charge was as brave.

Overnight the shelling and machine-gun fire continued to enfilade the trenches and, as casualties mounted, the Germans continued their

Private Keyworth wearing his
Victoria Cross.

counterattacks. Captain Figg, when his line was enfiladed by rifle and very
heavy shellfire, continued to lead his men to hold their ground and shore
up his flank until relieved. He too was awarded a Military Cross, part of his
citation reading 'For seventeen hours his conduct was a brilliant example to
the hard pressed men around him, and more than anyone in the battalion he
contributed to the successful retention of the position won'.

In the course of the fighting the battalion lost five officers killed and three
wounded along with fifty-two other ranks killed, 252 wounded and ninety-
six missing. The commanding officer specifically praised the work of the
battalion stretcher-bearers, who worked all night under heavy fire to bring
the wounded to safety.

Despite their initial problems the 23rd Londons attacked at 6.30pm
and two platoons of D Company under Lieutenant Wood and Company

Sergeant Major Hammond 'went over the parapet as one man' and at a cost of fourteen casualties successfully secured the portion of enemy trench at J7. Despite congestion in the British trench, the rest of the battalion was able to go forward by double platoons and by 8am all were in the German line. Congestion in the communication trench slowed down the feeding of extra support troops, but this was overcome by sending the men across the open ground between New Cut and Scottish Trench. Telephone lines were laid by the initial platoons as they advanced so the commanding officer of the battalion was in touch with his men within three minutes of their capturing the first German line. At about 8.45am it became clear that the captured trench was being enfiladed by rifle and machine-gun fire from the left and, though attempts were made to suppress this by the battalion machine guns firing from Upper Cut, the firing continued. Then the shelling began in earnest and the telephone wires were cut and could not be repaired. Throughout the night casualties mounted, especially as the shelling from across the canal enfiladed the trench with shrapnel and high explosives at an angle of about 5 degrees from the rear. The battalion was relieved next day, at 3pm, by the 20th Battalion, London Regiment and marched to billets at Le Quesnoy. Total casualties were 499, including three officers killed and ten wounded.

Following the failure to break through at Givenchy, the Battle of Festubert was called off, although the French offensive around Arras went on for some weeks. The initial successes of 142nd Brigade had also been their undoing. The advance took them within range of German heavy guns south of the canal, which began quartering the ground with shells. It was afterwards suggested that the Germans had intercepted British trench telephones (quite feasible) and knew the ground to be attacked, so had pre-registered their guns on their own trenches. Whatever the case, as the divisional history says:

they then encountered a fierce and deadly enfilading fire from the German guns, and particularly from a heavy battery posted near Auchy-lès-la-Bassée, far to the south and out of reach of the guns of our Division… Supports were brought up, including the 20th Battalion, which was then in divisional reserve, and desperate efforts were made to extend our gains, but tremendous losses were suffered by the men crowded in the captured trenches. Nothing could be done to keep down this enfilading fire, and by the following morning much of the captured trenches had been knocked to bits and had to be abandoned, but a considerable part of their front line was retained and taken into our own trench system.

The sophisticated system of fire control and the retention of some artillery to be directed by corps at exactly this kind of threat had not yet been developed and the attackers suffered accordingly.

On 31 May the 6th Gordon Highlanders (part of 20th Brigade, 7th Division) 'took over the trenches at Gavenchy' (sic). On the night 3/4 June, at 9.42pm, the engineers exploded a mine under the German salient at I4 and C and D companies, preceded by bayonet men and bombing parties, advanced around the resulting crater and into the German trenches. C Company pushed on down the German trench for 50 yards beyond I2 and built a barricade across the trench. D Company, on the left, advanced to I3 and joined up with C Company across the angle. There was little opposition and fifty dazed prisoners were taken and a machine gun captured. With the assistance of 55th Field Company Royal Engineers the position was wired and consolidated and two of the battalion machine guns brought forward and dug in.

At dawn the Germans launched a vigorous counterattack, using trench mortars and grenades, to which the Gordons could make little reply as their small stock of bombs was soon exhausted and the Germans did not expose themselves to rifle fire. They were compelled to withdraw towards I4 and eventually, at about 3.30pm, to evacuate the trenches, leaving behind the captured machine gun. They had lost one officer killed (Lieutenant Frank Farquharson) and five wounded, twenty-seven other ranks killed and 104 wounded and five other ranks missing. The battalion was withdrawn to billets on the night of the 4th.

June 1915 was stiflingly hot, with sudden thunderstorms that flooded the trenches and billets. On 10 June the 8th Royal Scots relieved 2nd Queen's and part of the 16th Canadian Battalion in the trenches north-east of Givenchy village. That night a trench raid of twenty men of A Company led

Private William Angus tending the wounded Lieutenant Martin under fire in no man's land.

by Captain F.W. Watson with fifteen bombers led by Lieutenant J. Martin was carried out against a crater held by the Germans. The result of the raid was inconclusive, so next night the same attack was carried out again, but this time the Germans were waiting. While the attack was in progress the Germans exploded a mine halfway between the lines and the attack was abandoned. On their return to their trench the troops discovered that Lieutenant Martin was missing.

Early next morning Lieutenant Martin was spotted lying close to the German parapet and observed to move slightly. An immediate rescue was discussed and an initial plan to wait until dusk before launching a raid in force was quashed as, it being another very hot day, it was thought unlikely Martin would survive that long. Lance Corporal William Angus, 8th Highland Light Infantry (attached to 8th Royal Scots), volunteered to go out. His decision was undoubtedly influenced by the fact that Lieutenant Martin was from the same battalion, which had been broken up to provide reinforcements to other Scottish Territorial units. Under cover of rifle and machine-gun fire Angus managed to reach his lieutenant unobserved and succeeded in rousing him. Lieutenant Martin, supported by Angus, then set off for the British line, but by now the Germans were alerted and began a throwing a large number of bombs. The two men got back, but Angus was severely wounded in the process. He was immediately recommended for the Victoria Cross, which was gazetted on 2 July 1915. It read:

Lance Corporal William Angus, The Highland Light Infantry; 12th June 1915.
For most conspicuous gallantry and devotion to duty at Givenchy, on 12th June 1915, in voluntarily leaving his trench under very heavy fire and rescuing an officer who was lying within a few yards of the enemy position. Lance Corporal Angus had no chance of escaping the enemy's fire when undertaking this very gallant action, and in effecting the rescue he sustained about forty wounds from bombs, some of them being very serious.

The burnt remnants of Angus' service record show that he received bomb wounds in an arm, his right leg, thigh and foot, the left side of his body and in his left eye, which later had to be removed. Various eyewitness accounts appeared in the Scottish press. A long and vivid one (here much reduced) appeared in the *Dumfries and Galloway Standard* of 7 July 1915. Having searched all night for Lieutenant Martin his men saw him at dawn, half buried close to the German parapet. His feeble movements and groans attracted German attention 'for the ugly neck of a periscope, with its ghoulish eye, reached over the trench and leered at the poor wounded soldier below… Hell itself can produce nothing to match the dreadfulness of that horrid periscope.' After explaining how, despite the danger to Lieutenant Martin, a British bullet eventually smashed the periscope, the writer went on:

> In agony, poor Martin appealed to the enemy for a drink of water and what do you think those unspeakable cowards did? They threw at him an unlighted bomb. Can brutal inhumanity go further? …they left him there in the cruel glare of a cloudless June sky – a bait to lure another Scottish soldier to his death.

The men volunteered as one to rush the position at dusk but they were spared this by 'one of the most brilliant acts of courage the world has ever yet seen'.

The soldier went on to describe the position:

> The Germans were on a bare, dry knoll about 70 yards from us… It was obvious that for more than half the distance between the trenches every square inch of ground was commanded by their rifles; there was no shelter whatever from their fire or their view. In front of our lines for thirty yards or so there grew the self-sown corn of last year's harvest, rank with weeds, and affording good cover.

Despite a warning from a visiting Canadian officer that 'you are going to certain death' a soldier (whom the writer names as Atkins, adding 'you will hear this hero's real name soon if you have not heard it already'):

> leapt over our parapet on his forlorn hope. Clinging to the ground, and using every precaution that training and skill have given to the soldier,

he crawled forward on his task… at last he reached the German parapet and still the enemy waited (hoping, perhaps, for yet another victim). He touched the Lieutenant's arm, whispered in his ear, raised him up a little, and placed a flask of brandy between his teeth. Together they sat up and waited for a matter of two or three seconds to gather strength for the ordeal before them. At this moment the Germans lobbed a bomb just over the parapet with a grim explosion, raising a storm of dust. Now or never it must be. Hand in hand the wounded officer and his man rise to their feet, the strong man guiding the weak as best he can.

It was here, the writer says, the Germans made their big mistake – instead of relying on their snipers, they threw more bombs and the dust and smoke hid the two men from both sides. Eventually:

Out into our view there stagger two poor wounded individuals, stumbling, running, falling, crawling. Down they go, then up again, on and on. The German rifles shoot wildly; still on they go, and our line of fire is clear. Our rifles now, one blast from the machine gun and it is all over; they are safely in our lines, and once again a stout heart and a cool head have enabled a brave good man to achieve what seemed impossible.

William Angus, aged twenty-five, had been a professional footballer playing for Wishaw Thistle, Celtic and Carluke Milton Rovers before he volunteered for the army following a recruiting rally at Carluke. When Angus, by then a sergeant, married Miss Mary Nugent at a ceremony at Carluke's Roman Catholic Chapel on 12 January 1917, one of the guests was Lieutenant Martin, the man whose life he had saved at Givenchy eighteen months earlier. Both men survived the war and remained in contact until Martin's death in 1956, after which his family continued the tradition of sending a telegram on 12 June each year saying 'Congratulations on the 12th'. Angus died in 1959, two days after the anniversary. The final telegram was delivered to him in hospital.

Private Angus carrying back Lieutenant Martin and winning the Victoria Cross, 12 June 1915.

The Second Action of Givenchy, 12–16 June

At the end of May 1st Canadian Division, which had already suffered heavy casualties at the 2nd Battle of Ypres in April and during the Battle of Festubert (15–25 May), took over the Givenchy sector from the canal to the Orchard. As the Canadian official history notes:

> The narrow divisional sector – the 4th Corps' frontage was a little over two and a half miles – required only one brigade in the front line, and units in reserve found relaxation in the pleasant Béthune countryside beside the banks of the canal.

The Canadian front extended from the canal, up the gentle slope and round the eastern end of the village (now mostly ruined, though some houses still stood as shells) to the vicinity of the Orchard. North of them were 7th Division and north of them again were 51st Highland Division. Having moved in from the low-lying Festubert sector, the Canadians were delighted to find themselves on higher ground where proper trenches could be dug and communications and support trenches were available. No man's land varied from 500 yards wide on the right down to 75 yards east of the village where a semi-circular sandbagged parapet, known as the Duck's Bill, protruded towards the enemy's line. Opposing them were the 14th Division with 134th (Saxon) Infantry Regiment holding the line around Givenchy.

On 2 June 1915 General Sir Edwin Alderson, commanding the First Canadian Division, visited the village. His attention was drawn, when passing what remained of the church, to a small statue fixed to one of the remaining walls. It represented St Joseph holding a lily and, apart from the loss of Joseph's lower right arm, was in excellent condition. Despite his rank, and regulations about looting, he quietly unfixed it and carried it back

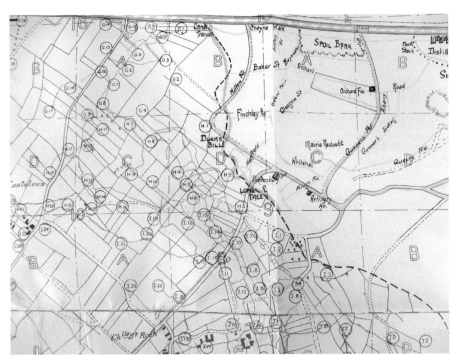

German positions around Givenchy in 1916 by letter and number. North is at the bottom of the map.

with him. Three days later he wrote a note which he secured to the back, and which remains there to this day. It reads:

Picked up outside the Givenchy-les-la Bassée Church in France on the 2nd June 1915. This Church is entirely destroyed by German shells and is still shelled daily. Only a small portion of one of the end walls is left standing and on this wall is a Crucifix, practically untouched. Our trenches run all round the Church, and what is called 'The Keep' (a fortified house) is just north of it.

Alderson kept the statue with him throughout the war and when he died in India in 1927 it passed to his widow, who died in 1950 aged ninety-six. Everything then passed to Alderson's nephew, Paul Griffith, who wrote to the village curé, Abbé Haverland, and arranged to have the statue returned, asking that the congregation remember his aunt and uncle in their prayers.

Lieutenant General Sir Edwin Alderson, commander of 1st Canadian Division at Givenchy, who rescued the statue from the wreckage of the church.

The wooden statue of St Joseph
returned to its rightful place in the
modern church.

The second church was destroyed during World War Two, and the statue
was finally remounted on the wall of the third church when it was completed
in 1960. It remains there, near the altar, with Alderson's original note on the
back: a precious relic of the original church.

The higher ground east of Givenchy, stretching across to Violaines and
the Aubers Ridge, dominated the ground to the south. When Joffre asked
for British assistance with an attack he was planning in Artois, specifically
an attack south of the La Bassée canal near Haisnes to take place in June,
it was decided that clearing the higher ground was a prior necessity. The
original attack was planned for 11 June, but postponed when the French
were forced to delay their proposed attack until the 16th. 7th Division were
to attack from Givenchy itself and to the north towards Rue d'Ouvert, with

Early summer, 1915. The last few ruins, looking east from Givenchy church.

1st Canadian Division attacking along the north bank of the canal and 51st (Highland) Division attacking Rue d'Ouvert from the north.

Givenchy 1st Canadians VC action

The Canadians had learned the lessons they had been so hard taught at Festubert only a month earlier and organised their artillery carefully. They made sure that they expended enough ammunition to ensure that the enemy wire facing them was properly cut. Brigadier General H.E. Burstall (commander of the Canadian Divisional Artillery) insisted that the opinion of the infantry commanders be consulted and fired more than the allowed number of shrapnel shells to ensure it happened. As a result, one of the serious obstacles to the attack, at least on the Canadian front, was dealt with in a satisfactory manner.

In order to deal with the German front line machine guns, three 18-pound guns were dragged, in secret, close to the British trenches; two only 75

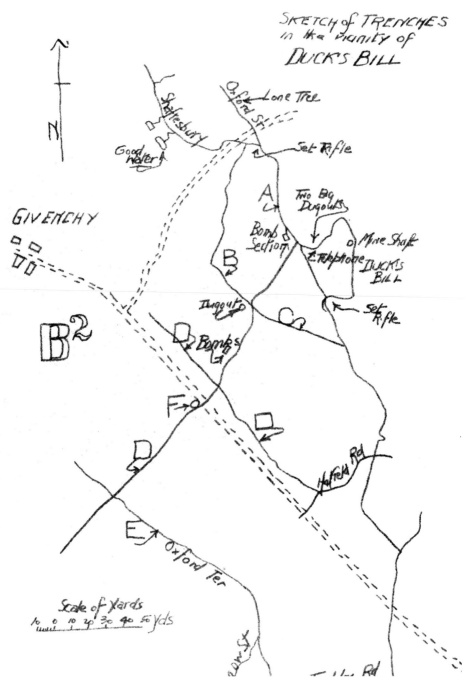

Givenchy – sketch map of Duck's Bill, 1915.

yards from the German positions near the Duck's Bill and one in a ruined farmhouse some 300 yards from the enemy's H3 position.

An assembly trench was dug in secrecy and by mid-afternoon on the 15th the 1st Canadian Infantry Battalion, which was to make the assault, was in position. Though the wire cutting had been excellent, the Germans had very quickly worked out from it where the assaults were likely to take place and arranged for their own guns to drop a heavy barrage on the assembly trench and the village, causing many casualties. Nevertheless, when Zero Hour came at 6pm, the leading company (No.4) was ordered to advance, without check, supported by 3 Company, with 2 and 1 companies in support as a local reserve.

At 5.58pm 176 Tunnelling Company (which had only taken over the sector thirteen days before and worked furiously to drive the tunnel forward) detonated 3,000 pounds of ammonal some 32 feet short of the German defences, though it was hoped the size of the charge would compensate.

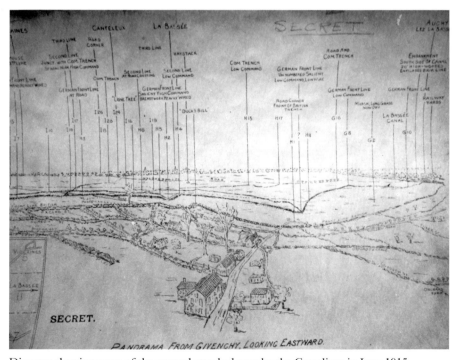

Diorama showing some of the ground attacked over by the Canadians in June 1915.

Another tunnel slightly further south had to be abandoned because of the level of the water table. The detonation caused a crater 75 feet in diameter and 15 feet deep, wrecking a good portion of the German line and a German shaft being dug near H2.

The leading company dashed forward through the dust cloud caused by the mine explosion, followed immediately by the support company with two machine guns. The barrage had cut the wire effectively and the two 18-pounders had demolished large parts of the German parapet. The mine explosion appeared to have cleared parts of the trench and killed many of the defenders. Bomb-throwing parties advanced behind and on either flank, but the right flank party lost an officer killed and eight men injured in the mine explosion and the reserve bomb depot on the right was buried. The mine detonation seems to have set off the grenades in the depot on the left. At H2 the German front line was quickly captured to a point south of the

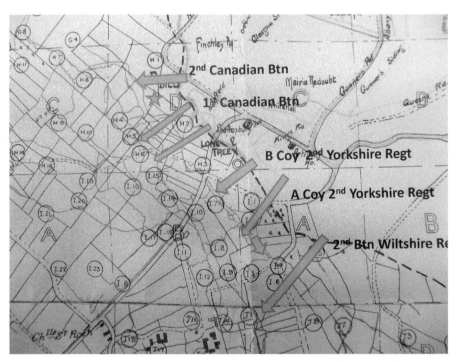

The Second Action of Givenchy, 15 June 1915. The star marks the point where the mine was exploded near Duck's Bill.

mine crater, but on the left the advance was checked by machine-gun fire at the junction between the Canadians and the Yorkshire battalion on their left. H3 itself seemed to be strongly held, with a number of machine guns which the other Canadian 18-pounder had been unable to engage for fear of hitting their own troops, and heavy fire cut down the advancing Yorkshiremen and made an advance impossible.

Having gained the German front line, 4 Company advanced without stopping up the communication trench and across open ground towards the German second line between H6 and I13 and to the north of I13, while 3 Company came up in support and began consolidating the front line. The machine guns in H3, however, having stopped the advance on their immediate front, were now turned upon 4 Company as it advanced, causing heavy casualties. The bombing parties, meanwhile, cleared the trenches to the right, probably as far as H5.

At 7pm the last of the local reserve, 1 Company, was sent forward, and at 7.15pm the Germans began counterattacking from the south around H5 and also from I14 on the left using rifles and hand grenades and supported by the machine guns in I13, which enfiladed part of the left flank and could fire obliquely across no man's land to the rear. The two machine guns brought up by 3 Company were placed on the left flank south of H3 to support attempts to capture it. Captain Frederick William Campbell (whose 47th birthday it was) took charge of one of 1st Battalion's Colt machine guns, which had lost its tripod, and, supporting it on the back of Private Howard Vincent, fired over a thousand rounds at virtually point blank range to hold off the German counterattack. He was eventually hit in the thigh and forced to abandon the gun. Crawling down the trench he was found by stretcher-bearers who got him back to safety. Though he received prompt first aid and was quickly evacuated to a Base Hospital at Boulogne, he died there four days later.

As the German counterattack developed, there was violent hand-to-hand fighting and bomb throwing, but the loss of the reserve bomb dumps now became critical and the supply of grenades dried up. Casualties mounted, the advanced position eventually became untenable and men fell back on the captured German front line. Communication across no man's land was difficult because of the machine-gun fire from H3, and a number of messengers were killed before a sergeant from 4 Company finally got across

Captain Frederick William Campbell winning the VC on his 47th birthday, 15 June 1915, firing his machine gun in no man's land. The artist clearly didn't know about Private Vincent's part supporting the gun.

at 8.15pm with a request for help. At just after 9am, Acting Major George Smith, the senior officer left in the German trench, was forced to order a withdrawal. With what men he could gather he dashed across no man's land under heavy fire and was killed just as he reached the British line. In the meantime a company of 3rd Canadians was ordered to advance to support 1st Canadians and to take forward additional grenades (at 7.30pm), but the trenches were crowded with dead and wounded troops and their advance was delayed so that they actually cleared the British parapet at about the same time as Major Smith decided to bring his men his men back. A party of men under Major Osbourne actually reached the German front line in the face of heavy rifle and machine-gun fire, and both rifle grenades and bombs thrown by hand, but they too were forced back, Major Osbourne being wounded.

Total losses to the 1st Canadians were ten officers killed, five wounded and two missing, fifty-eight other ranks killed, 215 wounded and fifty-eight missing. Among the wounded was the commanding officer, Lieutenant Colonel Henry Campbell Becher, who succumbed to his injuries shortly after and is buried at Beuvry Communal Cemetery.

Captain Frederick William Campbell, 1st Canadian Infantry Battalion, was buried in Boulogne Military Cemetery. On 23 August 1915 he was awarded a posthumous Victoria Cross, the citation reading:

> For most conspicuous bravery on 15th June, 1915, during the action at Givenchy.
>
> Lieutenant Campbell took two machine-guns over the parapet, arrived at the German first line with one gun, and maintained his position there, under very heavy rifle, machine-gun, and bomb fire, notwithstanding the fact that almost the whole of his detachment had then been killed or wounded.
>
> When our supply of bombs had become exhausted, this Officer advanced his gun still further to an exposed position, and, by firing about 1,000 rounds, succeeded in holding back the enemy's counter-attack.
>
> This very gallant Officer was subsequently wounded, and has since died.

Private Howard Vincent was awarded the DCM, which was gazetted on 6 September 1915. The citation read:

> For conspicuous bravery and devotion to duty on 15th June 1915 at Givenchy. In a position where a machine-gun tripod could not be used Private Vincent held the gun on his back under a heavy fire while an officer fired over 1,000 rounds. Afterwards he dragged the heated gun through a fire swept zone and saved it from capture.

South of the 1st Battalion, on the slope down to the canal, the 2nd Canadian Battalion, with two reinforcing platoons from the 3rd Battalion, had seized the mine crater but could get no further forward. A company of the 3rd

Battalion was sent forward to assist them shortly before 9pm, but was unable to advance beyond their front line because of enemy fire which was sweeping the parapet with bullets and shrapnel. When it was realised that 1st Battalion had already been forced to fall back, the crater position had to be evacuated too. The 2nd Battalion had suffered 366 casualties including twenty officers.

On the Canadians' left, two battalions of 21st Brigade, 7th Division, stood ready to go forward. Their war diary for the 15th reported:

> Brigade Headquarters moved to Windy Corner and all final preparations for the assault were completed. The day was warm and bright and a slow bombardment of the enemy's trenches went on all day. Parties of the Bedfordshire Regt. were sent to repair all communication trenches where they had been blown in. During the day Sunken Road and Oxford Street were cleared of our infantry to facilitate bombardment of enemy trenches by our guns.

At around 12.30 the Germans began a fairly heavy bombardment of the front line, causing some casualties among the troops. During the afternoon a company of Cameron Highlanders took over the defended points around the village, allowing the Yorkshires to move forward into the trenches alongside the Wiltshires and, by 4.30pm, both battalions were in position. On the brigade's right, immediately north of the Canadians, the 2nd Battalion, Yorkshire Regiment (the 'Green Howards'), who had suffered heavy casualties at Neuve Chapelle in March, had taken over the section of trenches east of Givenchy on 14 June, in preparation for their part in the assault scheduled to take place the next day. Battalion HQ and billets were at Windy Corner, A and B companies manned the firing trench and C Company was in Givenchy Keep and Mairie Redoubt, with reserves back near battalion HQ.

At about 3pm on the 15th A and B companies lined the fire parapet ready for the assault, each with a front of about 200 yards, and C and D companies supported them from the communications trenches. Battalion HQ moved up to the support trench behind the front line. The machine-gun section was with A and B company ready to move forward. Whether the movements had been spotted or not is unclear, but the Germans bombarded the village

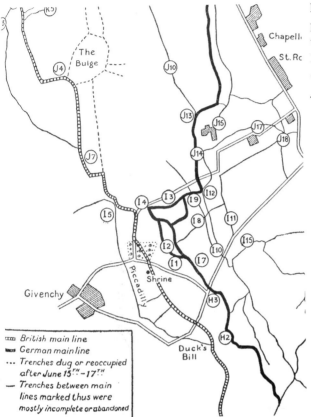

Details of the German positions in the area where the Green Howards and 2nd Wiltshires got badly cut up in the attack of 15 June 1915.

heavily and, even though the trenches were described as good, the battalion suffered a number of casualties, especially D company.

After what was described as a 'heavy artillery barrage', the two companies climbed out over the parapet and started to advance in two lines. They were met by 'a tremendous rifle and machine gun fire' and by particularly accurate shrapnel. B Company came under very heavy shellfire even as they clambered up and suffered heavy losses. A Company got clear of the parapet, but almost immediately came under very heavy machine-gun and rifle fire. Both companies advanced across no man's land under an intense hail of bullets. B Company, despite advancing in good order, was unable to make much progress and could not get to close quarters with the enemy. Cambridge undergraduate Lieutenant Malcolm Hewley Graham, who had given up his medical studies to enlist at the start of the war, was shot through the neck as he led his platoon forward. The men who had managed to get furthest forward were attacked with bombs as soon as they got within range. Of the five officers and 180 men who advanced, only one officer and thirty-one men made it back.

At 6.40pm the commanding officer of the Yorkshires received a verbal message that A Company was in the German trench, but this was not verified at the time. The brigade war diarist thought it possible that some men got into the trench and into the crater. A Company had, in fact, managed to get some men over the German parapet despite heavy losses, shooting down a number of Germans as they bolted from the trench. Their second line suffered heavy casualties as they advanced, but a small section of men under 2nd Lieutenant Arthur Belcher not only got into the first German trench, but also managed to penetrate almost as far as their second line. Second Lieutenant Lloyd-Jones, leading two sections of bombers, pushed down Sunken Road and reached the edge of the crater, but all the men, with the exception of Lloyd-Jones himself, were killed or wounded. Helped by two wounded men, he managed to hold off a counterattack by a company of Germans by throwing bombs until three sections of the battalion came up to support him. Lacking support, the company was unable to press the attack and withdrew to the first line, where it held out for three hours before being compelled to withdraw as it got dark. A Company lost all five officers and about 130 men of the 170 who went forward.

Captain William H.G. Raley was known to have died, though his body was never recovered. Captain Guy Lister Nevile, aged twenty-nine, was initially reported missing, although it was later accepted that he had been killed. Lieutenant Graham, killed leading his platoon, was brought back and buried beside Givenchy Church. Unfortunately any grave marker was lost in subsequent fighting and he is commemorated on the Le Touret memorial, as is Lieutenant Gerald Hadow, who survived the attack unscathed but was killed by a shell on his way back to report to headquarters. Second lieutenants John Oscar Pritchard-Barrett and Allan Pyman were also killed.

On the Yorkshires' left were 2nd Wiltshires, and at 6pm the battalion attacked the line I12, J14–J13. On quitting their trenches, the leading companies (C and D) were subjected to heavy frontal and enfilade fire, the latter from I4–I9. As the advance progressed it was enfiladed by machine-gun fire from both flanks, on the right from the foot of the small rise between I12 and I3, and on the left from machine guns concealed in the grass somewhere west of J13. B Company followed in support of C and D and managed to occupy part of the German trench between J9 and I5.

A Company was in reserve in Scottish Trench, having been kept in reserve intact, with orders to make a reconnaissance towards Violaines after the position had been captured – a grossly optimistic mission given what actually occurred. The advancing line of troops reached a point about 50 yards west of the German trench at J14, by which time there was only one officer left unwounded in the two leading companies. At 7.05pm half of A Company went forward to endeavour to push on the attack, which had been held up. This half company, with half of D Company, then advanced, and was subjected to enfilade fire from the crater. The men could not advance beyond the disused old German trench.

By 9pm these men had occupied the old German trench, with C and D companies in front of them, and the trench J7–I5. They were in touch with the Grenadier Guards on the left of J7. Groups from C and D companies were returning to the old German trench from the front.

Orders were now received to attack the German line at 9.15pm, in conjunction with 2nd Bedfords (who began moving up at 7.30pm to dig communication trenches, and were assembled in Scottish Trench and New Cut trench to await developments) and the Yorkshires. The time was subsequently altered to 10pm. In order to form up for the attack, the companies which were holding the old German trench and being enfiladed from the right were ordered back to Scottish Trench, with orders to form up behind it to clear the field of fire of the company holding J7–I5. The order to attack was subsequently cancelled as far as the regiment was concerned, and instructions were received to hand over the trenches to the Bedford Regiment and return to Windy Corner, which was accomplished around midnight.

Casualties had been heavy and mostly incurred by C and D companies. C Company lost 100 men of the 180 who had gone forward, and had no officers left. D Company had one officer left uninjured.

Captain Edric Hugh Barnstey Richardson (C Company) was killed before he had gone more than fifteen yards from the British trench. Second Lieutenant John Halsted Cortis (D Company), who had joined the battalion less than a fortnight earlier, and who had volunteered to take the place of a sick brother officer, was killed 80 yards from the German trenches. Second Lieutenant James George Gee Janasz (D Company), who was attached to the battalion from 3rd Dorsets, was killed 200 yards from the German lines. Second Lieutenant Gerald Morton Stamford (C Company) was also killed. None of their bodies were recovered. Seven other officers were wounded.

Total casualties among the other ranks were twenty-five killed, 127 wounded and forty-eight missing, though the war diarist noted that 'the majority of the 48 missing most (likely) were killed in front of the German trench.' A note later in the diary added 'During the action of 15th 16th, the Germans used incendiary bullets, and also sniped the wounded in front of their trenches'.

16 June

Despite the abject failure on the 15th, 7th Division Headquarters insisted on the attack being renewed, though they conceded that the battalions that had suffered so much on the first day should not take part. Instead, 3rd Canadian Infantry Battalion were to go in over the slope south of the Duck's Bill down to the canal, 2nd Battalion of The Royal Scots Fusiliers were to attack over the ground where the Yorkshires had failed and 2nd Bedfords were to attack north of the crater. No.10 Trench Mortar Battery was in support on the right and No.3 Trench Mortar Battery opposite the crater, with the machine guns of 20 and 21 Brigades also supporting the attack. The Royal Scots Fusiliers' four machine guns were brought up to the front line so they could fire directly at the German parapet opposite.

A thin barrage that had lasted until 4pm intensified for the last three quarters of an hour, prompting a heavy German counter-bombardment, which hit the trenches hard, particularly around the Orchard. The Germans seemed to know exactly what the plan was (possibly through tapping the field telephones), and two minutes before the attack was due they opened heavy rifle and machine-gun fire along the top of the British parapets. At

4.45pm A and B companies of the RSF tried to get over their parapet and advance. Many men were shot down making the attempt (or even in the trench itself), and by the time the first wave reached their own wire they had suffered 50 per cent casualties.

Thirty-five-year-old Second Lieutenant Alfred Eliot Somers Robinson, a long-time soldier who had enlisted in 1894 and been commissioned in April 1915, led his platoon with great gallantry and actually reached the German wire before he was shot. Twenty-eight-year-old Lieutenant John Laxon Leslie Sweet also got close to the wire before he was killed, but very few of their men got that far.

The company of the Bedfords had a little more success: advancing by platoon they managed to get to the crater, but came under very heavy rifle and machine-gun fire as they crossed the raised lip. A spirited fight then took place in the crater itself, with the Germans throwing hand grenades at close quarters and the Bedfords throwing them back. Corporal Robert Milne distinguished himself by throwing back every bomb that landed near him until he was wounded. By now the company had lost two officers killed, the commanding officer, Lieutenant Powell, had been wounded twice, and the company sergeant major once, along with about half the men dead or wounded. There was no sign of the Royal Scots Fusiliers and casualties were mounting, so Powell ordered his men to fall back. Twenty-one-year-old Second Lieutenant Robert Bowness Gibson, who had been in France less than a month, took charge. He managed the withdrawal with great skill and got his men out in perfect order. This ended the attack in this sector.

1/4th Cameron Highlanders, with the second attack about to commence, had moved up to support the Royal Scots Fusiliers. Their war diarist recorded:

The orders to the Camerons were to occupy trenches as the Fusiliers went forward and support them as required. The ground was being heavily shelled and the battalion had over 30 casualties from shell fire on the way up. The Scots Fusiliers were unable to make progress but over half the battalion was out in front of the trenches. B Coy occupied half of the fire trench which was empty. C & D remained in the support trenches.

At 5.30pm, the commanding officer of the Royal Scots Fusiliers, Acting Lieutenant Colonel J.W.H. Pollard, acting on his own initiative, decided that to press on with the attack would involve 'a totally useless sacrifice' and cancelled it. As the survivors of the RSF began to come in over the parapet after dusk the Germans continued shelling the trenches and the village, causing further casualties.

The situation was the same on the Canadian part of the battlefield. The official history recorded:

> The new assault was made on all three divisional fronts at 4.45pm on the 16th, after a two-hour bombardment – all that ammunition stocks would allow. Yet again the enemy was fully prepared, and nowhere did the assaulting troops gain a permanent hold on the opposing front line. As soon as the barrage lifted the Germans manned the parapet, and the 3rd Battalion, this time unaided by mine or advanced field guns, met such a hail of rifle and machine-gun bullets that its leading waves could not cross no man's land.'

Casualties to 21 Brigade over the two days had been heavy, though the commitment of only parts of the Bedfords and RSF to the attack and Colonel Pollard's decision to abort any further assaults on the second day undoubtedly saved many lives. 2nd Bedfords lost five officers and eighteen men killed, two officers and seventy-two men wounded, with twenty-seven men missing. 2nd Yorkshires lost five officers and thirty-two men killed, five officers and 250 men wounded and one officer and 128 men missing. 2nd RSF lost four officers and twenty-one men killed, two officers and 121 men wounded and fifty-two missing. 2nd Wiltshires lost four officers and twenty-five men killed, five officers and 128 men wounded and forty-seven men missing. Even 1/4th Camerons, who had been in support, lost thirteen men killed, three officers and thirty-three men wounded and seven missing.

Almost all the missing were in fact dead. Virtually all were regular soldiers and their loss in such a futile attack made their deaths even more tragic. The old regular army was on its last legs, and only the growing presence of Territorial Force battalions was keeping it going. It seems highly likely that the Germans knew exactly when, and where, the attacks were coming, probably through their ability to intercept telephone calls at a distance. The two-day barrage must also have helped to confirm where the assaults were to take place, without breaking down the network of underground bunkers the Germans had constructed to protect their troops. Probably the only British success was the blowing of the mine on the first day; the Royal Engineers had been able to compensate to some extent for it being blown short by increasing the amount of explosive used.

Shortly after 21st Brigade's failed attack, Lieutenant General Sir Henry Rawlinson, commander of IV Corps, which included 7th Division, visited the battlefield. In a letter dated 21 June he described what he had seen and thought:

> things are pretty busy in the La Bassée area at the moment and do not seem likely to quiet down – our last attempt was as you know unsuccessful though in places we managed to capture the enemy's first line trenches but the hostile fortifications were such that our (artillery) preparation, well directed as it was, had not the desired effect on the enemy and on the majority of the front he was able to man his parapets before the infantry could deliver their assault – we hear from those who actually gained the German trenches that they found them from 7 to 10 feet deep with dugouts driven into the bottom of them 6 feet and more below the ground level – into these 'cellars' the garrisons must have withdrawn during the bombardment so that when the moment came for the assault they were able to rush out and line their trenches without having suffered to any serious extent from the hellish bombardment we'd given them…

Commenting on the fighting Rawlinson noted 'one cannot expect any human creatures to go on charging barbed wire under heavy rifle and machine gun fire, for ever' giving the lie to the standard 'Lions led by Donkeys' theory that the generals neither knew nor cared about what their men had to endure. He had also been out to inspect the ground they fought over:

> I went down yesterday to have a look at the field of action – you never saw such a scene of desolation and destruction – opposite Givenchy

there is hardly a yard of ground that is not a shell crater, every house is flat and all the trees have been cut to pieces and killed – on the Givenchy ridge where the fighting has been heaviest there (is) nothing but a series of waves of earth and stones, flung about in all directions by the mine craters and big shells, but the Bosches stick to their ground with the utmost tenacity and without killing them it is most difficult to force them from their trenches.

On 24 June 6th Gordon Highlanders were back at Givenchy holding the trenches from the Orchard, south of the Sunken Road, to J7. There was little to report save that the Germans detonated a mine immediately south of the Sunken Road, near I4, on the 28th. Casualties in the six days were three other ranks killed and nine wounded.

On 30 June 1915 the 2nd Battalion, Oxfordshire and Buckinghamshire Light Infantry, took over part of the Givenchy sector from the 2nd Border Regiment. Though they had been in the area since the start of the year and had been in the trenches at Le Plantin, this was their first time in Givenchy itself. They described their position as:

In the section occupied by the Regt, 2 cos are in the front line in good first line trenches. The new 2nd line was in the course of completion. One Co in support near canal, the other also in support in vicinity of Orchard and Old Keep. Enemy about 200 yards distant on the canal bank but then forms a large re-entrant, extreme point about 600 yards away until opposite extreme left their trenches only 50 yards away. Some heavy shelling from a southerly direction of extreme left of front trenches on evening of 1st. Some intermittent shelling at times.

They were relieved on 4 July by 2nd Royal Irish Fusiliers, having suffered one man killed in the artillery bombardment on the 1st (Lance Corporal Henry Frederick Mount) and another on the 4th (Private Elias Froggatt), with one man wounded.

The battalion was back at Givenchy on the 9th, having been acting as reserve battalion at Le Preol, though this had not kept all the men away from Givenchy, as 200 per day were detailed for fatigue parties for the mining operations there. 'Only one man killed when at this work', noted the war diarist. Between the 9th and the 13th, when they were withdrawn to Bethune, the battalion lost only two officers wounded, though they were periodically bombarded with shells and rifle grenades.

On 20 August it was realised that the Germans were extremely close to the charge that had been laid the previous day in Duck's Bill No.2 tunnel, so it was decided to blow the charge prematurely. A double explosion proved that the Germans had either been in the process of tamping their charge, or were waiting for the British to start working again before detonating it. 'Either way', noted the war diarist with some satisfaction, 'it must have caused casualties to the enemy'.

The Germans continued their policy of raiding 2nd Division's trenches. On 25 August the 2nd Battalion Ox and Bucks were holding the trenches north of Givenchy when, at 4am, the Germans blew a mine which blocked the last 20 feet of gallery of No.1 Mine in the Rabbit Warren. Sappers John Goury and George McKenzie were trapped at the face, and other men were overcome by gas that engulfed the passage. Sapper Andrew Getty organised the rescue of the officer in charge, Lieutenant Williams, and of his relief, both of whom had been gassed, then of Corporal Thompson, who had succumbed while working with him. He then endeavoured to rescue the men trapped at the mine face. He helped a serjeant arranging air-pipe lines to clear the gasses, after making certain there was no hope of rescuing the men at the face. Sapper Joseph Fox twice entered the mine gallery, first to assist in the rescue of Lieutenant Williams, and then to try to rescue the four men trapped in the mine itself. He was eventually overcome by gas himself and had to be dragged out, but as soon as he had partly recovered he insisted in going on with his work, until ordered to stop by an officer. The two men trapped at the face were never recovered; of the other two trapped men one was brought out dead at the time, while the body of the other was recovered later. They are both (Sapper Frederick Ernest Payne and Sapper James Hobson) buried in the Guards Cemetery at Windy Corner.

As this was going on underground, on the surface the Ox and Bucks fought back gallantly and the Germans gained no ground at all. They bided their time and the 26th passed quietly, but shortly after midnight on the 27th 'the enemy made a determined bomb attack on the Northern Crater at the

Sunken Road but were repulsed after considerable bombing on our side'. The German attackers got so close that several of their grenades actually entered the British trench, causing casualties, but gained no ground. The diarist noted that this was the first experience that the regiment's grenadiers had had, and that they had acquitted themselves well, in particular Lance Corporal William Watkins (10290) of C Company. Watkins was awarded the DCM, his citation reading:

> A small mine was exploded at the head of a sap. Lance Corporal Watkins, who was in reserve, on his own initiative collected two other bombers and hurried up at once to give assistance. Again, on the night of the following day at the same place, he voluntarily remained on duty all night, at times climbing out of the trench to enable him to reach the German trenches better.

The success of the defence was, in part, because the defenders had the new Mills Bomb, which was to become the standard British grenade for over fifty years. Even an unpractised thrower could hurl it 30 feet or more, and a trained bomber 50 feet or so. It became a crucial weapon in trench warfare.

The battalion lost thirteen men killed and twenty wounded over four days before they were relieved by 2nd Royal Scots Fusiliers on the 28th.

On 6 September 2nd Ox & Bucks were back at Givenchy, in the same section as before but now renumbered B3. There was a little bombing overnight but it was otherwise quiet until the Germans blew a small mine in the southern craters, which fortunately did little damage. During the evening of the 7th an unfortunate premature explosion of a British grenade in the trench injured two officers and an unspecified number of men. At 5am on the 8th the Royal Engineers blew a small mine, which collapsed a German mine and the craters, 'much improving our position at the sap heads'. At some point in the early morning a German sniper shot dead 34-year-old Captain Arkley William Neville Ponsonby, grandson of the second Lord de Mauley, an officer of the 3rd Battalion of the regiment who had been serving as aide de camp to Viscount Buxton in South Africa at the outbreak of war. He had rejoined his regiment and already been wounded at Ypres. His body was taken to Windy Corner and he was buried in the Guards Cemetery.

Other than that, it was a quiet day and the battalion were relieved by 1st Queen's.

The Battle of Loos (25 September to 18 October) took place across the ground south of the La Bassée canal on a 20-mile front to just north of Arras. Operations north of the canal were designed to distract and confuse the enemy. Other attacks were planned to take place much further south, around Rheims and Verdun (later abandoned), and the whole strategy was designed to take advantage of a perceived advantage in men on the front (132 British and French divisions opposed to 102 German) and to prevent the further movement of German troops to the Russian front. In the Loos area it was hoped that the German line would be broken quickly so the gap could be exploited by the reserves pushing forward to capture key rail junctions that supplied a large section of the German front.

Sir John French had agreed with the French proposal that Haig's First Army should attack south of the canal, despite Haig's opinion that it was unsuitable ground for a large-scale offensive. Haig thought the attack should go on north of the canal towards Violaines and La Bassée, but was overruled.

I Corps operational orders dictated that the offensive was to begin on 25 September following a preliminary bombardment that began on the 21st. 'North of the La Bassée Canal the enemy will be engaged vigorously, in order to prevent him withdrawing troops for a counter attack. Wherever the enemy gives ground he must be followed up with the greatest energy'. Instructions for the diversionary attack north of the canal were for 5th Brigade, which was holding Givenchy, to attack the enemy's trenches opposite and advance on to the line Chapelle St Roche to Canteleux.

Troops for the assault began taking over the trenches around Givenchy on the 23rd, as a heavy four-day bombardment of the German lines went on around them. The 2nd Highland Light Infantry were to be in the centre and spent the night of the 23rd firing rapidly in the direction of the trenches opposite, in the hope it would deter the Germans from repairing their damaged wire. It was very wet and the trenches were in a dreadful state.

For the attack itself the 9th HLI were to attack along the canal bank in conjunction with an attack by 6th Brigade on the south bank; 2nd HLI were in the centre; 1st Queen's were to their left and 2nd Ox and Bucks Light Infantry were on the far left. 2nd Worcesters and 7th King's

Liverpools were in reserve. The main attack at Loos was to begin at 6.30am following the release of a gas cloud, so the diversionary attack at Givenchy commenced at 6am following the release of gas at 5.50am. Though the German wire had been cut, and at first things appeared to be going well, it soon became apparent that the stillness of the air was holding the gas above the British trenches and not blowing it at the Germans. The troops, wearing their 'smoke helmets', moved forward and the Ox and Bucks advanced quickly through the German front line (it was later realised it had been deliberately abandoned, possibly from fear of a mine detonation) and into the second and third lines, where more resistance was encountered. 2nd HLI also got through the front line, but only got into the German support line after severe hand-to-hand fighting. Among their dead was Captain Charles Winsmore Hooper of B Company, an officer who had already been through the retreat from Mons, been wounded at Ypres and fought at Neuve Chapelle. His colonel wrote to his family that 'His Company all speak highly of his behaviour during the last action… I can assure you that his memory will always be kept in affection by us all.' His body was never recovered and he is commemorated on the Loos Memorial. 1st Queen's reached the German third line with few casualties and considered the attack 'was obviously a complete surprise'. At about 8.15am, however, the Germans began a bombing counterattack and it soon became apparent that not only were the British carrying nowhere near enough bombs to fight back (though each battalion took forward 200 or more), but also that many were the new 'Ball' grenade, which relied on a fuse that was ignited by striking a special wristlet, rather like a matchbox – and it was raining! The Germans, with their more powerful stick grenades, which had a longer range, gradually drove the men back to their own trenches.

On the canal bank things did not go well from the start. 9th HLI were ordered to attack at 6.30am (presumably to conform with operations on the south bank), and were in position with gas hoods properly adjusted when the gas was released. Instead of blowing eastwards it seemed to drift north-east and then suddenly, at 6.25am, a dense cloud coming in from the canal enveloped the trenches and disabled almost all the men in the two leading platoons, who had to be replaced. A patrol was pushed forward and came under fire, and only one man got back alive. The attack on the south bank having clearly failed, and having suffered about 120 casualties, mostly from their own gas, the battalion took no further part in the action.

Thirty-five-year-old Corporal Robert Booty, Royal Garrison Artillery, advanced immediately behind the infantry to bring up a trench mortar:

I had only just got over our parapet when I was struck in the right leg, but did not take much notice of it then; the distance was over 280 yards, and on this the Germans had 16 machine guns, each firing 260 rounds per minute. Add to this thousands of rifle bullets, and shells also in thousands, and then you have a fair idea of the advance to their trenches at Givenchy. On the way over, I was separated from my detachment owing to casualties, but I managed to get there, and as I got in their front trench I was set on with hand-bombs. I rushed up after the first one was thrown and clubbed the German on the head with the butt of a rifle. His head cracked like an egg. However, the other let go at me, and I am more than surprised that I am alive, as the bomb blew my clothes

No man's land, Givenchy, towards the end of 1915.

to pieces, and the right leg was burned and the right arm sleeve was in many pieces, even the stripes were blown off. I was knocked to the ground by the explosion, but got up and went for them again. I think on the second occasion I must have been mad, for I simply broke their heads up. After getting clear of these, I had more to contend with, and their bombs began to tell, as I was losing much blood, and just as I was giving up, some of our men came and put a finish to the lot. I was then lifted out of the trench and crawled back the 280 yards. It was a good thing for me that the fire was ceasing. I lay on a stretcher from noon on Saturday till 2am on Tuesday in a very bad state.

Corporal Booty made it back down the chain to 14th General Hospital and was transferred to the pre-war military hospital at Netley in Hampshire, from which he wrote the letter quoted, which appeared in the *Yorkshire Post and Intelligencer* on 20 October 1915. He made a full recovery from his wounds and was back in France on 3 March 1916. He survived the war.

Many others were not so lucky. The attacking battalions lost something in the region of 950 men killed, wounded and missing, having achieved nothing.

Tunnelling operations continued and there were signs that the tunnellers were learning their craft – and being crafty. Captain Edward Marie Felix Momber, of 176th Tunnelling Company, deliberately blew a small charge knowing that the Germans, who at this stage in the war were better able to respond quickly to such events, would rush forward and occupy the crater. They did so and began digging in, at which point he detonated two much larger charges and, it was believed, killed about fifty Germans, as well as doing substantial damage to their front-line parapet and deeper galleries. He was awarded the Military Cross.

On 29 October 1915 two sections of 180 Tunnelling Company took over a 350-yard section of the Givenchy front from two sections of 173 Company. On the right of their part of the front lay Orchard Mine, 20 feet deep with laterals branching from the main gallery to about 80 feet in front of the fire trench, with listening galleries about 50 feet apart in front of the lateral tunnel. Seventy yards to the left of Orchard Mine lay Red House shaft, 37 feet deep with a main gallery running about 20 feet, which then forked into two branches extending out about 120 feet, to be about the same distance as the listening posts from Orchard Mine, to which they were connected by a Winze shaft dug down to connect with the Orchard shaft lateral.

Next to the left, by 55 yards, lay White House shaft, which was 23 feet deep, then five inclined galleries dug down from the front line itself called the Warren, and finally, on the far left, another inclined gallery known as Look Out mine. None of these were connected by laterals and the galleries from White House were barely ahead of the infantry's advanced posts. It was decided to push out the White House galleries, dig connecting laterals and try and push Look Out gallery forward with a view to getting under the German salient.

On 8 November Germans were heard walking through their passages from Look Out mine gallery and a 1,000lb charge of gun cotton was fired. On 11 November the Germans fired a mine in front of the Warren, but caused no casualties. By 25 November the tunnellers had completed the lateral at White House, making ventilation and the removal of sand bags a lot easier.

During the night of 29/30 November two German deserters reported that two large mines had been charged under the British trenches and were to be fired at dawn. Questioning elicited the approximate position of these mines and it was decided to fire two large charges at the head of the galleries in the hope of breaking any adjacent German ones. Accordingly, one charge of 2,000lb of gun cotton and one of 1,400lb of ammonal were detonated at 4.20am on the 30th. At 7am the Germans fired one mine slightly to the right of the British detonations, but there were no casualties among either the infantry or tunnellers.

On 21 December the Germans sprang another mine north-east of the White House galleries. No damage was done and it was decided that they had probably been responding to a strange tapping sound that the British had heard there themselves that sounded like mining. It is not clear if whatever caused it was ever explained.

It was now winter proper, and the slightest problem with pumps or drainage could cause flooding. A shell burst in the front-line trench cut power to the pump and the water level rose and could not be reduced. Water levels in White House meant that parts of the galleries were flooded, but fortunately all important works could be reached from other entrances.

On 21 December the 7th Suffolks, part of 35th Brigade of 12 (Eastern) Division, took over part of the line in Givenchy from 9th Essex. The Germans were shelling Gunner Siding and two men were killed. Next morning, at 11am, the Germans welcomed them with a barrage of rifle grenades along the whole of their part of the front, to which the battalion responded with alacrity. That evening an experimental gas attack was to be made along the front of 35 Brigade and 5th Royal Berkshire Regiment, who were in the trenches alongside them. During the morning a rifle grenade fell on a gas cylinder in the Berkshires' trench, cracking it, which caused the gas to leak. Eight men were poisoned, three men were shocked and five wounded. Special instructions were issued during the day regarding the gas operations, including the instruction that bombers in the forward saps had to wear their smoke helmets. At 9.05pm, as the gas was being discharged, the Germans lit fires along the parapet of their trenches and saps (this was supposed to cause the gas to rise), fired red flares and opened up with their machine guns. Their artillery opened up at the same time and remained heavy until 10.25, concentrated on Berkeley Street and King's Road. No.3 Sector HQ also took several hits. After a pause the barrage began again at 12.30am and lasted until 1.15am, concentrated on Mairie Redoubt. A third barrage struck Mairie Redoubt and Gunners Siding between 4.30am and 6am. Mairie Redoubt was badly damaged, with large sections of the parapet blown down. Five yards of the parapet of the fire trench was demolished in No.1 Sector, but rapidly repaired. In No.2 Sector a further five yards of parapet were demolished in the fire trench; more damage was done to Berkeley Street and Regent Street trenches, but the support trench avoided too much damage, most of the shells just missing the trench itself. In No.3 Sector the fire trench escaped much damage, but there was intermittent damage to the support trench. King's Road took a lot of damage, especially in the vicinity of Willow Road, but this too was repaired overnight.

Listening posts were sent out from each sector when the bombardment started. The posts in 1 and 2 sectors reported that the Germans were busy repairing their parapets, but the post in 3 Sector was twice buried by enemy shelling and never got close enough to find out. Two special parties to ascertain the effects of the gas cloud were unable to operate because of the brightness of the night generally and the German use of searchlights and machine guns. It was noted that the bombardment cut several of the telephone lines between the sector HQs and the back area, and it was recommended that the protection of communication lines be reviewed.

On 29 December the Germans fired a mine near White House that collapsed 30 feet of one gallery but caused no casualties. Work on clearing it began the next day, when it was also noted that the Warren galleries had all been connected by a lateral tunnel that greatly increased ventilation. Listening posts were being pushed out into no man's land in the hope they would be able to detect preparations for a mine so far out, that the detonation of a 700lb charge would not affect the lateral itself.

A fascinating glimpse of Givenchy at the end of 1915 appeared in an article entitled 'A Young Cornishman's First Visit to the Trenches', published in *The Cornishman* newspaper on 23 December. Though the writer is not named, it seems likely he was a member (probably an officer) of 251 Tunnelling Company, Royal Engineers, a unit recruited mainly in the Duchy of Cornwall, and which had very recently moved into the Cambrin sector, immediately south of the La Bassée canal.

Accompanied by another officer and a section of Tunnelling Royal Engineers, I left the grimy war torn town of B(ethune) and headed up the muddy, poplar fringed highway that leads to G(ivenchy). The road was torn and pitted by shell fire and transport traffic until it almost resembled a cart track on the Karvo. On either hand was a countryside of indescribable desolation. Where there had once been green smiling pastures and well tilled fields, was now a dreary waste of weeds and rubbish, an unkempt wilderness of yellow grass and cantankerous undergrowth. Here and there piles of debris, heaps of brick and plaster and protruding beams marked where the homely cottages of the peasantry once stood. Now not a peasant was to be seen. They had fled before the terrible, all destroying tidal wave of war, and the little homes that had sheltered them for years had been pounded to shapeless heaps by the roaring guns of the merciless invader. Everywhere was solitude, dreariness and ruin. All the familiar sights and sounds of the countryside were wanting; the defiant cock crow, the lowing cattle, the twittering sparrows; everywhere an aching, lifeless desolation.

After driving for about two miles along the highroad, we came to the village of G(ivenchy), around which some of the most sanguinary fighting of the campaign had taken place. But what had once been a village was now simply a grotesque collection of shot-riddled partly demolished walls. Nowhere was there a building that could properly be called a house. The tide of battle had swayed uncertainly about this place for many months, and practically ever since the commencement of hostilities it has been in the fire zone. Shrapnel has torn off every roof, common shell has perforated the red brick walls, and high explosive has wrought havoc and ruin everywhere. Only a few mutely protesting pieces of wall still stand. In one place the end of a house had been blown away, leaving most of the side walls standing, and I saw a broken twisted bedstead hanging through a gaping hole in the bedroom floor. Everywhere great holes gaped in the brown earth and on every side were hastily made trenches, sand bagged defence works and barbed wire entanglements, which had been used by the contending armies. On the outskirts of the village, where the road turns sharply to the right, is that blood soaked spot which has on many occasions run red with the blood of heroes and which will be known as long as the British army lasts as 'windy corner'.

The lorries could not proceed much beyond this place, and the remainder of the journey had to be done on foot. We were now quite close to the firing line, and tired, dirty mud-caked Tommies were straggling down, presumably on light fatigues. The guns on both sides had now commenced roaring defiance at one another, paying the grim compliments which the irrepressible Mr Atkins has facetiously termed the 'morning hate'. The uproar was deafening. The tearing crash of discharge, followed by the duller boom of the bursting shell, made a truly awful and nerve shattering din. One German shell burst in a field about fifty yards away, and we involuntarily ducked as a shower of earth and stones flew around us. A little further on we saw a pool of blood in the road with a red, saturated rag close by, showing where some luckless soldier had fallen victim to the sniper's bullet. (Hit in the knee our guide afterwards told us).

Shortly after we left the road and turned into a deep communication trench which wound its sinuous way to the firing line. A wooden track had been put in to facilitate drainage, and the earth banked up on either side gave good protection from the enemy's fire. Presently we reached the reserve trenches, then the support, and a little further on found ourselves in the firing line itself. In spite of all preconceived ideas it seemed a strange and wonderful place. There had been a hard frost during the night, and there was no mud. Every few yards a grim, silent khaki figure, greatcoated and begloved, stood watching the German trenches sixty yards away through a periscope. Day after day they stand thus, always watching, always waiting, always alert. In the dug outs behind were more khaki figures ready to spring out and take their places at the slightest sign of a hostile movement.

It is a wonderful world, this trench world. For many months the two armies have been facing each other here with but slight alterations in their respective positions, and always they have been digging, altering, improving and repairing till now the uninitiated might wander for a day in this twisting, interwoven maze without finding a way out.

It was my privilege in the afternoon to witness a bombardment of the German lines. For two hours the air was alive with roaring, whizzing, screaming, hurtling projectiles. The big howitzer batteries a long way in the rear first opened fire, and this seemed to be the signal for every reeking tube along our front to add its quota to the hail of lead and steel. The dull roar of the big shells mingled with the hoarse shriek of the trench mortars, and the hissing scream of rifle grenades made a deafening, ear splitting bedlam of sound, which made one's brain reel. Crouching beneath this infernal canopy of rushing death the senses gradually became numbed and deadened. The German trenches were seemingly being pounded out of existence. The air was thick with flying mud and sandbags, and the fumes from the bursting shells hung like a yellow pall over their lines. Yet I was told no great material damage could be done in such a short time, that most of the German troops were back in the comparative safety of their dug outs, and if an attack had been attempted it would have been met with a deadly withering hail of rifle and machine-gun fire. The German batteries made a half-hearted attempt to reply, but their fire was weak and inaccurate compared to our own.

When the firing stopped, which it did as soon as the darkness started creeping down, the silence that ensued was, for a little while, almost as awful as the deafening din of the bombardment. Soon the evening merged into night, and the star shells soared like blazing comets in the sky, flamed their sickly light over the serried, sandbagged lines, and curved their dimming radiance back to earth. These were often followed by a little desultory splutter of rifle fire at some too venturous head that showed above the parapet. Although anything in the nature of a continuous bombardment is unusual after dark there is always some intermittent 'strafing' going on. A really peaceful night is almost unknown. In the firing line there is always a tense alertness for no one knows the hour or the minute when a surprise attack may be attempted, and comparative serenity be transformed into a flaming hell of bursting bombs and stabbing steel.

German spies sometimes worm their way across the stretch of 'no man's land' between the firing lines and creep into our trenches. Stumbling through these zig-zag Stygian alleys at night a grim white face is thrust into one's own out of the blackness, a sharp, peremptory voice raps out: 'Who are you?' and one's answer has to be quick and satisfactory or it's a case of being manhandled back to the nearest company headquarters for identification. There is always the crack of a rifle or the spasmodic pop-popping of some well concealed machine gun from some part of the line, and at intervals the whirring scream of a trench mortar projectile overhead, followed by the crash of its bursting, which reverberates away into the night.

Behind the firing line there is a subterranean town of dug outs. These have evolved from a hole in the earth into underground rooms of respectable proportions. They accommodate the troops not actually engaged in the firing line, and as Tommy usually contrives to have some sort of fire, winter conditions in the trenches are not quite so terrible as formerly. Everywhere one goes there is a smiling cheerfulness and an unshakeable confidence in ultimate victory.

Chapter 3

1916

1916 saw a very gradual quietening down on the Bethune–La Bassée front, as the focus of British operations shifted further south with the taking over of part of the Somme front from the French in April and preparations for the offensive there that would begin in July and absorb much of both sides' attention until November.

In February the Germans launched an offensive against the French at Verdun, an important strategic point on the River Meuse which, for historic reasons, the French were bound to defend. It lay in a salient and the Germans hoped that by attacking it they would draw more and more French troops into the battle, where they could be destroyed by superior artillery. In fact both sides threw in more and more reinforcements and the battle dragged on until December, with approximately 700,000 casualties in total.

Partly to relieve the pressure on Verdun, and partly forming part of the only concerted action by the three main allies, the British and French launched the Battle of the Somme on 1 July, along a 25-mile front. For much of the northern part of the attack, though many British units reached the German trenches in small numbers, the attack failed as a whole because reinforcements could not get across a no man's land being swept by machine guns and artillery. There were some successes in the centre, but it was only on the southernmost part of the British assault, where they were assisted by French troops, that any serious advances were made. The British army suffered 60,000 casualties, nearly 20,000 of them killed, on the first day. The need to keep up pressure on Germany in order to assist Verdun resulted in the focus of the attack being switched to the southern area, and in a series of attacks over the following months the Germans were gradually driven back six miles. British and French casualties reached over 600,000 and the Germans over 460,000, but for the Germans these were experienced soldiers they could ill afford to lose.

On the Russian front the Russians gathered themselves for a great offensive on the Galician front as their part of the grand strategy. General Brusilov planned a rolling series of attacks starting in Galicia and gradually extending to the whole Russian front, as Austria and Germany frantically moved their reserves huge distances to counter the breakthroughs. The date of the offensive was brought forward to take pressure off Verdun and, on Brusilov's own part of the front, his strategy worked perfectly. A phased series of assaults saw the Austrian line collapse and German reinforcements rushed to their aid. Unfortunately Brusilov's fellow generals failed to cooperate by launching their attacks and his own were gradually throttled. Though he regained much of the ground lost in the south in 1915, broke the back of the Austrian army and caused the Germans to transfer troops from Verdun, Brusilov's offensive also cost the Russians dearly in terms of casualties. The initial success also persuaded Romania to enter the war as an

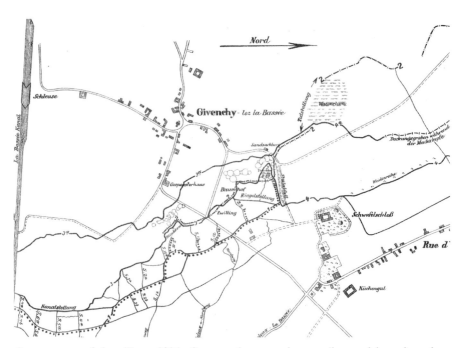

German map of the village, 1916. *Gespensterhaus* translates as 'haunted house'; perhaps the Germans were unaware that it was a lookout, but had seen movements at night as the observers changed shift? (With thanks to Sebastian Laudan)

ally, but her army was swiftly shattered by a sudden German attack. Much of the country fell into German hands.

In Britain, following much soul-searching, conscription was introduced in January. Though it would take months to train new troops, the army could at least now be sure that reinforcements would be forthcoming.

Though 1916 was to be a quieter year on the Bethune part of the front as a whole, Givenchy itself remained the focus of small-scale but intense actions, both on the surface and underground. Two more Victoria Crosses were won on the same day in June.

On the surface, apart from the usual daily shelling, the occasional trench raid in either direction and the ever-present danger of snipers, things were relatively calm – or at least relatively calm for Givenchy. 'Givenchy shelled at intervals throughout the day', 'Quiet morning till about Noon, when the Germans shelled Le Plantin and also Givenchy Keeps' and 'much activity with rifle grenades in Scottish Trench; nothing else of note' are typical of the comments one reads in the contemporary war diaries for January.

Mining activities continued unabated, even with the winter rains causing problems with flooding. On 13 January the Germans sprang another mine in front of Orchard Mine, but there were no casualties or damage to the British galleries. Officers of 176 Company Royal Engineers reported the noise of mining heard from their dug-out some 10 yards behind the front-line trench, and an inclined gallery was driven down from the dug-out itself and another straight down from a sap in no man's land. As if to prove that it was not just underground that the tunnellers were vulnerable, on the same day a trench mortar shell caught second lieutenants V.H.M. Barrett and H. Ball in the trench, wounding Barrett and killing Ball, who was carried down and buried in the Guards' Cemetery at Windy Corner.

Lance Sergeant Charles Quinnell, of 9th Battalion, Royal Fusiliers, was one of the many men sent to work with the Royal Engineer miners at Givenchy. He described the mines and the work to the Imperial War Museum:

As you walked along the trench all you saw of the mine was a wooden framed doorway about four feet high and two wide. Behind it was a staircase that went thirty feet underground and opened up into a room about eight feet by eight. In the centre of that room was a four-feet-square shaft, and over the top of that was a wooden windlass and a rope. The shaft went down another twenty feet or so. At the bottom of the shaft there was another doorway facing the German lines, and that was the entrance to the tunnel. The tunnels were a continuation of this wooden framework that went straight ahead under the German lines.

He described how the miners dug out the clay, which was put into a sandbag and passed along the tunnel before being hauled up by the windlass to the upper chamber, then passed by hand up the staircase by a chain of men who, at the surface, threw them over the top. When work stopped a man was always left at the face of the shaft with a stethoscope, listening for the Germans working. While they could be heard it was known to be safe; only when they stopped was the detonation of a German charge likely. On one occasion the mine filled with water, and despite the best efforts of the pumps could not be cleared. The water level continued to rise up the shaft. The puzzled RE officer eventually went out into no man's land and discovered that the Germans were pumping water out of their shaft into a crater immediately above the British passage. He cut the German hoses and the problem was solved.

In February 13th Battalion Royal Welsh Fusiliers seem to have had a reasonably sharp time of it, but it was their first time in a serious hot spot, having only come out to France the preceding December and their previous trench experiences having been quite deliberately in quiet sectors. They reported artillery bombardments, a bombardment by rifle grenades, some successful sniping of their own (claiming one human victim and some smashed trench periscopes), a gas alarm that turned out to be false, some fairly vigorous patrolling on their own part into no man's land and the explosion of an enemy mine that caused the men to open rapid fire on the enemy parapet. The entry for their first brief tour in Givenchy reported 'During our tour in trenches communications improved, parapet strengthened and stores for bombs and SAA (Small Arms Ammunition) built.'

The press at home reported faithfully the Official Communiqués issued by the army in France and, though they undoubtedly gloss over some of the events on the ground, the frequency with which Givenchy is mentioned in

1916 is far, far less than in 1915. A communiqué of 9 March reports 'Today the enemy sprang a mine near Givenchy but made no infantry attack'; on 26 March 'Enemy exploded a mine yesterday north of Givenchy but did little damage' and on 8 April 'Last night and today there has been some mining activity about… Givenchy.' The routine of three or so days in the front line trenches followed by spells in reserve, all the while suffering spasmodic shelling and the occasional raid, continued.

In the spring of 1916, 254th Tunnelling Company, which had just returned from Gallipoli, took over tunnelling operations. They managed to drain some of the flooded workings. Their listening posts began to report sounds of German working close to E Sap, Shallows and Bond Street, and it was decided to attack them on 20 June using charges placed in E Sap, which was quite shallow, then Bond Street, where the galleries were deeper. Unfortunately the detonation of the shallow charge broke the wires to the deeper one, which had to be blown 12 hours later. This bigger charge blew through the side of the crater formed earlier and sent tons of debris on to the German trenches; timbers from the enemy workings could be seen protruding through the crater side. However, unknown to the British, the German miners opposite, 295 Pioneer Mining Company, had deeper workings that had not been so badly affected.

During 20 June 2nd Battalion Royal Welsh Fusiliers took over the Givenchy left section from 4th Suffolks. They had been visited in their billets by the CO of the mining company, who had carefully explained that recent British work, including the explosion of two small mines and a camouflet, had handicapped the German workings and that it should be six to eight weeks before they could pose a threat again in the sector. After a quiet day on the 21st:

At 2.05am the enemy exploded mine of the right of Givenchy Left, under B Company's front line, wrecking completely of the line and doing considerable damage to the support line. At the same time a very intense bombardment was put up by the enemy on the front line, support line and Battalion Headquarters of all calibres up to 8. This lasted for 1½ hours, after which the enemy attacked with about 150 men and entered our first trench, but were promptly ejected by

The Royal Welsh Fusiliers counterattack at Red Dragon Crater, 22 June 1916.

the small remnant of B Company left after the mine explosion and bombardment.

Writing about the incident afterwards in *The War the Infantry Knew*, Captain E.C. Dunn described dawn, under heavy bombardment from the enemy guns, revealing B Company HQ and two centre platoons buried in the ruins of their trenches. The barrage boxed part of C Company and shelled the reserve line and communications, then a large group of Germans wearing white armbands, presumably so they could identify each other in the semi-darkness and confusion, began to advance in three lines. Unfortunately for them the armbands also made them easier for the few defenders to see, and they opened fire with rifles and Lewis guns, though there were only eleven men unburied by the explosion. The Germans, possibly not expecting any resistance, became confused, hesitated and then tried to work their way forward round the edge of the crater. One man came in behind B Company's little band, but was identified by his armband and shot at close range, crying 'Oh, Mutter' as he was hit. Two men immediately climbed out and stripped him of his revolver and other souvenirs. Second Lieutenant Arthur Chaplin Banks killed four Germans before he was killed himself, dashing out into the crater to tackle three Germans in the crater on his own. One of the Germans stabbed him in the abdomen before he was himself shot and bayonetted by Sergeant Roderick.

Captain Stanway, who had just received another assurance from the tunnellers that no problems were anticipated, was in C Company HQ when there was 'a most colossal bang, and the whole area just rocked from one end to the other.' The barrage came down and he realised what had happened. When the shelling lifted and the Germans came forward he ordered his men up on to the parapet where they knelt to open fire. There was a big gap on his right where the Germans were getting through and he sent Lieutenant John Lawrie Walter Craig with a few men to try and plug the gap. Stanway continued to gather men and organised a further party to push out into the gap on his right. Here they found Lieutenant Craig being held prisoner by a large German who was standing over him – but not for long. They joined up with some men of the Divisional Labour Battalion and sealed the gap.

Captain Harrison MacDonald Blair was initially reported missing, but was dug out alive after 24 hours. Two more officers, Company Sergeant Major Pattison and forty-seven other ranks were missing, eight men were known to be dead and thirty-four wounded. The remnants of B Company were relieved by A Company of 5th Cameronians.

Captain Blair survived the war and also detailed his experiences that day in *The War the Infantry Knew*, explaining how he had gone up to the line accompanying Second Lieutenant Trevor Allington Crosland, the Harrow-educated young 19-year-old being excited about his first visit to the front line. The company commander he relieved explained that there had been no sound of German mining activity, but Blair was not reassured and had an uncomfortable feeling of foreboding, which grew as the night went on despite the lovely peaceful night: 'Perhaps it was the almost uncanny stillness, too quiet to be natural in that unpleasant part of the line'. He ordered his sergeant major to have ready-prepared boxes of bombs placed on the fire steps and insisted his company be made up to the full complement of trained bombers. Having taken what precautions he could, he was planning to have a drink at the company dug-out and to turn in, but decided against it when a brother officer declined to join him and went forward, instead, to one of the saps and spoke to the sentry. Everything was still. As he stepped off the fire step 'I felt my feet lifted up beneath me and the trench walls seemed to move upwards. There was a terrific blast of air which blew my steel helmet Heaven knows where.' He awoke in the dark (he estimated he had been unconscious for an hour or so) to find himself buried up to his neck and quite unable to move. Men shouting unintelligibly (he later realised they were Germans) were running past him and came close to kicking his head. Bullets were flying everywhere; he heard a hunting horn, more firing and then things gradually calmed down. As dawn rose he realised that Lance Corporal Morris, with whom he had been talking in the sap, was lying next to him with both legs broken and in great pain. He gradually worked an arm loose, pulled out his pocket knife and began to dig some cover for them both, though he still couldn't move his leg. Because they'd been forward in the sap as the mine exploded, the two men were in a horribly exposed position between the lines, so he carefully built a small parapet that hid them from German snipers. They lay out in the heat of the day with no relief.

They were spotted by some Cameronians, who tried to come to their rescue but were shelled, and Blair's attempts to wave them back finally drew the Germans' attention and they began machine-gunning them. Thankfully the digging and parapet provided sufficient cover to avoid them being hit.

Blair continued to dig, partly to improve their cover and partly because it gave him something to do, but the sun beat down and by the early afternoon both were in a bad way. Morris became so distressed, through pain and thirst, that he threatened to put his head up in the hope of being quickly killed, but Blair punched him in the solar plexus and dragged him back. As evening approached his pain ebbed somewhat and Blair realised that a rescue party should come out during the night (unless the Germans got to him first). However, it was midsummer and it was not until 10.30pm that it got dark enough for men to venture out from the trenches. At about 11.30 he heard a voice whispering in English, and a party of Cameronians crawled forward and gave them the first water they had had all day. Blair had to be dug out, and it was over two hours before the two men were got back to the British trench. Blair was later diagnosed as having a fractured skull.

There were, naturally, a number of medals awarded. There was a DSO for Captain (acting lieutenant colonel) Stanway; Military Crosses went to Lieutenant J.L.W. Craig and Lieutenant M. Williams; Sergeant C. Rush was awarded the DCM for immediately reorganising his men and leading the counterattack, and Private J. Lane won one for setting a fine example by jumping out of the trench and killing several Germans in the open before returning. There was a bar to his existing DCM (won in March 1915) for Sergeant P.B. Roderick for immediately attacking and driving the Germans from the trench and then following them into the crater, routing a group of forty Germans, then searching all night for his wounded officers. There were Military Medals for Corporal D. Davies and Lance Corporal George Richard Knight, as well as for privates Maurice Vyse (who died of wounds less than a month later), Michael Walsh, A. Jones, F. Bond and P. Morgan.

The official correspondent of the *Daily News* sent a vivid report back from GHQ dated 24 June, which was carried by many newspapers over the next few days. It was obviously cleared by the censors of MI7, the intelligence department that dealt with the press in France, but the facts as given seem pretty accurate. It reads, in full:

The Royal Welsh Fusiliers taught the enemy a wholesome lesson the day before yesterday. The official communiqué speaks of it as a 'very gallant and successful affair' and there are perhaps few regiments out here that have better earned official praise, not merely by this single exploit, but by a consistent staunchness and fine behaviour under all conditions. The particular incident in question began with the explosion by the enemy of what is probably one of the largest mines yet used by either side upon this front. At all events it made a crater about 120ft across, while the area of debris is over 300ft. This is believed to be at least one third larger than any former mine used in this region, and it is estimated that the enemy must have used many tons of explosives.

The scene of the affair was the Givenchy Hill, which is only a hill as the term is used out here, to signify some sort of elevation in the ground. In this case, the hill is at its highest not more than 30 or 35ft above the surrounding country; but in this flat region any eminence has importance.

The mammoth mine was exploded at a few minutes before 2am on June 22, accompanied by the usual heavy bombardment which, beginning shortly before the mine was fired, continued, first on the front trenches until the infantry attack was delivered and then, after the usual formula, on the communication and support trenches so as to interfere with the bringing up of reinforcements. The explosion, as may be imagined, was terrific. The mine, which was very deep, was between the old pearl–craters and our front line, the front of which was smashed in. The infantry then came on to attack and, presumably, to hold the ground.

Everything goes to show that the attack had been long prepared and carefully organised in every detail. The enemy attacked in three columns abreast, at equal distances apart, each party led by its own officers.

The enemy reached our trenches, or rather, they reached the hither edge of the great crater at the point where our front trenches had been. On both sides, however, quite undemoralized either by the explosion or the bombardment, the Welshmen were waiting for them; and then there seems to have followed some really great hand to hand fighting, in which a small detachment of one of the Pioneer battalions rendered good service. The Germans, as is their way on such occasions, were armed with bludgeons, daggers, and pistols. Our men had their bayonets and rifles, and there is no doubt that, in their hands, the regulation weapons demonstrated their superiority. What the enemy losses were it is impossible to say. They had made very good arrangements for getting their dead and wounded away, but they left enough to leave no doubt about the severity of the handling they got; and with all their tons of explosives and elaborate preparation, they failed to gain an inch of ground. In 15 minutes from the time they reached our front line they had been thrown back again and were caught both by machine-gun and artillery fire as they went.

There were many conspicuously gallant deeds in the dreadful mêlée. One of the officers of the Fusiliers is known to have killed four of the enemy before he was shot himself. A private, having broken his bayonet, is said to have 'laid out' two of the attackers with his fists. A machine-gun had been blown from its position by the explosion and lay in front of our lines, whence the Germans were carrying it off. Two men of the Fusiliers went out for it, and both gave their lives. But they saved the gun, which is safely in our hands. An officer was buried by the debris of the explosion; he was pinned down and partially covered by the wreckage. The part of him exposed was invisible to the Germans, but they saw our men trying to rescue him, and, guessing the situation, they played a machine-gun on the spot, making it impossible for anyone to approach and evidently seeking to kill the man, through the interposing sand, as he lay. They failed, however, and after he had remained there all day, as soon as dusk fell he was brought in by our men, and is now in hospital bruised and hurt by the explosion, but unwounded.

Work by 254 Tunnelling Company had continued since their detonations on the 20th, principally in driving forward under no man's land from the Shaftesbury Avenue shaft. It had not gone very far, but the detonation of the huge German mine nearby broke some of the timbers near the shaft itself, causing the roof to collapse and trapping five men who were working at the face. Relays of men began digging to release them and, after 24 hours,

Sapper William Hackett remains with his injured comrade in the collapsed mine and wins the Victoria Cross, 22 June 1916.

succeeded in making a small entrance to the chamber they were trapped in. Three men scrambled out but a fourth, twenty-two-year-old Private Thomas Collins of the 14th Battalion, the Welsh Regiment, who was attached to 254 Tunnelling Company to fetch and carry, was too big and too badly injured to squeeze through the narrow gap. Sapper William Hackett, aged forty-three, who had worked as a coal miner in Nottinghamshire for twenty-three years, knew he couldn't leave his comrade alone. Saying 'I am a tunneller and must look after the others first', he stayed with Collins to await rescue when a better passage could be cleared. As the rescue party retired their tunnel collapsed, and although teams of men worked for four more days, Hackett and Collins could not be saved and they remain buried under the fields just outside the village.

Hackett's courage was instantly recognised and on 4 August 1916 the *London Gazette* carried the following citation for his well-earned Victoria Cross:

For most conspicuous bravery when entombed with four others in a gallery owing to the explosion of an enemy mine. After working for 20 hours, a hole was made through fallen earth and broken timber, and the outside party was met. Sapper Hackett helped three of the men through the hole and could easily have followed, but refused to leave the fourth, who had been seriously injured, saying, 'I am a tunneller, I must look after the others first.' Meantime, the hole was getting smaller, yet he still refused to leave his injured comrade. Finally, the gallery collapsed, and though the rescue party worked desperately for four days the attempt to reach the two men failed. Sapper Hackett well knowing the nature of sliding earth, the chances against him, deliberately gave his life for his comrade.

As the initial attempts to rescue the trapped miners got underway, another Victoria Cross was being won on the surface above them. The company of Royal Welsh Fusiliers that had borne the brunt of the fighting was withdrawn as soon as was practicable, to be relieved by a company from the 1st Cameronians which, in turn, was relieved by a company of 5th Cameronians (Scottish Rifles) who were rushed up from their billets in Le Preol, into which they had moved the previous day. As they worked on consolidating the crater, the officer in charge, Second Lieutenant David Stevenson, the sapping officer, was shot in the head by a sniper and believed killed. Lance Corporal (acting Serjeant) John MacLaren Erskine, a trainee draper who had enlisted on 10 August 1914, had already risked himself twice bringing in wounded men, but thought he saw his officer move and went back out into the crater to rescue him. He lay beside his officer while others dug a shallow trench out to them, but Stevenson was discovered to be dead once he was got back into the fire trench and his body was taken back down the communication trench. He was buried in Gorre Military Cemetery, next to the chateau.

Erskine was awarded the Victoria Cross (also gazetted 4 August 1916), the citation reading:

Whilst the near lip of a crater, caused by the explosion of a large enemy mine, was being consolidated, Actg. Serjt. Erskine rushed out under continuous fire with utter disregard of danger and rescued a wounded serjeant and a private. Later, seeing his officer, who was believed to be dead, show signs of movement, he ran out to him, bandaged his head, and remained with him for fully an hour, though repeatedly fired at, whilst a shallow trench was being dug to them. He then assisted in bringing in his officer, shielding him with his own body in order to lessen the chance of his being hit again.

Erskine only found out about his VC by reading about it in a newspaper while at a base depot. He wrote to his mother saying that he knew he had been recommended for a medal, but having heard nothing he had assumed the whole thing had been forgotten. John Erskine was killed on 14 April 1917, leading his company into an attack after his commanding officer had been killed.

Acting Serjeant John MacLaren Erskine protects the body of Second Lieutenant Stevenson while his comrades dig towards them and wins the VC, 22 June 1916.

The German mine that produced what became known as Red Dragon Crater, in honour of the Welshmen who drove off the German attack that followed the explosion, was reckoned to have been the largest detonated by the Germans on the Western Front. The crater dominated the landscape and it was estimated to be 120 yards long and between 70 and 80 yards wide and 30 feet deep. The detonation was felt across the whole divisional area.

Wreaths laid at the opening of the Tunnellers' Memorial, Givenchy, 2010. The approximate position of William Hackett's entombment is indicated by the white cross in the field.

Work continued to repair the damage of 22 June and consolidate the crater under a barrage that lasted several days. 5th Cameronians provided fatigue parties until the whole battalion relieved 2nd Royal Welsh Fusiliers in Givenchy left section on the 27th. A constant barrage was being kept on the German lines and wire in front of them. At about 7am the Germans exploded a further mine in the vicinity of F Sap, blowing in part of the fire trench, but, possibly because a British barrage came down almost immediately, no attempt was made to rush the position. A desultory exchange of rifle grenades went on all day until, at about 5pm, another mine was blown by the Germans in the same area, followed by a heavy barrage that again blew in parts of the trench. Once more British artillery responded with a barrage and, again, there was no attempt by the Germans to follow it up. A patrol sent out into the crater in the early evening found it to be about 50 yards in diameter and 40 feet deep. The patrol was sniped at on its return, but fire returned by 5th Cameronians was reckoned to have killed two Germans and the sniping ceased. Sapping out to the crater began overnight.

The battalion war diary reported on the 29th:

The trenches are in a very bad state owing to bad weather and the concussion from mine explosions. Large quantities of stores are being carried up nightly, and the work of rebuilding the trenches is being carried on. Some of the men are complaining of trench foot, and arrangements have been made for the washing of feet and the changing of socks. In spite of the fact that two mines have been exploded in the one day and that conditions are severe, all ranks are cheery and optimistic.

There was fighting on both flanks on the night of 29/30 June as the British launched a raid against the Germans further north and the Germans raided the British lines south of the canal, but in front of Givenchy itself fighting was restricted to a long exchange of rifle grenades between the lines and an artillery bombardment of the enemy trenches and a slow but constant artillery attack on gaps in the German wire. During the day on the 30th two officers made a daring daylight patrol through the northern craters and obtained some useful information. At 5pm the Germans blew a small mine close to the surface near F Sap, doing comparatively little damage. It was thought the Germans were trying to blow a line of craters right along their front as a defensive measure.

For the next couple of days the German wire was subjected to a steady bombardment designed to cut their wire, with a view to a possible trench raid. It was also reported that a German mine was being dug under one of the saps and the garrison here and in the trenches nearby was reduced to a minimum. On 3 July the battalion suffered a grievous loss. Lieutenant Colonel Robert Douglas, who had brought the battalion out to France, was sniped in the head while using a trench periscope in B Sap. He was killed instantly. The same evening the battalion was relieved by 2nd Royal Welsh Fusiliers and went into billets at Le Preol. Colonel Douglas was buried next day in the Bethune town cemetery with the six senior NCOs from the battalion acting as pall bearers and the pipers playing *Flowers of the Forest*. General Landon, who commanded 33rd Division, was present, along with other senior officers of the division and brigades.

Following the detonation of Red Dragon mine things again quietened down. Repeatedly the war diary for 254th Tunnelling Company records 'Little enemy mining activity', though they were at one point working on seven separate tunnel faces! It was, for the British miners, a time for repairing existing shafts and galleries, installing new pumps and digging further lateral galleries so that a network of tunnels ran under the front line and out into no man's land.

At the start of October 1916 the 15th Battalion of the Royal Warwickshire Regiment moved up to the sector from the Somme as part of the 13th Brigade of 5th Division. They were billeted in Le Touret and, after a day or so of rest, were ordered to take over the Givenchy left sub-section and the Old British Line (OBL) from 11th East Lancs, which they carried out on the afternoon of 4 October.

The 15th settled in on 5 October, described as 'quiet', with the battalion HQ in the OBL and D Company in the front line on the left, A Company in support in the OBL and B Company in front on the right with C Company in support, also in the OBL. The trenches were noted as well boarded with good (though old) breastworks. There were a few snipers about, but there were no casualties. The men were in the line for five days, but didn't suffer a single casualty, and they were withdrawn to the Village Line around Windy Corner, being replaced by 2nd King's Own Scottish Borderers.

After another quiet few days the battalion were back in the Givenchy left sub-section on the 17th, but this time were more active, undertaking regular patrols into no man's land. At 6pm on the 17th Second Lieutenant P.H. Hollick went out with one NCO and one man to reconnoitre the enemy wire and trenches. They reported the enemy wire was very old in places and reinforced by looped trip wire. The ground was difficult to traverse and scattered with gooseberry and concertina wire. They managed to get right up to the German trench, which they reckoned was very lightly held, and they thought that all the enemy Very lights were sent up from one spot. Next night Second Lieutenant C.I. Herbert went out with one NCO and three men to try and identify weaknesses in the enemy wire and confirmed the previous night's report. Hollick went out again on the 19th, reporting that the ground was very difficult; he and the NCO and man with him had been forced to cross a waist-deep dyke. They had found the wire in reasonable order, but had been able to reach the trenches undetected 'proving that they are not very alert or are very thinly posted'. At the same time (6pm), a fighting patrol of two NCOs, five men and a Lewis gun team went out under Second Lieutenant Herbert, with the intention of wiping out a German patrol and taking a prisoner. They intercepted a numerically superior enemy, probably a German raiding party, who challenged them in broken English and then started throwing grenades. The British retired under covering fire from the Lewis gun, which caused casualties among the Germans, forcing them to withdraw. Herbert's party made it back to the British trench, leaving one man missing in no man's land. Another patrol went out the following night to look for their missing comrade, to no avail, though they did report that it appeared the Germans were now keeping geese to warn of anyone approaching. After two more quiet days, when they were subject to aerial reconnaissance but little else, the battalion was withdrawn to billets in and around Gorre Chateau and was replaced in the line by 2nd King's Own Scottish Borderers.

During their six days at Gorre, when many men found themselves back at Givenchy fetching, carrying, digging and assisting both the infantry garrison and the tunnellers, the good news came in that the man who had gone missing on Lieutenant Herbert's patrol had been found alive by the KOSB; he had been alone in no man's land, hiding up in shell holes by day and surviving on iron rations for six days.

The battalion went back into Givenchy on the evening of 28 October for another six days; daytimes were reported as quiet, but patrolling resumed on the second night. A twelve-man patrol under Second Lieutenant Hollick went out to investigate the state of the ground for future operations, but reported that the dykes were swollen and the ground impassable. On the 30th Hollick took out another patrol and managed to find a route across no man's land. On 1 November a fighting patrol of one officer, two NCOs and twenty men, backed up by another officer and two Lewis gun teams, went out to try to catch a German working party. They lay out until 1.30am, but there was no sign of any Germans and they withdrew. On 3 November, after a day in which the Germans shelled the OBL, the battalion was relieved by 2nd KOSB.

On 9 November they were back in Givenchy, but this time in the right section, relieving 2nd Battalion KOSB. A, B and C companies were from north to south in the firing line with D Company in reserve. The weather was bright and the days quiet, but on the night of the 13th a patrol of one officer and four other ranks went out to find information about enemy positions and came back with no casualties. As the evenings were drawing in patrols went out earlier in the evening. On the 14th two patrols went out; at 6.30pm Second Lieutenant Garwood took a patrol out to reconnoitre approaches to the German trenches, but their presence was detected and Garwood was hit. His NCO satisfied himself that Garwood was dead and brought back the remaining five members of the patrol unharmed. Gerald Garwood's body was never recovered and he is commemorated on the Loos Memorial to the Missing. Despite this loss a further patrol went out at 8.25pm to investigate a suspected track and came back unchallenged with the news that it seemed to lead to a pond. The battalion was relieved on 15 November by 2nd KOSB and returned to Gorre Chateau.

On 22 November the battalion went back into the line in Givenchy left section and was relieved by 14th Royal Warwickshires on the 29th. They ran no patrols in the period and in the six days they were there only Second Lieutenant P.H. Hollick and one other rank were wounded.

In December 1916 there was a renaming of the sub-sections around Givenchy, with the old Festubert right sub-section being renamed Givenchy left sub-section. 14th Warwicks held the section over Christmas, and saw heavy shelling on Christmas Day when they lost two other ranks killed and three wounded to artillery fire.

Among the men of 15th Warwicks was Private Harry Drinkwater, who was secretly writing a diary. He'd never been to the area before and was astonished at being able to relieve the line in daylight. He wrote:

> Before we had done it almost on our hands and knees and after dark, hardly daring to whisper and glad when the rotten job was over and here we were, marching along the road and whistling. We soon struck a main trench called Barnton Road and into this we dropped. The floor was in good order; duckboards all along. Underneath, we are told, is anything up to three feet of mud and water. After we had been walking up the trench some three parts of a mile, we were somewhat surprised to see cooks boiling water for tea and a little further on, men walking about apparently in the open and further on still a huge breastwork was erected which apparently went as far as we could see right and left.

Barnton Road ran from just south of the village of Festubert, up to the old front line that skirted the bottom of the slope down from Givenchy and the ridge, but Drinkwater's description gives a clear picture of the general level of inactivity on the front at that time.

Even on a quiet front the men were ordered to fire 500 rounds per Lewis gun per night. No one seemed to be quite sure why, but it was done every night: the gun on one flank would fire its quota and the remaining guns would fire in sequence down the line.

Amazingly, Harry recorded, there was still one French inhabitant in Givenchy village. On Christmas Day 1916 he reported the arrival of parcels, which came up by limber and were thrown into the road to be sorted into those for companies and then for platoons. The men opened their individual parcels and commenced munching on cake, fruit and chocolate:

Dinnertime, 12 of us had a bust. Two shoulders of lamb had produced from somewhere and taken to the only inhabitant of the village; some old dame who was a good cook and had got a room left in her cottage. To there we repaired armed with jack knives and plates. Givenchy was one of four villages scattered along the main road. Each village could best be described as a pile of ruins. There was not a cottage intact among the whole lot. Since 1914 they had been subject to bombardment and in many places the ruins were becoming overgrown with moss and grass. How this old woman preferred to remain under such circumstances of loneliness and desolation it is difficult to imagine. Her house was partly blown down and at any moment, a shell might finish it but she lived on, the only inhabitant. We sat down on anything we could find in the cottage and finished off the lamb. We had little else but the meat. There are no vegetables in this district.

No one knows who the lady was. Most previous descriptions say that the village was completely destroyed, but the occasional photograph suggests there were still some buildings half standing below the slope on the road to Windy Corner. The battalion war diary says that on 25 December they were in support, which presumably means in the vicinity of Windy Corner. Drinkwater had previously mentioned that there were damaged houses, their contents disturbed by British troops, in Festubert, and that occasional attempts were made to find and remove the few local people who were believed to be eking out a pathetic survival in the ruins of their cottages right up close to the front line. Perhaps she was in one of these.

Chapter 4

1917

The main focus of British offensive activity in 1917 shifted away from the Somme, where the Germans unexpectedly pulled back to the Hindenburg Line in March, to around Arras in April to June and then towards the Ypres salient, where on 7 June British tunnellers, who had been working in great secrecy for two years, blew the top off the Messines Ridge with nineteen huge mines. The follow-up attack, supported by an enormous artillery barrage, drove the Germans from the ridge and cleared the way for a further offensive around Ypres itself. This went ahead on 31 July and, though initially successful, it became bogged down in the autumn rain and mud that became the Battle of Passchendaele. Operations lasted until November when, eventually, the scattered ruins of Passchendaele village astride the ridge of low hills that surround Ypres were captured. Fought in unimaginable rain and mud, the battle cost nearly 650,000 casualties. In November, in conditions of great secrecy, a large force of British tanks was assembled near Cambrai and struck against the German trenches that surrounded the town. Initially there was great success, but a surprise counter-attack by the Germans negated many of the gains. The tank had, however, proved itself as an assault weapon.

In Russia, revolution broke out in February and the Tsar was forced to abdicate. The Duma (parliament) formed a provisional government which pledged to continue the war. The hard line revolutionaries set up their own Workers and Soldiers Councils (Soviets) and, at least at first, the two groups worked together. Determined to stand by its commitments, the Duma appointed Brusilov as commander in chief, but even his genius couldn't prevent Russia's last offensive of the war, launched on 1 July, from collapsing in the face of strong German resistance. Many troops, fed up with the war, simply refused to advance, and when the Germans and Austrians counterattacked they faced little resistance. The Soviets began to agitate for peace and the provisional government vacillated until it was finally overthrown by Lenin's Bolshevik Party in November. Russia was now out of the war and Germany could turn her forces westward.

There was one point that gave the Allies hope. The United States, which had tried hard to be neutral, was finally pushed into declaring war on Germany in April following the declaration of an unrestricted war on shipping in British waters by German submarines. Her army was tiny, but her population vast; though there was only a trickle of American troops into France in 1917 it was clear that many, many more would be arriving in 1918.

1917 was the quietest yet on the Bethune front. The whole line between Ploegsteert (Plugstreet) down past Armentières and along past Neuve Chapelle, Festubert and to Givenchy became known as a quiet sector. It was so quiet that it seemed the ideal spot, when Portugal entered the war in 1916 and sent a 55,000-strong Expeditionary Corps to France, to deploy the troops when they began arriving in early 1917. Their presence in the area was to have important consequences in 1918.

1st battalion the Royal West Kents, (part of 13th Brigade, 5th Division) had been in and out of the line in the Givenchy right sub-sector since the middle of January, but their spells had been fairly uneventful apart from some artillery and trench mortar exchanges with the enemy. On 6 February they were back again, with A Company in the right front trenches, B Company left front and C and D companies each with two platoons in the redoubts and two platoons in reserve at Windy Corner. On the 7th the companies swapped round, with D relieving A and C relieving B. At 4am on the 8th a heavy bombardment fell on D Company and at 4.30 'the enemy entered D Sap. The fighting that followed was very confused and the enemy soon withdrew leaving 1 man killed. Several more casualties are believed to have been inflicted on him.' The Kents lost two men killed, two more died of wounds, six wounded and two missing. At eleven o'clock the next evening a deserter made his way across from the German lines; he was from Alsace-Lorraine and 'seemed more French than German'.

After two quiet days the battalion carried out a major raid against the Germans opposite. This was not in retaliation for the German raid; it had been being planned since they first went into the trenches in mid-January, but had been postponed after the corps commander had decided that it was

Plan of the Royal West Kents'
trench raid, 10 February 1917.

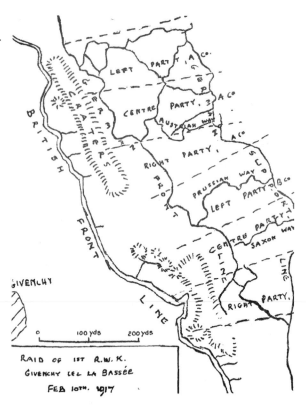

to be out carried in daylight with no preliminary bombardment to alert the enemy. During the intervening tours the ground had been reconnoitred and routes across the crater field noted (there were over fifty craters in no man's land in this one sector). Once the routes were decided on, the trench mortars began cutting the wire as part of their daily bombardments and during the periods in reserve selected parties from A and B companies were given training in bayonet fighting, wire cutting, advancing over rough ground and the use of grenades and rifle grenades. Trenches were marked out with tape at Gorre Chateau so the men would understand the layout of their targets, and maps were issued to the officers. For the first few hours in the line A and B companies had a final look around and then were relieved.

At noon on the 10th the two companies took over the line ready for the off at 2pm. Final arrangements were made, including the issue of 100 body shields and additional grenades to be carried in special carriers. Extra ammunition was issued to be carried in bandoliers, small flags were given out so the men could signal their positions, old-fashioned gas hoods were issued instead of the new box respirators, to prevent any falling into German hands, and the men were joined by two parties of miners from 254 Company RE, whose job was to identify and damage as many German mine shafts as could be located. Additional batteries had been brought up and twinned with batteries already in place so they could register their guns on their lines without giving away their positions, and for a few days beforehand the corps artillery had carried out counter-battery work at the same time each day as the raid was to take place, in the hope it would keep the enemy gunners from immediately retaliating once the raid went in. Advanced company headquarters were dug by the engineers in the saps and thirty-six additional stretcher-bearers and three medical officers were brought into the line. Temporary dressing stations were built behind each company front line and two more were next to the usual one in Herts Redoubt.

The morning was quiet; so quiet that it was thought that the Germans might have got wind of the attack from the man posted missing on the 8th, who, it was assumed, had been captured. A few shells were fired at the village at noon, but there was no sign of other activity. Zero hour was at 3pm and at precisely that time the barrage opened up and A Company, commanded by Captain William Ralph Cobb, and B Company, commanded by Captain John James Scott, went over in three parties each, with two waves to each party. There was very little resistance and both raiding parties pressed ahead quickly. The men had been equipped with phosphorus grenades, which were thrown down dug-outs. The few Germans encountered in the front line put up little resistance and were either shot or captured. As a result of the lack of resistance, the raiding parties got ahead of the plan and dashed into their own creeping barrage, causing several casualties. The enemy trenches were found to be in a wretched state. The leading party, led by Serjeant George Lines, got furthest ahead and 'must have inflicted very heavy casualties', but unfortunately Lines was badly wounded. Although an attempt was made to get him back, he died en route. He was buried later at Gorre Chateau cemetery. Having achieved all their objectives, B Company began to withdraw earlier than planned, causing A Company to think they'd missed the signal, and they too withdrew. The two raiding parties had captured one officer and twenty other ranks unwounded and several wounded men, all of the 264th Regiment. They penetrated the enemy lines to a depth of 300 yards over a front of half a mile, destroyed four mine shafts and bombed out ten dug-outs, several of which burned for hours. As a result of the raid several Germans deserted over the next couple of days. Casualties to the raiders were eleven men killed, fifty-four wounded (almost all slightly), three wounded and missing and two missing. The figure appears to apply to the Royal West Kents only, as Captain William Douglas Madore, the officer who led the 254th Company tunnellers, died of wounds in the evening at Lone Farm dressing station. The war diary noted that the artillery barrage had been excellent and commented that it was not the fault of the gunners that so many men had been made casualties by men advancing too quickly into it. Sergeant Donhoe of A Company was awarded the DCM, which appeared in the *London Gazette* of 26 March. The citation read:

For conspicuous gallantry and devotion to duty during a raid on the enemy's trenches. He handled his men with great judgment and carried out his work with conspicuous success. Later, although wounded, he carried on and personally accounted for several of the enemy, including an officer.

On 17 February 15th Royal Warwicks (part of 13th Brigade, 5th Division) relieved 14th Royal Warwicks in Givenchy left sub-section and were there until the 23rd, another quiet period relieved by periodic patrols into no man's land. Two were to check reports that the Germans were working on a new trench, which turned out to be incorrect. The third, an eight-man patrol led by Second Lieutenant A.C. Caldicott, which went out on a similar mission, came across a German working party putting up wire near Old Man's Corner and turned their Lewis gun on them, dispersing them. They got back with no casualties themselves.

On 1 March 1917 15th Royal Warwicks were again in the Givenchy left sub-section, but operating on an extended front. Again it was a quiet period by day, but on 4 March Second Lieutenant G.W. Wilson, four other ranks and a Lewis gun team, attempting to find gaps in the German wire and to test the time it would take to reach the enemy line, were discovered and subjected to heavy machine-gun fire. They withdrew and tried again, but came under renewed fire. Grenades were thrown so the men withdrew to the British trenches. A further attempt was made later, but the Germans were still on the alert so the whole thing was called off. No casualties were recorded. Next night a patrol under Second Lieutenant A.F. Page set out with the same objective, and this time the patrol halted 20 yards from the wire while Page went on alone. He found the enemy wire to be 'about 2 feet high, continuous, well staked and very strong'. An hour was spent listening but there were no sounds of activity and the patrol withdrew. They reported that the ground was rough and covered with grass and debris and it took 40 minutes to get across. On the 6th, Page took over a patrol of four men and a Lewis gun team to again examine the German wire and try to ascertain the position of their sentries. They left the British trench at No.29 post and were almost immediately fired on, but after posting the Lewis gun team Page and four men went forward and, halfway across, saw a German party working on the wire with a larger support party nearby. They avoided them and approached the wire further away, but while they were lying listening, the Germans threw a bomb into their wire about 30 yards to their left and a flare was sent up to their right. By its light they saw the heads of two sentries silhouetted above the parapet. Having verified that the wire was intact and very strong they withdrew and directed the Lewis gun to fire on the wiring party, which withdrew. They returned, after a two-hour patrol, with no casualties. The battalion was relieved on 8 March, having suffered only one other rank killed (28-year-old Drummer Frank Redhead) and one wounded in the whole six days in the line.

In May 1917 the first troops of the Portuguese Expeditionary Corps began to deploy along the front south of Armentières and east of Bethune. On 11 May the 34th Battalion became the first Portuguese unit to enter the line. Gradually other units joined them after a period of training in trench warfare by British units, so that by November they held a 12-mile length of the front from north of Festubert to south of Bois Grenier near Armentières (much of it matching the line held by the Indian Corps in 1914/15). Though the British senior officers seem to have considered them second-rate troops, they performed well in their early contacts with the Germans. Much time

Harley Street from Windy Corner, looking towards Givenchy, 1917.

and effort was spent by British units in helping them acclimatise to trench warfare and learn the techniques required to fight and survive.

In June 1917 2nd Division came back to the sector after a long period of fighting on the Somme and at Vimy Ridge. The presence of a new division prompted the Germans to begin a series of probing patrols and raids, the unlucky recipient of the first being 1st King's Liverpools on 25 June when, following a heavy artillery bombardment that lasted over three hours, the Germans put down a shrapnel barrage behind the Liverpools' trenches, effectively boxing them in (and reinforcements out), then launched an attack by stormtroopers at three points. The Liverpools were in the line near Red Dragon crater and the attack on their left companies was driven off by rifle and Lewis gun fire. C Company, next to Red Dragon, were a lot closer to the German line and here the Germans got into the British trenches. It was raining heavily and there was much confusion; Captain Francis Finlay Ryan, CO of C Company, was killed early on leading a few men in a counterattack on a party of Germans who were bombing their way down the trench; parties of Germans managed to get 150 yards into the defences and were approaching Mairie Keep. Fortunately two young second lieutenants, Stuart

Lockhart and Reginald Stuart Tarran, were in Gunners Siding with the support platoons and led a spirited counterattack that drove the enemy back, capturing several of them, and re-established the front line. The battalion lost Captain Ryan and ten other ranks killed, with seven other ranks missing, but they captured thirteen German prisoners and others were believed to have been killed or wounded.

For months after the Red Dragon explosion the Germans seemed to have calmed down their mining activities, allowing the British to expand their defensive mines and galleries more or less unmolested, but in May 1917 the sound of working was again heard, but was so faint it was, at first, assumed to be on the surface. Gradually it was realised that it was fresh German tunnelling, and that it was getting closer. The geophones tracked their every advance. Eventually the sound of quiet talking was picked up and it was realised the workings were close. A charge of 9,000lb of ammonal was laid and the tunnel 'tamped' with a series of earth barricades to ensure the full charge blew in the right direction, but before the tunnel was tamped a 'seismomicrophone' was left behind with the charge and the leads taken back to the surface. With this in place the tunnellers listened until they were sure the Germans were working with fifteen feet of the charge, then blew it on 10 August. It resulted in a large, elliptical crater immediately south of the old Duck's Bill crater and within a day the Germans had begun putting defensive posts on their side of the crater lip. In response the 17th Royal Fusiliers mounted a sortie of their own to the British lip of the crater following an artillery barrage, drove the Germans back and established three posts along the lip, which they surrounded with barbed wire, placed Lewis gun sections in and then withdrew, with the loss of three other ranks killed and six wounded. The battalion had been formed at Warlingham in 1915 and so the crater was named Warlingham Crater in their honour.

The Warlingham explosion was the last blown by the British on any front and the Germans only fired three more small ones, which did no damage, in September and October when the tunnelling war effectively ceased. But no one knew that then, and a long listening watch continued to the end, while the tunnellers' work gradually shifted to other defensive excavations.

At the beginning of October, 25th Division took over the sector and were there for seven weeks. The centre section of their line, which straddled the

La Bassée Canal looking towards Pont Fixe, 1917.

canal and included Givenchy, was held by the 75th Brigade comprising 11th Cheshires, 8th Border Regiment and 8th South Lancs. As the divisional history noted:

> An immense amount of labour had been expended in strengthening and improving the system of trenches with tunnels, deep dug-outs for machine guns and their detachment and strong fortified posts... In all probability it is no exaggeration to say that the Givenchy sector was the best and most scientifically defended portion of the whole British front.

It was a quiet period, with only the inevitable artillery exchanges, occasional trench mortar bombardments and two trench raids in the whole seven weeks. Typical of war diaries for the period is the one for 1st Battalion, the Wiltshire Regiment, for the period between 11 and 16 October:

> On the afternoon of the 11th the Battn relieved the 10th Cheshire Regt in the line. The relief was effected without casualty. On the right was the 2nd S Lancs of 75th Bde, and on the left the 8th LN Lancs Regt. The Battn's line was extended from Wolfe Road (A 9 d) to northern end of Warwick South Island, (A 3 a 8.6). Three Coys held the front line and one was in Support in Gunner Siding, The Avenue

and Upper Cut. During this time the Battn remained in the line: the enemy's attitude throughout was very quiet, and his line appeared to be held lightly, particularly at day: his artillery was not active except on the neighbourhood of Givenchy Church which was shelled almost daily with 77mm and 5.9' shells. Enemy's trench mortars only fired occasionally, chiefly upon the right Coy's Sector, and the greater part of these fell in rear of the front line. A special labour platoon was formed for purposes of work in the line, and these men and all available men of Coys were employed upon the maintenance of front, support and communication trenches. The work was particularly urgent as on the approach of wet weather portions of the trenches began to collapse: to combat this a large amount of revetting was taken in hand and the work continued throughout the Battn's tour. In addition the trenches were kept well drained. The Regimental snipers had few targets, but some hits were claimed: good retaliatory fire was opened by the Stokes mortars in this Sector whenever the enemy's mortars opened, but our artillery generally was inactive. Officers' patrols were out each night and succeeded in locating a few of the enemy's posts and Machine Guns, but no identification was obtained.

Much of the time was spent training men from the Portuguese division to the north by taking battalions into the British line for a few days. At the end of October 25th Division was moved to the Somme and it was replaced by 42nd (East Lancashire) Division, which had previously fought at Gallipoli and which had, since its arrival in France in February 1917, been in the line at Epehy, Ypres and, most recently, on the edge of the flooded coastal sector at Nieuport.

42 Division's time in the sector was mostly spent building reinforced concrete shelters and emplacements or reinforcing what defences they could with the same materials. The system of defended localities (known as keeps) was reinforced, even more heavily wired, mutually supported with machine-gun fire and connected, where possible, by shell-proof underground tunnels with deep dug-outs and command posts. The value of this work was later acknowledged in a letter from Major General Jeudwine of 55th Division

in a letter to Major General Solly-Flood of 42nd Division following 55th Division's defence of the area in April 1918.

Throughout their period in the sector the Divisional Royal Engineers (427, 428 and 429 Field Companies) worked at improving the defences. It was so quiet that the engineers were able to carry out most of their work by day. They noted the importance of Givenchy 'To the north (of the canal) the tactical feature – on which our retention of the whole sector depends – is the Givenchy ridge'.

427th Field Company left an excellent description of the system in the war diary:

> The trench system is elaborate. The majority of it is revetted with A frames or pickets with hurdles and floored with 'duckboards'; the trench drains under the trench or 'duckboards' discharge north of the canal at fairly frequent intervals into the main drains and south of the canal merely hold the water till it drains away. The trenches in general are too narrow, the traverses are too small and the parapets not divided from the trenches by berms. The front line is in good order, although subject to trench mortar fire... North of the canal the posts alone exist, situated at the heads of the communication trenches, the lateral trenches having been filled in with wire or destroyed by the enemy's shell fire. Both south and north of the canal the close support line is abandoned, shallow and damaged by shell fire. The main support or reserve line is in fairly good order. Communication trenches are numerous and cannot all be fully maintained accordingly. Trench mortar and machine gun emplacements are also numerous. Trench railways run forward as far as the support line.

427th took over the work already started by 106th Company RE, including the completion of two pairs of 6in trench mortar emplacements, each equipped with an ammunition store for 150 bombs, a firing recess and a gun pit. The sides were strongly lagged with steel rails set vertically in concrete and holding up one-inch boarding, with a concrete floor. Tunnelled dug-outs were provided for six men and tunnels were also created for ammunition stores. The pits themselves were provided with roller screens that could be worked from inside the pits, but they didn't work efficiently and were replaced by rigid screens that hung on the side of the pits and could easily be hoisted, using pulleys, into position.

An attempt was made to tunnel a deep battalion HQ in a big spoil bank to the north of the canal, but water was encountered at 14ft which could not be got rid of except by the building of a complex drainage system, and the project had to be abandoned. A battery position for ten machine guns was built and work was started on concrete field-gun emplacements, though the onset of a sudden thaw meant this work had to stop while men were put to work clearing trenches, laying new duckboards and revetting the trench sides. Many of the concrete emplacements flooded and the side walls collapsed. Tunnelled dug-outs were built, including one in Orchard Road which was too shallow, because of water levels, but was completed because it was felt to be better than what was there previously. New fire steps facing to the flank and rear were built in the trenches in the defensive positions on the left of the Givenchy position. The three companies relieved each other on these projects and when not working on strictly defensive positions there was a great deal of work done providing shell-proof billets around Windy Corner, improving the tramways that ran from the RE forward dumps near Windy Corner up the main communication trench and Harley Street, and extending the line back to Pont Fixe and the canal and building concrete command posts for the artillery. A new tram line between Moat Farm and Mairie Redoubt was completed and, where a previous line crossed the trench at Gunner Siding and impeded movement, a moveable span was laid over the trench. Extensive work was done on the Village Line installing concrete shelters and repairing the trenches and the obstacles in front of them.

Careful positioning of the divisional machine guns meant that every possible inch of ground over which a German attack on the village might be expected was covered by direct or indirect fire. Two guns cunningly placed in the railway embankment south of the canal covered the ground above Death or Glory sap as far as Red Dragon Crater, and four guns at Festubert Keep could sweep, by indirect fire, the ground north of Givenchy. Concrete pill boxes were carefully sited – one consumed over 200 tons of reinforced concrete before it was considered strong enough.

The crater field, Givenchy, 1917.

251 Tunnelling Company had also dug an extensive network of deep dug-outs, linked by underground passages. A long tunnel, known as Bunny Hutch Subway, was dug from the mine system at Bunny Hutch Shaft, in the front line, to the slope behind the ridge where it came out near Moat Farm Keep. The mining officers' dug-out was off the tunnel and a spiral staircase went up to the Caledonian Road communication trench with a sloping incline, called Piccadilly, forward to the surface at Piccadilly support trench. Just behind the support line, along the crest of the Givenchy Ridge, a deep set of dug-outs, capable of holding two battalions and complete with tiers of bunk beds, was created, linked by passages and, being 40ft deep, impervious to the largest shells. It connected Givenchy Keep and Mairie Keep, which were 300 yards apart, with entrance shafts at each. Three inclined shafts led up into the support lines to facilitate easy exit by the garrison if an attack took place. Three vertical shafts, steel lined, with a concrete cap reinforced by railway tracks, provided fresh air to the system and contained the pumps necessary to keep the water levels down in the passages. Power was supplied from a power station at Pont Fixe.

Though it was generally quiet, there was always the chance of a sudden raid. 1/10th Manchesters (the 'Oldham Terriers') took over the line from 4th East Lancashire Regiment on 10 December and had only been in the front line for an hour or two when the Germans, knowing a relief had just taken place, bombarded their trenches with gas, preliminary to an attack. Frederick Gibbon wrote in the 42nd divisional history:

Practically every man in the post in Red Dragon Crater, occupied by men of 'C' Company, was affected by the gas, and most had been put out of action when the Germans attacked. But though choking, blinded and reeling – and well aware from lectures on the subject that exertion under such circumstances is likely to be fatal – every man who could stand made for the parapet, and with bombs, rifles, and Lewis guns put up a memorable fight, one after another sinking back into the trench to die from the poison. But they held their post and beat the Boche, and every man who took part deserved recognition. Private Walter Mills, realising the deadly nature of the gas and the danger of the post being lost, sprang at once to the top of the trench and fought magnificently to save the situation. Though suffering acutely from the gassing he remained there, throwing bombs and beating off the attack,

Private Walter Mills, 10th Manchesters, who defended the sap at Duck's Bill with grenades until overcome by gas, 10/11 December 1917, and was awarded a posthumous VC.

and fell back to die just before victory was assured. He was selected for the posthumous award of the VC and four other men of the company received the Military Medal.

Sergeant Maurice Bradbury described the fight in one of a series of articles in *The Oldham Standard* in 1919:

There was plenty of snow on the ground at the time and it was bitterly cold in the trenches. The 10th had commenced a tour of duty in the front line on that day, and had only been in an hour or two when the gas came. It was too much of a surprise and came too rapidly for the men to have any real chance and they were casualties before they realised what had happened. That night will stand out as one of the most glorious in the annals of the 10th Manchesters, for there was not a man there but was a hero. The advanced post were the first to succumb to the effects of the gas and there casualties became general, and when everything and everybody were upset the Germans came over the top and tried to reach our lines. Men suffering from gas leapt to the parapet and hurled bombs or fired their rifles, knowing full well that it was certain death to exert themselves in the least and that their only chance of life was to remain perfectly still until they were carried away. Men died that night on the parapet almost in the act of firing but the Germans never reached our lines, and the attack was a failure, thanks to the self-sacrifice and bravery of those Oldham lads. It was that night which brought the battalion its first V.C., which was awarded to Private Mills who gave his life in keeping the Germans back.

Private Walter Mills, 375499, who had served with his battalion since it first went abroad in May 1915 (to Gallipoli, where it fought with distinction), and who had, before the war, been a piecer at the Greenacres Spinning Co. in Oldham, was carried back from the crater but died as he was being transported. He is buried in at Gorre British and Indian cemetery, only a few miles from where he fought and died. His Victoria Cross was gazetted on 13 February 1918, the citation reading:

On 10–11 December 1917 at Givenchy, France, after an intense gas attack a strong enemy patrol tried to rush British posts, the garrisons of which had been overcome. Private Mills, although badly gassed himself, met the attack single-handed and continued to throw bombs until the arrival of reinforcements and remained at his post until the enemy had been finally driven off. While being carried away he died of gas poisoning but it was entirely due to him that the enemy was defeated and the line remained intact.

The grave of Private Walter Mills VC, Gorre Chateau cemetery.

Gorre Chateau cemetery, where so many men killed in Givenchy lie.

Life out of the line

It should be obvious to readers of this account that the ordinary soldier did not spend the bulk of his time in the front-line trenches, or even in the support lines further back. The longest spell in the Givenchy front line was twenty days, by 2nd Battalion, the Welsh Regiment, in January and February 1915. At Givenchy it was common to spend three or four days in the front line, alternating with a similar spell in the support line at Le Plantin or Windy Corner. As Harry Drinkwater has suggested, there were still a few original French inhabitants clinging on in the wreckage of their homes, and there were certainly enough buildings left to provide billets for troops. During the early part of the war, troops could bathe and swim in the canal quite close to Pont Fixe, and in the quietest year, 1917, there was a newspaper vendor at Windy Corner selling the latest British newspapers. Not much further back, on the road to Gorre, where the supporting artillery was sited at the Tuning Fork, there were fully functioning cottages by the roadside, whose owners still managed to till their small gardens and hang their washing out on lines strung between the battery positions. Many civilian men still cycled to work in the Bethune coalfield nearby. Gorre had a civilian population, including a café that sold the ever popular dish of egg and chips. The French authorities made a conscious decision not to evacuate the civilian population, mainly because the coalfield required the labour, but also because of the huge number of refugees from earlier in the war. In the Portuguese sector to the north it was stated quite flatly by a British officer that the women (whose menfolk were away in the army) 'sold themselves for milrais (money)'; no doubt similar comforts could be obtained by British troops.

Even when pulled back behind the firing line, the soldier had plenty to keep him busy. The battalions in reserve at Windy Corner could train on a miniature rifle range and training and lectures were arranged in the buildings there. Much of the time was spent, however, in providing carrying parties up to Givenchy itself or labour for the Royal Engineer Field Companies or Tunnelling Companies in the vicinity. Further back, there was a constant demand for road building and the digging of defensive lines, and the unloading of railways and barges. There was little time for rest, but it kept the men busy and out of trouble.

Gorre Chateau, 1917. It provided billets for troops throughout most of the war, but was destroyed in April 1918.

Drunkenness and associated violence were a problem. The two soldiers who shot and killed Company Sergeant Major Hughie Hayes at Pont Fixe had clearly been drinking, and a lance serjeant of the Welsh Regiment was killed at Gorre in April 1918 after a soldier discovered a stash of wine and returned to the chateau drunk. The army knew that it could never stop soldiers from drinking and tried to arrange other entertainments as a distraction. As well as regular sporting contests (football and boxing were particularly popular, but cricket, rugby, hockey and shooting competitions also took place), both within the battalion and against other units, each division usually had its own theatre company. 25th Division had its own Pierrot Troupe, who were installed at the Municipal Theatre at Bethune. Their divisional historian wrote:

> Their daily performances gave the greatest of pleasure to thousands of men of all units within reach, and the employment in this manner of a few talented men, some professionals, some amateurs, was amply justified by their cheering effect on the troops during the winter

months. The importance of providing good wholesome entertainment of this description for the troops in competition with the estaminets cannot be overemphasised.

As well as the theatre Bethune boasted 'a first class restaurant, an excellent officers' club, a well stocked Expeditionary Force canteen and several cinemas', as well as attractions of 'a more dubious nature', which included a brothel for officers and another for 'other ranks'.

Robert Graves was billeted in the town in June 1915 and described it as:

a fair sized town about seven miles behind the front line. It has everything one wants; a swimming bath, all sorts of shops, especially a cake shop, the best I've ever met, a hotel where you can get a really good dinner, and a theatre where we have Brigade 'gaffs'.

It hadn't changed very much by 1917. In December the quartermasters of 42nd Division were able to buy 'oranges, apples and nuts, and even beer at a price', as well as locally reared pigs which they fattened before slaughter. Harry Drinkwater recorded a visit to the town in October 1916.

It is forbidden to walk about in daylight so we made for a teashop and then stayed till dusk. We had some excellent French pastries and tea. At dusk we made our way out and had a look around town. It's a fine show and assumed most natural conditions except no lights were showing. Most requirements could be bought. We went into a local cinema that was still showing. Afterwards to a café for egg and chips and then back here to Gorre. All troops had to be clear by nine o'clock and civilians indoors.

Troops lucky enough to be billeted in Bethune were usually in the old Tobacco Factory near the railway station, the Montmorency Barracks to the west or the 'Ecole des Jeunes Filles' (Girl's School) to the east, which in the first two years of the war retained some of its former pupils and which later became the ambulance station. Here there were showers and baths, a much-needed relief from the mud in the trenches. Early in the war (certainly up to the beginning of 1916) troops were also billeted in the Orphanage. Robert

Graves who, as an officer, was billeted in the Rue de Bruay with a refugee family 'of the official class' in the summer of 1915, had it explained to him by their daughter that her lessons were constantly being interrupted because the Germans knew there were British troops billeted there and shelled the place regularly.

Even the vicinity of Givenchy could be reckoned quiet. Harley Street, now the D166 which runs from Cuinchy to Festubert via Windy Corner, apparently came alive at dusk, at least in late 1917. According to the 42nd divisional history:

With divisional baths and a reading and recreation room in full swing, the street was a crowded thoroughfare, and when night fell limbers and wagons passed through in an unending stream. Men lounged in the doorways of ruined houses, smoking, passing remarks on things in general and critical comments on drivers and animals. The air hummed with the buzz of conversation, broken now and again by snatches of popular ditties from gatherings of convivial souls.

But even when it was apparently quiet, the war was never far away. When the Canadians made their brief visit to the area in June 1915 an NCO of the Royal Canadian Dragoons reported two incidents in a letter:

I had a humorous and at the same time hair-raising exploit this afternoon [7 June 1915]. We came out of the trenches on Friday evening, and came along eventually to this village, through which there was a dandy canal, broad, clean and deep; and as the day was hot, we had a bathing parade this afternoon. While we were swimming around enjoying ourselves the Germans started chucking shells across; one fell in a field about 100 yards away, which only made the fellows look, as they have got so callous; but about half a minute later one fell on the bank and wounded five, and three more fell near us in the water in quick succession. Well! You should have seen the scatter! I broke all records for the fifty yards dash to the bank, picked up my clothes, and streaked naked over a hedge, railway, and about three fields before I stopped and looked around; all I could see was naked bodies darting in all directions;

I simply had to laugh. Well, they dropped another half–dozen shells and then stopped; that is only an afternoon's pastime for the Germans. But I have a nastier one than that to tell you about. On the way back from the trenches on Friday we stopped in a village about two miles back from the line; mind, this was fully inhabited, that's where we think the authorities make a big mistake. Anyway, we stayed until Saturday night, then a spy either gave the news away or an aeroplane saw us, and the shelling started; they fell all around us. I was standing talking to my best chum, a fellow from the wilds of Canada, in the street, and a shell fell just beside us. He pitched forward into my arms and gasped: 'Goodbye, I'm done!' I laid him on his back, and did all I could for him; but he died with his jugular vein severed and a gaping hole through his lungs. While I knelt over him, another burst near, and I ran across, as there had been some women near; when the dust had cleared I found two women, a girl about sixteen, and a little baby about nine months, all mangled, lying dead. We carried them into a house and covered them with sheets and placed my chum beside them… I made a cross, put all particulars on it, and made a wreath of beautiful flowers, which I got in the garden of a house ruined by a shell; then yesterday, Sunday, a party of a dozen of us went back and buried him under a beautiful pear tree in a quiet place, and as we turned away I don't think I ever saw a more beautiful picture than that quiet grave.

The NCO's mate was almost certainly Private William Reader, aged forty and a veteran of the Boer War who had been born in Kent. He was reinterred in Brown's Road military cemetery after the war.

Chapter 5

1918 and After

The last year of the war (though the thought it was to be so would have caused great merriment at the beginning of the year) suddenly saw Givenchy back in the limelight and strategically significant for the first time since 1915. Russia had effectively left the war in late 1917 and in November the Bolshevik Party took control of the government in a virtually unopposed *coup d'état*, eventually being forced to sign an imposed peace treaty on 3 March. Over the course of late 1917 and early 1918 British intelligence identified fifty-two German divisions moving westward from the Russian Front. Though the Americans had entered the war the previous April and troops were arriving in France in growing numbers, there were not yet enough to significantly change the balance. An extra fifty-two German divisions (though not all were sent to France) might make all the difference, and Haig and his staff knew that German offensives were coming, although not where. The Germans struck on 21 March against 5th Army and 3rd Army between Arras and La Fère, south of St Quentin. Following the heaviest bombardment of the war so far, and under cover of a heavy fog, troops of the German 17th, 2nd, 18th and 7th armies advanced along a 40-mile front, fighting their way through the lightly held Forward Zone and into the Battle Zone, driving back the badly stretched battalions of 5th Army. The Germans used tactics developed on the Eastern Front, using small groups of men to infiltrate gaps between the British defences and leaving the isolated defended posts to be mopped up later. By the end of the second day 5th Army was in full retreat, but it continued to fight and the Germans never quite broke their line, which fell back, regrouped and fought on. Reinforcements were rushed to support, including French divisions, and the advance was gradually slowed. On 28 March the Germans tried to break through to the north of the rapidly expanding salient to capture Arras, but 3rd Army were well dug in and the attack was repulsed with heavy losses. On 4 April the Germans began a drive to capture the strategically important rail junction of Amiens, but were frustrated by the Australian 35th Battalion and the British 14th and 18th Divisions at Villers-Bretonneux. The offensive came to a halt. It was clear that further German offensives would be launched along other parts of the line.

At Givenchy things had changed greatly since 1915. The vast increase in fire power provided by reorganisation of the artillery, coordinated fire plans, plenty of ammunition and the issuing of the Lewis light machine gun to the front line troops meant that the whole sector could now be defended by just two battalions rather than by the three (sometimes four) that had been required previously. British tunnellers had won the war underground and there was no sign of any German mining activity; indeed, the British miners had built a series of deep tunnels and dug-outs that could shelter the defenders against the heaviest artillery the Germans could throw at them. The defensive strategy being adopted along the whole British front of defence in depth, with a lightly held front line of posts, a secondary line of strong points and a final battle zone where the enemy could be engaged from a proper defensive line could not be adopted in so small an area, but the saps became the front line, the old continuous front-line trenches were in large part abandoned and filled with barbed wire to create an additional obstacle, the series of keeps and redoubts became the second line and the support trenches became the battle zone. Fighting was now carried out by individual platoons with specific defensive or offensive roles, and was planned to be much more flexible in response to German tactics that also involved a more flexible assault in small groups.

The village itself had virtually disappeared; the church could still be located by the mound of rubble it had become, and Mairie Redoubt identified where the maire's office had stood in peacetime. Of the rest, no wall stood more than a few inches high and the fields where the haystacks had burned in December 1914 during the Manchesters' attack were nothing but a sea of mine and shell craters. But Givenchy was still atop its gentle rise, and still dominated the country behind the British lines for miles around – and the Germans had not forgotten.

On 15 February 42nd Division was relieved by 55th (West Lancashire) Division, which became forever associated with Givenchy. Their memorial

Major General Arthur Solly-Flood, who commanded 42nd Division in 1917/18 and vastly improved the Givenchy defences.

was built there after the war. The division consisted of Territorial Force units from West Lancashire, though by 1918 the number of former Terriers in the ranks had been much depleted, and reinforcements were coming through from the men conscripted in 1917. Though the division had been ready to go to war as a formation in August 1914, its infantry units had been sent out to France piecemeal to reinforce the BEF and its artillery was sent out in October 1915 to fight with the 2nd Canadian Division. In January 1916 the disparate units in France were reconstituted as a division, and it conducted its first operations as a whole south of Arras in February. In July 1916 it moved south to the Somme and fought in the battles of Guillemont, Ginchy, Flers-Courcelette and Morval, before being sent to the Ypres salient in October. It was in the salient for a year and took part in the early stages

Major General Hugh Jeudwine, who commanded 55th Division at Givenchy in 1918.

of the Third Battle of Ypres at Pilckem Ridge and Menin Road Ridge. In October it moved to Cambrai and, following the successful tank attack there in November, faced the full might of the German counterattack. Outflanked when the division on its left flank fell back unexpectedly, the 55th fell back too and was subject to an official court of enquiry. The commanding officer, Major General Sir Hugh Sandham Jeudwine, mounted a spirited defence, including the fact that there had been no heavy artillery assistance from III Corps as he had requested, but the division's reputation suffered badly in the eyes of the higher command and it was sent back behind the lines for intensive training.

Jeudwine was furious and determined that this humiliation would not happen again. Jeudwine was a bit of a martinet, but he had definite ideas of what was required and gave clear orders as to what was expected:

Infantry continued their training and, even in the line, every man in front or support line, was expected to fire at least five rounds a day if it was in any way possible... every day the garrison of every post was tested and timed in getting from its mined dug out or shelter, where it had one, to its fire trenches, and where the performance was unsatisfactory the test was carried out again and again... (each) platoon was trained to be the fighting unit, competent to carry on its own in any circumstances of defence or counter-attack... A standing order was issued that every officer and man in the division was to put on his box respirator at 10 o'clock every day and wear it till 10.15 no matter what he was doing. Several exercises were carried out actually in the positions to be occupied, so that everybody, even the most junior of officers, knew not only the exact spot he was first to go to, but such details as what ammunition was to be carried, where reserve ammunition would be, what rations were to be taken, how communications ran, and how to obtain touch with the front line, what tools were to be taken and exactly how and with what stores each limbered wagon was to be packed. Especial attention was paid to getting men fit, but the most important training of all, and the one to which the greatest attention was given, was with the rifle, the bayonet and the Lewis gun... every company was expected to have its 30 yard range if possible of 8 targets, and every man had to fire 10 rounds a day, no matter what his employment might be. Special attention was paid to rapid fire, and a battalion was expected to try and to attain an average of 12-15 aimed rounds per man per minute. Bayonet courses were established close to billets. In Lewis gun training, particular attention was devoted to remedying stoppages and continuous supply of ammunition, so that fire should not be checked. Machine gunners were trained on similar lines. The aim was to give every man skill with his own weapon so that he might have confidence in it and to develop to the utmost the volume of fire.

The takeover of the 42nd Division positions proceeded quietly, but the Germans were soon aware that new troops were opposing them and mounted probing attacks and raids. 1/4th Loyal North Lancashire Regiment took over from 1/8th Lancashire Fusiliers on the canal on 14 February, with three companies on the north bank and one on the south. They spent the first couple of days repairing and improving the defences and sending out night patrols, but on the 17th:

> At 3 15 am a silent raiding party of the enemy rushed the crater [Warlingham Crater] posts of the Left Company [D] under the cover of smoke bombs. The enemy were quickly ejected and the situation restored. Two enemy dead were left in the crater. We had one officer [Second Lieutenant Westwood] wounded and 3 OR's missing. 2 Other ranks wounded.

It was almost certainly a raid to test the responses of the new garrison and to capture prisoners for identification purposes. The next couple of days

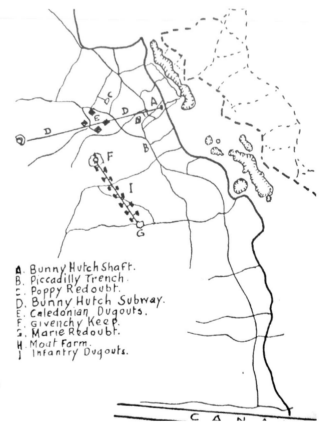

A. Bunny Hutch Shaft.
B. Piccadilly Trench.
C. Poppy Redoubt.
D. Bunny Hutch Subway.
E. Caledonian Dugouts.
F. Givenchy Keep.
G. Marie Redoubt.
H. Moat Farm.
I Infantry Dugouts.

The network of defensive tunnels under the village, 1918.

were quiet, but the Fusiliers did push night patrols into the enemy front line for 200 yards without encountering any troops; one patrol tried to rush a German wiring party, but it got away. They were relieved in their part of the line by 1/4th King's Own Royal Lancasters on 20 February. The battalion history says of this period 'Trench life at this period was comparatively uneventful, quiet periods alternating with intermittent shelling on both sides, while patrols scoured No Man's Land nightly.'

March 1918 passed quietly, but there was definitely something in the wind. Jeudwine kept up his relentless training schedule and the troops were 'stood to' regularly. The signal 'Bustle' was to be made in the event of an attack being anticipated. It was an uneasy period in the war as a whole. On 21 March the Germans struck against the British 5th and 3rd Armies on the Somme and, within a few days, had pushed them back miles, taking tens of thousands of prisoners. All leave for the men of 55th Division was cancelled on 25 March. As the Lys front was reckoned to be a quiet one, divisions that had been decimated further south were transferred there to recover and take reinforcements. 102 Brigade of 34 Division, for example, which was sent to Armentières on 30 March, had lost all its battalion commanding officers, seven company commanders, forty-four other officers and 1,422 other ranks, all of whom had been recently replaced, leaving units which had not trained together, did not know each other and did not know the ground they were to fight over. 40th Division, which took over the line to their south, had sustained similar levels of casualties.

Then there were the Portuguese. Nine months in the line had not been good to them. Though there had been little fighting, apart from the odd trench raid in which they acquitted themselves well, disease and a daily dribble of battle casualties had badly affected both their numbers and morale. Reinforcement had been virtually impossible because of a shortage of shipping, so 2nd Portuguese Division was well below strength, being 399 officers and 7,059 other ranks short on 30 March 1918. Many battalions were commanded by captains, companies by subalterns and platoons by sergeants. The established strength of a battalion was thirty-seven officers, but one had as few as thirteen (Infantry Battalion No. 12); others had between sixteen and nineteen officers and the most up-to-strength (Infantry Battalion No. 17) had only thirty. Likewise, the other rank strength of a battalion should have been 1,083, but the strongest (Infantry Battalion No.15) had 678 and the weakest (Infantry Battalion No.10) had just 577. Morale was at rock bottom and there was a battalion mutiny on 4 April. Such was the concern of the British, that it was agreed that the Portuguese would be withdrawn from the line on 9 April and British troops would begin to replace them. To this end 166th Brigade of 55th Division moved north across the La Bassée canal and prepared to move into the line over the next couple of days. Patrols pushed out from Givenchy during the first days of April managed to get hundreds of yards into the enemy positions without encountering any Germans; it all seemed very quiet.

On the morning of 9 April there was a thick and persistent fog that reduced visibility to ten yards in places. At 4.15am the Germans opened a barrage of gas and heavy explosive shells along the whole front. The Givenchy sector was being held by 1/4th Loyal North Lancs on the northern side of the village and 1/4th Kings Own Royal Lancasters were holding the slope down to the canal south of Warlingham Crater. In reserve were 2/5th Lancashire Fusiliers, with two companies at Windy Corner and the remainder at Gorre Chateau. Facing 55 Division was 4 Ersatz Division, part of General Kraevel's IV Corps, which had left the Eastern Front in January and moved up to the sector on 5 April, which was to attack Givenchy itself; north of them was 43 Reserve Division, which had moved from Russia in February and north of them again was 18 Reserve Division, which had moved south from Ypres.

The whole thrust of the German offensive, which extended on the first day as far north as Armentières, was to break through the Portuguese and 55th Division, push back the Divisions (40th and 34th) around Armentières and cross the River Lys and its tributary the River Lawe before the end of the first day. With flanking attacks along the canal and round the north of the village, which would capture Windy Corner and advance rapidly towards Bethune, Givenchy could be isolated and mopped up at leisure. Before British reserves could be deployed, Bethune was to be seized and, north of the Lys, the ultimate objective was the strategic rail junction at Hazebrouck, the capture of which would cut the lines north to Ypres and force the British to withdraw to the coast. It was an ambitious plan, but its success depended upon 55th Division being as poor as German intelligence assessments suggested.

Givenchy defences 1918; a forward sap.

One of Jeudwine's peculiarities was his insistence that every platoon should write a brief description of its actions during each battle, to be written by the senior surviving member. This sometimes means we have eyewitness accounts written by privates and lance corporals in the official divisional papers and they are used here, where appropriate, to illustrate the course of the fight.

At about 5am the artillery barrage began to concentrate on the keeps and support lines, before moving again after about an hour to hit the sapheads, the main lines of resistance and the communications trenches. The Germans seem to have been unaware of the deep dug-outs and communications tunnels, and didn't concentrate fire on them. At around 8.30am two battalions of the 360th Infantry Regiment launched an assault on 1/4th KORL south of the village.

The most advanced British post was Death or Glory sap on the canal bank itself, and Sergeant Frank Dawson later described its defence:

We were holding a very important flank position on the left bank of the La Bassée Canal and in front of Givenchy on the 9th April 1918 called Death and Glory sap (number 3 Platoon). A stiff barrage of all calibres including numerous gas projectors began at 4am, and we all stood to with our gas masks on for fully 3½ hours, gazing with much eagerness into No Man's Land but could not see far beyond our own wire owing to the deep mist, which hung thickly in the air. Shells were falling pretty freely all around but none found its berth in our little sap, for which I can assure you we were truly thankful and we all kept a good lookout in anticipation of a Bosche attack. I was joking with the men on one of the Lewis Gun Posts when my brave comrade Sgt Birkett shouted 'they're here' and every man with one accord and eagerness placed his rifle to his shoulder to comply with 2nd Lt Dane's order 'up Lads and at 'im' (15 rounds rapid fire). We displayed some fine shooting, and held our opponents at bay for fully 3 hours with rifle and LG fire. In the meantime we lost a dear old lad, L/Cpl Bennett. Our left Lewis Gun team proved its worth and did much severe hand to hand fighting, finding out that the Bosches had endeavoured and gained possession of our CT trench, they at once made a block in the trench but owing to accuracy of a few Bosche bombs, lost the whole of their team with the exception of one man, Pte Gayler. At any rate we were too wide for our rivals later on, and 2nd Lt Raeside along with other men such as Cpl Hogg, L/Cpl Round kept the Bosche at bay with bombs, in which attempt the gallant officer was sniped and died. In the meantime we got rather troubled with our own shells, and 2nd Lt Dane asked for volunteers to take a message down to CHQ. Cpl Hogg and L/Cpl Round went with the message and though opposed many a time with great odds, arrived at their destination and soon were back again with an answer.

Things afterwards cooled down a bit, and movement being seen in our wire, Sgt Birkett went out and behold 17 prisoners were taken by him also a M Gun. I took them down to Battn HQ but on my journey I was encountered with one Bosche fully armed but I soon proved myself too good for him and took him down the CT trench with me along with the others. On returning everything was pretty normal, our survivors cheery and we enjoyed a good square meal sent up from the cookhouse, about 11am thanks to the cooks and our worthy CQMS.

Things remained normal until about 6 pm when we enjoyed ourselves more than anything else, killing the retreating Bosche or at least severely punishing him once more with our rifle and L G fire. Thanks to the coolness of all our 3 Officers 2/Lt Raeside, 2/Lt Dane and 2/Lt Pemberton, and all our NCOs and men who on that day scored a decisive victory for their Platoon, Company and Battalion and not least the gallant 55th Division.

The mist was so thick that the usual SOS flares fired to call down artillery support could not be seen (even by the men who fired them). Second Lieutenant Lionel Andrews was in Bayswater Trench with part of A Company when:

At 8.30 approx it was rumoured that the SOS had been sent up from Death and Glory sap, but owing to the mist all visual signals were rendered useless. A few minutes later Bosches were seen from Bayswater about thirty yards in front and at the same time it was found that they were in rear of us also. The writer then got hold of a few men and went out over the back of Bayswater to investigate. The trench leading to Spoil Bank OP was found to be occupied by the enemy but they were soon bombed out. We then drove the remainder of the enemy towards Spoil bank, till we found that we were under fire from our own people in Spoil Bank Keep, so we returned to Bayswater.

Finding that the right flank of Bayswater was uncertain I got together a small party and got connection with Cheyne Walk, eventually getting to Coy HQ where we met others of the Coy who had worked their way up from Spoil Bank Keep.

Not having definite news from Death and Glory sap about 10 o'clock I went with a party of 6, along Cheyne Walk to the sap and found the garrison there still holding out in spite of casualties (which included 2 Lt Raeside whose loss was keenly felt by every man in the company). The garrison in the sap was reinforced about midday and during the afternoon did excellent work with rifle and lewis gun, firing at numbers of the enemy returning to their own trenches from the neighbourhood of Warlingham Crater. At least 30 hits were observed during this time, the range being from two to three fifty yards.

Other Germans worked their way along the wire to the north and began to cut their way in. At 8.35am the Moat Farm garrison heard something through the fog and issued a challenge, to which came the reply 'Me Portuguese. Beaucoup bombard'. Thinking they might be Portuguese miners, who had been working on the defences, the garrison held their fire, but the mist lifted momentarily to reveal Germans in full pack. The order to fire was immediately given and both Vickers machine guns, two Lewis guns and every rifle that could be brought to bear opened up. According to Sergeant Atkinson they continued to shout 'Come and help Tommy, we are Portuguese', but the firing was kept up. Having driven them off temporarily the garrison fired an SOS rocket, but the mist was so thick the garrison itself could not see the flare, let alone any watching artillery observers. Shortly

Givenchy defences 1918; Moat Farm Keep.

afterwards enemy grenades were thrown into the strong point and a machine gun opened up from close range. This was on the roof of the cookhouse and was manned by two Germans, who were rapidly despatched by rifle and revolver fire. A Lewis gun was placed to cover the farm entrance and a runner sent out to find headquarters and to report that the post still held out. The Germans seemed quite unaware of the tunnel entrance leading into the heart of the defences, which was right behind them.

The value of the tunnel system in both providing cover and moving men between the posts was immense, but few of the accounts mention it, concentrating on the fighting once the men got to the surface. Lance Sergeant Robert William Jones of 16 Platoon, D Company, 2/5th Lancs Fusiliers, dictated his story of the day to his friend Sergeant Patrick Friel of the same platoon:

I was one of twenty of a working party under 2nd Lt Wells which went up to Bunny Hutch on the night of the 8/9th. At 4.30 on the morning of the 9th the enemy commenced a vigorous bombardment at which time the whole of the party was working in the tunnel. The Gas Sentry gave the gas alarm and we immediately 'Stood To'. Acting under the orders of 2nd Lt Wells we lined the ridge on top of the tunnel when he received the information that the Bosche had broken through on the left. We saw the Bosche coming down Cavan Lane and we immediately opened fire on him. Some enemy took cover by the pill box and we threw bombs at him. The next thing that happened we took one prisoner and almost immediately forty-six others and two officers surrendered. Some of the party were sent down with the prisoners, 2nd Lt Wells and about four of us proceeded down New Cut Extension. After going down the trench about 300 yards I saw a German machine gun in working order. I mounted it and fired at some retreating enemy. I noticed two or three to fall. I stopped with the gun until it was growing dark when I was sent down with a batch of prisoners about twelve midnight. I handed the prisoners over and I was sent to Village Line where I remained till we were sent to Gunners Siding about 4 or 5 days later.

Despite the best efforts of the defenders, the Germans were infiltrating small groups of men through gaps in the defences. By 9.30am the Germans had a machine gun among the rubble of the church. Others were closing in on Orchard Keep. Sergeant Whiteside was in Mairie Redoubt, which overlooked the slope down towards the keep:

> On the morning of this day 11 platoon was holding Mairie Redoubt. After a severe bombardment we were made aware that the enemy was attacking forward positions and had approached as far as Orchard Keep on our right. We first sighted the enemy approaching by way of Hatfield Road. Rifle and Lewis gun fire were opened on the enemy and casualties were inflicted. One German carrying Lewis Gun was killed and the recaptured gun brought in.
>
> Between 2.30 and 3pm we received a message from 2/Lt Thorp saying that the Germans were lying in front of Orchard Keep, asking us to direct fire in front of Orchard Keep. This order was immediately complied with and as a result the enemy were seen to retire in large numbers to their own position behind the craters.

Lance Sergeant G.J. Moon of 12 Platoon was in the keep itself:

> On the morning of April 9th/18 No 12 Platoon was holding Orchard Keep… The morning being very misty the Bosche were upon us, in front of the wire and bombing from the communication trench …The Platoon Commander (2/Lt Collins) gave the order for rapid fire, and casualties were inflicted. The officer mounted the parapet and killed three of the enemy – shot with his revolver. Whilst this was taking place immediately on our front, a party of about 50 Germans passed down Orchard Road on our right. During this local engagement our numbers had considerably diminished and being heavily outnumbered the Platoon Commander decided to withdraw for about 100 yards just in front of Gunners Siding. Here were reinforced by 9 Platoon and a few of 'B' Coy. A stand was made at this point, rapid fire was maintained and bombs were thrown. From this position 2/Lt Collins rushed out with 2 Mills Bombs in his hands to attack an enemy machine gun team

which had already got into position. He succeeded in killing four and wounding three of the team and putting the gun out of action. After accomplishing this feat he returned to his men, placed a Lewis Gun in position and directed fire upon the approaching enemy inflicting casualties. By this time it was obvious that the enemy attack had been broken and disorganised. We fell back on Gunners Siding and here a bombing party was organised and succeeded in bombing the enemy out of Gunners Siding into Orchard Road and with the rifle fire bearing upon him from Mairie Keep, Wolf Road, and Gunners Siding they were compelled to retreat. Fire was directed on the retreating enemy and shortly afterwards the few remaining men of 12 Platoon went up to occupy Orchard Keep. At dusk a machine gun team and a few isolated Germans came in and gave themselves up.

Second Lieutenant Joseph Henry Collin, aged twenty-four, was awarded a posthumous Victoria Cross, which was gazetted on 25 June 1918. His citation read:

After offering a long and gallant resistance against heavy odds in the keep held by his platoon, this officer, with 5 only of his men remaining, slowly withdrew in the face of superior numbers, contesting every inch of the ground. The enemy were pressing him hard with bombs and machine gun fire from close range. Single handed 2nd Lieut Collin attacked the machine gun and team. After firing his revolver into the enemy, he seized a Mills grenade and threw it into the hostile team, putting the gun out of action, killing 4 of the team and wounding two others.

Observing a second hostile machine gun in front, he took a Lewis gun, and selecting a high point of vantage on the parapet whence he could engage the enemy gun, unaided he kept the enemy at bay with fire until he fell mortally wounded. His heroic self-sacrifice was a magnificent example to all.

The Germans were now approaching Gunners Siding trench, which ran down the slope towards the canal to the east of the Givenchy–Cuinchy road. Here a solitary anti-tank gun, which had been damaged in the barrage and could only be kept working by levering the breech open with a pick-axe handle after every shot, fired 180 rounds of shrapnel at close range. A Company, 2/5th Lancashire Fusiliers, was one of the reserve companies at Pont Fixe. No.1 Platoon (Second Lieutenant Clarke) and No.2 Platoon (Second Lieutenant Morrison) held the posts in the Village Line. No.3 Platoon (Second Lieutenant Scroggall) and No.4 Platoon (Company Sergeant Major Chadwick) were in billets at the Brewery. Captain William H. Wild was commanding officer.

> At about 7am the enemy were reported in Windy Corner but, since the morning was very misty, they were difficult to detect. On hearing that the enemy had reached this position two platoons were sent to Windy Corner to reinforce D Company. Mr Clarke and Mr Morrison becoming casualties, Sergeant Williams and Sergeant Lee carried on as platoon commanders and once again all ranks distinguished themselves by courage and initiative. No sooner than these two platoons had been despatched to Windy Corner than the enemy were reported as working down Cheyne Walk, which was held by the King's Own Royal Lancaster Regiment and orders were received to send reinforcements, so two sections were sent up Cheyne Walk. After the reinforcements had been out about five minutes a prisoner was sent down to Company HQ and then to Battalion HQ. This was the first prisoner to be taken.

Company Sergeant Major R. Walker, B Company, 1/4th King's Own Royal Lancasters, had been fighting near his company HQ, but weight of numbers had forced his small party to separate. Learning that the bulk of the company were in Bayswater and Cheyne Walk he made his way there and rallied the men.

> After this I, along with two other NCOs collected some bombs and made our way up Bayswater, and into Orchard Road. The first German we saw there was attending to one of our wounded. The wounded man told me that this Bosche had been with him ever since the Germans entered the trench, when the other Germans retired this particular one

would not go back with the rest. He said he wanted to be taken prisoner as he was fed up. He could speak English a little. After this the two NCOs and myself made our way into Oxford Terrace and there met Lt Schofield of the 2/5th LFs (who was afterwards awarded the VC). He told me that the Germans occupied our Front Line, so we got together a party of the LFs who had then come up to reinforce the King's Own and bombed the trench occupied by the Bosche. Before many bombs had been thrown 123 Germans had surrendered to the bombers. This cleared the front line of Germans with the exception of two who we found in a snipers post the next day, at the junction of Orchard Road and the front line. These two we utilised for carrying down wounded Germans of whom there was a good many lying about, along with many dead.

Second Lieutenant Schofield had twice been refused by the army because of bad eyesight before being taken on as a clerk and being commissioned from the ranks. His Victoria Cross, the second of the day and the second time two VCs had been won in Givenchy on the same day, was gazetted the same day as Lieutenant Collins's. The citation read:

For most conspicuous bravery and devotion to duty in operations against the enemy at Givenchy on the 9th April, 1918.

He led a party of 9 men to a strong point, which was reported strongly held by the enemy.

A party of the enemy about 100 strong attacked his party with bombs. 2nd Lieut Schofield disposed his men so skilfully, and brought such rifle and Lewis gun fire to bear, that the enemy took cover in dug outs. This officer himself then held up and captured a party of twenty.

With the help of other parties, this position was then cleared of the enemy, who were killed or captured. He then collected the remainder of his men, made his party up to ten, then proceeded towards the front line, previously sending back a message to his Commanding Officer as to the position, and that he was proceeding to take the front line. He met large numbers of the enemy in a communication trench in front of him, and in a drain on right and left. His party opened rapid rifle fire, and he climbed out on to the parapet at point blank machine gunfire, and by his fearless demeanour and bravery forced the enemy to surrender.

123 of the enemy, including several officers, thus surrendered to 2nd Lieut. Schofield and his party. A few moments later he was killed.

Schofield's captain wrote to his mother:

No doubt you will have heard of your son's death on the 9th April. It is difficult, almost impossible, to tell you of his bravery and cheerfulness under the very abnormal conditions we were fighting under on the 9th. I am not exaggerating when I say that of the many brave, fine men I have seen in action out here your son stands out almost alone. The officers and men, not only of this battalion, but of the neighbouring ones, too, are full of tales of him, and his extraordinary pluck. During the day I sent him with a small party of ten men, to work up a trench and clear it of the enemy. He did this, and sent me a message saying he had met a large party of the enemy, much further up than I thought he would be able to go. I was luckily able to send another party to reinforce him, but when the party arrived your son had already taken forty prisoners with his original forces... the next thing I saw was 123 prisoners, 'sent down by Mr. Schofield', as their escort proudly informed me. This was almost immediately followed by the news of his death. He had been hit by a machine gun, and just murmured, 'Send someone to help me down', and passed quietly away. It was all over very quickly and I thank God that a brave, cheerful soul was spared any long drawn out pain. All day long he was laughing and joking about his work, and told one of my officers 'that I don't need my revolver, I just shout at them and out they come, calling Kamerad'. I reckon that he took some 170 prisoners off his own bat in that one day, by sheer pluck and initiative... Personally, I have lost not only a fine officer, but a cheerful, good comrade and friend, by his death.

By a series of small counterattacks such as those led by Second Lieutenant Schofield, the Germans were gradually cleared back. Many surrendered and the troops found light machine guns and other equipment abandoned.

The grave of Second Lieutenant J.H. Collin, VC, in Vieille Chapelle new military cemetery.

The grave of Second Lieutenant J. Schofield, VC, in Vieille Chapelle new military cemetery.

Sergeant John Colman, who had originally gone to France in 1915 with the 9th Norfolks, but transferred to the Machine Gun Corps, went forward with the attacks and personally collected five abandoned German light machine guns and distributed them among the infantry. He went from gun to gun, clearing stoppages as they occurred, so as to keep up the rate of fire. Sergeant Holt also acquired 'a light machine gun, this gun was then put in action by myself… where I had every chance of getting the enemy from the left flank'.

The retiring Germans, the mist having lifted, presented a splendid target. 'The next thing we saw was the enemy retiring and they were as good a target as they had been in the morning a blind man could have shot them', wrote Sergeant Lawton. 'Several of the enemy were then observed making their way to their own lines, then all that was left of the garrison opened rapid fire, inflicting heavy casualties on him', wrote Private Jackson. 'After the mist cleared I examined our wire and we must have killed 200 Bosche… I think the 9th April was the best day's sport I have had in this war' wrote Second Lieutenant Dane.

Apart from a few saps and stretches of the front line too badly damaged to be immediately reoccupied, the village was back in British hands. Sergeant Lawton summed up the day's events:

> Night is now upon us, we gather together what men of our Coy. was left. 17 men all told and formed a bombing post in Orchard Road. Things have quietened down and we get time for a little rest and a smoke which we thoroughly enjoy. The bit of good news is that the ration party is coming up with our food it being 24 hours since we last had anything hot, the only thing we got was some potatoe (sic) biscuits off the Germans we captured. Then we have a little sleep while one or two keep a sharp look out and so ended the most memorial (sic) day in my life, the things I saw and did on that day I shall never forget.

Elsewhere on the 55th divisional front things had gone almost as well, though it had been touch and go. The Portuguese to the north had collapsed spectacularly, exposing the division's northern flank. Fortunately 166th Brigade, which had been scheduled to start replacing them in the line that day, was almost ideally placed to form a protective flank stretching from north of Festubert back to the River Lawe, a line that was not broken. Further north the Germans had, after heavy fighting with a hastily despatched British force that had blocked their path, just about managed to reach the Lawe, but were not across it. 40th Division to the north of the Portuguese had been badly outflanked and lost heavily as the units that could fought their way to the River Lys, and the Germans were beginning to infiltrate men across. 34 Division still held Armentières, but in a difficult to defend salient from which they were preparing to withdraw.

The close of the day's fighting found 55th Division, with the assistance of the 154th Brigade of 51st Division, holding a front of about 11,000 yards from the La Bassée canal to the west of the Lawe canal, 2,000 yards north-east of Locon, from where it was prolonged, though not continuously, by troops of 51st Division. Between 700 and 800 prisoners had been taken, and about seventy machine guns.

The 55th Division remained in the line until it began to be withdrawn on 14 April. Things were going badly north of the River Lys and across the

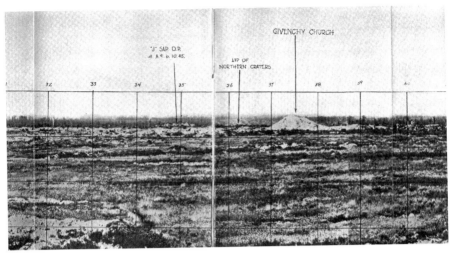

GIVENCHY CHURCH

'J' SAP O.P.
at A.9. b. 10.45.

LIP OF
NORTHERN CRATERS

32   33   34   35   36   37   38   39   40

Givenchy, 1918. What was left of the village.

River Lawe, and there was noone to replace them. There was some fierce fighting north of Festubert and along the flank held by 166 Brigade, but Givenchy, apart from a persistent artillery attack, remained quiet. 164th Brigade was the last of the three brigades to be relieved, on the night of 16/17 April, by 3rd Brigade of 1st Division. In the meantime, there had been clearing up to do. On 10 April Corporal Patrick Wyre, 1/4th Loyal North Lancs, heard that a patrol had been called for:

> and I again volunteered, and after reconnoitring we approached Givenchy Church, and found many dead Germans and an officer who was slightly wounded in the arm. After we had brought him in and taken everything out of his possession he was found to be in possession of a 1st Class Iron Cross which was returned to him and he was then handed over to Battn HQ.

Communication trenches were cleared, parapets repaired and wiring parties were out at night. The whole time German artillery harassed the defenders. Attempts were made to locate and bury the dead. Most seem to have been buried in the King's Liverpool graveyard at Cuinchy, from which the bodies were subsequently moved to the concentration cemetery at Vielle Chapelle new military cemetery a few miles away. The bodies of lieutenants Collin and Schofield lie there, quite close to one another.

55th Division were so proud of their work in the defence of Givenchy and Festubert that they commissioned and produced a special booklet, which included all the telegrams of praise and letters they received from Field Marshal Sir Douglas Haig, a series of army and corps commanders, Lancashire mayors, members of the general public and even one from a 61-year-old soldier serving in France with the Labour Corps.

On 18 April the Germans resumed their attack on the southern flank of the salient they were pushing into the British line. They hoped to take Givenchy, cross the canal, capture Bethune and take Mount Bernachon, which dominated the forward, western point of their line. The bombardment began at 1am and was every bit as heavy as the one on the 9th. As before it ranged far and wide, hitting artillery batteries, headquarters and roads before shortening and raining down on the forward defensive positions and drenching the defences in gas. It was another misty morning, though

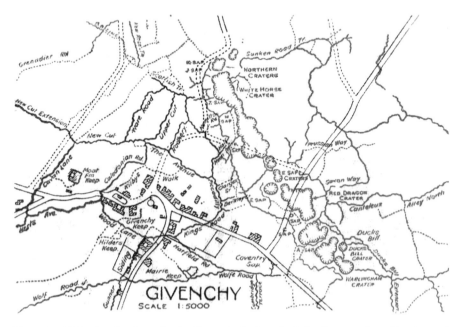

Givenchy, 1918, showing how the April attacks had pushed the German front line beyond the crater field, but not reached the village.

visibility was slightly better when, at 8am, six German divisions advanced against the two brigades of 1st Division (1st and 3rd Brigades) that were holding Festubert and Givenchy.

On the night of 16/17 April 1st Battalion, Black Watch, had taken over the Givenchy left sector. D Company was on the left with two platoons in Le Plantin South and two in Grenadier Road. C Company was in the centre holding New Cut, Ware Road and the old British front to Sap K. A Company was on the right to Berkeley Street. A counterattack platoon and the reserves for A and C companies were accommodated in the tunnel system. B Company garrisoned the keeps, with one platoon in Herts Keep, one platoon in Moat Farm and two in Givenchy Keep and Givenchy Tunnel.

At 10am on the 17th the Germans began a long, slow bombardment of the keep system, using heavy artillery, and at 1am on the 18th it intensified with shells of all calibres, including, it was said a 12in gun, raining on the village positions. At 8am the German infantry advanced to the attack, profiting from the knowledge they'd gained of the defences in their attack of the 9th. They now knew the locations of the tunnel exits and moved swiftly to capture them and seal off the counterattack platoons and the company reserves. 251 Tunnelling Company had intentionally sent up a large shift in order to act as guides to the Black Watch, who were not yet acquainted with the line and the ins and outs (literally) of the tunnel system. There were three officers – Captain Walker MC, Lieutenant B.E. Rees and Lieutenant Marsland – and thirty-nine other ranks. The tunnellers were all sent to special stations to assist the infantry garrison in case of attack, and at other times were engaged in their ordinary occupations of pumping, listening and maintenance. The battle positions were detailed with the knowledge and approval of the infantry company commanders. Captain Walker, one NCO and six other ranks were sent to Moat Farm; Lieutenant Marsland, one NCO and three other ranks were posted at Piccadilly Exit, with orders to close the exit by detonating a charge fixed to the inside of the gallery should the enemy attempt to enter by force, and Lieutenant Rees and the remainder of the tunnellers manned No.4 Shaft Penthouse and the sap leading to it, to protect the north side of Caledonian Road Penthouse and Moat Farm entrance. One NCO and four men were sent to the Givenchy Keep dugout system to act as guides and maintain liaison between the garrisons in Givenchy Keep and Mairie Redoubt.

The Germans, who had obviously done their homework analysing the failure of the attack on 9 April, shelled the vicinity of the Caledonian Road tunnel exits and the Moat Farm tunnel entrance very heavily, and advanced to the attack in great strength. The Caledonian Road Penthouse shelter area was subjected to an intense bombardment of heavy howitzer shells, estimated at 8 or 10in diameter. This knocked out those of the defenders who were manning the trenches, and one platoon of the 1st Black Watch was wiped out by a single shell. About twelve tunnellers, who were endeavouring to dig out the few survivors, were knocked out within two minutes by another shell. This had the effect of disorganising the surface defence of the Penthouse shelters, as those who remained on top of shafts were bombed down below into the deep dugout system.

One captain of the Black Watch, with fifteen other ranks, reached Piccadilly trench through the Bunny Hutch Subway but all were overwhelmed, with the exception of three other ranks who escaped to Caledonian Road dugouts, badly wounded, at 8am. After this the defence of Piccadilly Exit devolved on Lieutenant Marsland and four men from the tunnelling company. They held their position by rifle fire until there was danger of them being overwhelmed, when Lieutenant Marsland fired the demolition charge and closed the exit. The long stretch of Subway West of the Piccadilly Exit was then defended by a Lewis gun posted at a turn in the gallery.

Moat Farm was attacked as the Germans followed up close behind a creeping barrage and got to within 40 yards of the defences. At Moat Farm Entrance, Acting Captain Gerald John Sinclair, Black Watch, was holding the surface approach. As the garrison in Caledonian Road Penthouse was in difficulties, he organised an attack against the enemy in the vicinity of that point to relieve the pressure. He was killed in the attack, which fell back. Captain Walker, RE immediately reorganised the attack and led the remnants of the Black Watch from the Moat Farm Entrance in an easterly direction against Caledonian Road. He was hit in the leg by machine-gun fire, which fractured his shin bone and put him out of action. The attack failed and Captain Walker was assisted into the dug-out system by Sergeant Newell, RE. It was now about 9am and Walker, despite his injury, assumed command of the entrance. As the Germans started throwing grenades into the tunnel the defenders were ultimately beaten back from the stairway near the surface and retreated behind the gas door, where they erected a barricade of sandbags, from behind which they fired their rifles, thus denying entrance to the enemy.

With Walker and his men holding one end of the tunnel complex and Marsland the other, things began to get bad within the dugouts themselves. By early afternoon there were some 200 men down there, many of them wounded. Ammunition and bombs were running out and, after power to the pumps was cut, the water level started to rise slowly but inexorably. Sergeants Newell and Menadue later reported that the Germans had gas, either in bombs or in spray form, and threatened to use it in quantities unless the garrison surrendered. Captain Walker, though wounded, urged a policy of no surrender, but conditions continued to deteriorate. After a parley, the surrender was arranged at about two o'clock in the afternoon.

Lieutenant Marsland, who was captured, wrote a brief description of the action on his return to Britain at the end of the year:

The Germans attacked our lines and took them. I was in the mining system at the time and my instructions were to blow up from below at all cost a special stairway entrance to prevent the enemy from entering, and other officers were given several mine shaft entrances (on the surface in supports) to hold.

I waited at my stairway till the Germans came rushing down and let my serjeant shoot the first man then, as they all rushed down the stairway throwing bombs at us I pulled my fuses and ran and the explosion took place before they could enter. I expect all on the stairway were killed.

When I reached our dugout the place was full of wounded and every exit was in the hands of the enemy who were throwing bombs in and we were well past 40 feet below the surface. I posted the only Lewis gun we had to hold the main entrance and then started pulling wounded out of the water which was filling the place because the electric cable for pumps was cut.

I went to one of the shafts and walked into a German officer with 10 men before I saw them. Our conversation took place in Spanish. He told me to go to the surface and I answered that I could not leave my wounded in the water to be drowned. He said he could not deal with wounded but I told him I could send some of our captured men to do this and eventually I was allowed to send men to take them out.

Though ordered, on pain of death, to evacuate the underground system, three of the sappers managed to conceal themselves and so escaped. Captain Walker was put on a stretcher, which could not be taken up the spiral staircase, and sergeants Newell and Menedue carried him down to the Moat Farm Entrance. They were accompanied by two other sappers and, as they approached the entrance, Sergeant Menedue realised there were only two sentries on duty. He 'dealt with' them, allowing the whole group to reach Pont Fixe and safety. Captain Walker had to have his leg amputated. Sergeant Menadue, who had already won a Military Medal in 1916, and Sergeant Newell were awarded the DCM with identical citations, which read:

> For conspicuous gallantry and devotion to duty. This non-commissioned officer with another was in charge of a portion of underground defence that was overrun by the enemy; they, however, refused to surrender, and remained below with an officer who was unable to walk, having always in view the possibility of an escape during the confusion. Their anticipations were justified, and in spite of a heavy machine-gun fire and shell barrage they succeeded in carrying the wounded officer into safety and in rescuing six other men. The happy result of this enterprise was due to the courage and resource of these non-commissioned officers, who were equally responsible for its success.

Back on the surface, the most desperate fighting took place around Givenchy Keep, where the two officers, Captain Denys Cook and Lieutenant Alexander Kilgour, were killed in the first assault and where the garrison was reduced from two officers and forty other ranks to just one warrant officer and eight other ranks, but continued to hold out. Eventually a party of six men, under

Lieutenant Addison, DCM, was sent up to reinforce and the keep was secured.

Although the garrison of Moat Farm was much reduced, it held out throughout the attack under the command of Lieutenant Burton. D Company on the left came under intense pressure from wave after wave of infantry, and Second Lieutenant Walter Balmain was killed, but heavy rifle and Lewis gun fire held them back. Despite heavy casualties, D Company managed to hold its line. Company Sergeant Major John Ford, a highly experienced pre-war veteran who had been in France since August 1914, took command of some men who were falling back in a disorganised fashion in the face of the bombardment and got them into an extemporised line of defence, thus preventing a breakthrough.

A counterattack by the battalion, supported by platoons of C and D companies of the 1st Cameron Highlanders who had been sent up in support, was hastily arranged, supported by an artillery barrage. The speed of arrangement meant the barrage was ineffective and, although one platoon of the Black Watch under Lieutenant J.A. Smith reached the first objective, killing several of the enemy on the way, the C Company platoon of the Camerons under Second Lieutenant Burns started but was unable to make much progress and Burns himself was wounded. The counterattack was a failure.

The main part of the village was held at the end of the day but the Germans did manage to occupy Ware Road, Scottish Trench, Piccadilly, the saps, the craters and Avenue Trench.

1st Battalion Loyal North Lancashire Regiment was holding the trenches between Givenchy and the canal. The Germans made little headway attacking frontally, partly because of heavy and accurate machine-gun fire from the guns dug into the embankment, but were soon filtering into their northernmost trenches from the village itself and succeeded in reaching the main line of resistance before a vigorous counterattack by C and D companies successfully drove them back and only a few outposts remained in enemy hands.

On 19 April the commanding officer of 1st Battalion the Northamptonshire Regiment, accompanied by captains Pickering and Tetley, went up to Givenchy to reconnoitre in anticipation of an attack to retake the ground lost the day before. Their war diarist wrote 'The high ground in front of Givenchy was comprised roughly of a couple of lines of trenches, front about 450 yards and depth about 300 yards. This ground was very important as it overlooked surrounding country.' Maps and orders were issued for an attack the next day. The HQs of A and C companies moved up into the Givenchy trenches.

At 4.45am on the 20th, as dawn was breaking, A and C companies of the 1st Northamptonshire Regiment, A on the left and C on the right, attacked Piccadilly supported by a heavy barrage and by 5.05am had established their final objective. The war diary described a most efficient attack:

> The positions were fairly strongly held but many of the enemy retired on the approach of our men, but quite a large proportion of them were killed. 18 prisoners were taken and 5 more in the afternoon. The enemy opposed the advance with fairly heavy MG fire and after the position was taken there was a considerable amount of sniping with Light MGs and rifles at close range. The enemy also made some half-hearted attempts both on the left and right to bomb us out through saps leading from the craters in front which the enemy held. These attempts were easily repulsed… The men did this operation extremely well especially as the ground was absolutely new to all, and as the attack was at dawn it was most difficult to keep direction. No organised counter attack was made but in the evening (the) trench was rather heavily bombarded.

The front line trenches to the north-east of the village had been recaptured at a cost of two officers and forty other ranks wounded from A Company (though Captain Pickering was wounded too he remained on duty), Captain Joseph Pilkington and Second Lieutenant Caldwell missing and fifty-six other ranks wounded.

The German occupation of the old front line and the craters was a thorn in the side of the British defence of the village. Not only did the elevated crater rims (in a flat landscape a few feet in height is quite an obstacle) give the Germans observation over a large part of the defences, but they also prevented the British getting a clear view eastwards towards La Bassée. Plans were laid to drive the Germans back.

After a few days in billets in Marles-les-Mines, the 4th King's Own, having spent a pleasant day resting up in the woods around Vaudricourt en route, returned to the line at Givenchy on the evening of 23 April and took over the right sector, down to the canal. The Germans still occupied most of the old front line and the saps. On the 25th two fighting patrols went out to occupy the old front line between its junctions with Orchard Road and Finchley Road, but found it occupied by a strong force of the enemy and were driven back. A barrage was put down to enable a third party to rush the line, but it came down behind the target and the troops were unable to advance because of heavy machine-gun fire. It was clear that the old front line was being held in strength, so next day, at 4am, two platoons of A and D companies rushed the position under cover of an artillery barrage and succeeded in entering the trench. After some hand-to-hand fighting they were forced to withdraw.

On 26 April an early morning attack by two platoons of A and D companies again got into German positions, but were forced to withdraw after more hand-to-hand fighting. At 2.20pm two platoons of C and D companies, under cover of machine-gun and artillery barrages, attacked the saps and trenches on the left of the battalion position towards the top of the slope from the canal. Two platoons from 5th Lancashire Fusiliers attacked the saps and craters towards the northern end of the crater field at the same time, but unfortunately their supporting barrage did not come down and they failed to reach their objectives. The two platoons of 4th KORL did reach theirs –Second Lieutenant Herbert Hunter's men seized Berkeley Street trench, their section of the old front line and E sap, and Second Lieutenant W.M. Stewart's troops rushed from Coventry Sap and captured A Sap. Hunter was unfortunately killed at this point and, with the Lancashire Fusiliers unable to get forward due to strong German counterattacks, the platoons became isolated and surrounded on three sides. Having taken forty prisoners they made a fighting withdrawal to their own lines.

It was during this fighting that the final Victoria Cross was won in the Givenchy sector. Lance Corporal James Hewitson, 4th King's Own (Royal Lancaster) Regiment, was gazetted on 28 June 1918:

In a daylight attack on a series of crater posts, Lance-Corporal Hewitson led his party to their objective with dash and vigour, clearing the enemy from both trench and dug-outs. In one dugout he killed six of the enemy who would not surrender. On the capture of the final objective he observed a hostile machine gun team coming into action against his men. Working his way round the edge of the crater, he attacked the team. Five of them he killed outright; the sixth surrendered. Shortly after he engaged a hostile bombing party, which was attacking a Lewis gun point. He routed the party, killing six of them. These extraordinary feats of daring crushed the hostile opposition at this point.

Born in Coniston on 5 October 1892, Hewitson had originally enlisted in 8th (Service Battalion) KORL on 17 November 1914 and later transferred to 1/4th Battalion. He was promoted to corporal and received his VC from King George V in France on 8 August and survived the war. He returned to Givenchy in 1921, wearing his medals, for the unveiling of the divisional memorial. He attended old comrades' dinners regularly and continued to live in Coniston until his death in 1963.

Though there were alarms about possible new German attacks in May and early June, which came to nothing, possibly because good intelligence meant that their presumed concentration areas were saturated by an artillery barrage, the Givenchy front remained quiet. The attention of both sides had moved south again, firstly to the German offensive on the Aisne in late May, then their attack towards Compiègne in mid-June. On 8 August a joint Anglo-French counter-offensive began at Amiens, in which the Germans were driven back eleven miles in four days, beginning a series of assaults that started to push the Germans back along large parts of the front.

At Givenchy itself the continued German occupation of the crater field was still causing concern and plans were revived to drive them out, this time on a larger scale than the attempts in April. The assault was to be carried out once again by 4th KORL on the right flank from Warlingham Crater on the right to E Sap craters on the left, taking in Red Dragon Crater and the old road towards Violaines, and the 2/5th Lancashire Fusiliers taking the left flank as far as K Sap. There was to be no preliminary bombardment, but when it was fired, at five minutes after zero hour, it was provided by

55th Divisional Artillery, 84th and 158th Army Brigades RFA, two batteries provided by the 1st Division, Corps Heavy Artillery and 55th Battalion of the Machine Gun Corps. Rather than using just a few platoons of infantry, the two infantry battalions were to attack in full strength. Dozens of pages of orders had been written. The officers and NCOs had studied them and had been fully briefed and examined carefully. They had made models of the crater zone, after which the company commanders had lectured their men on the plan. The task fell to 1/4th King's Own Royal Lancasters, whose battalion historian recorded the story:

At 2.20am on the morning of 24 August, all companies were in assembly positions. Despite a very slight harassing fire no casualties were sustained. Wire cutting had previously been carried out by advance parties. The enemy was very quiet, sent up a few lights, and showed no sign of anticipating an attack. Supporting companies received hot breakfasts, and the assembled troops had sandwiches and chocolate. No noise was made in getting up food. Snipers crept out into position on spoil heaps, from which they kept down enemy observation prior to the attack, by firing on such targets as exposed themselves.

At 6am visibility became very poor, a slight rain falling. Our own Stokes Mortars fired intermittently on the crater areas up to the time when the rockets were fired at zero hour. One of our aeroplanes flew low over the craters, drawing only a very slight machine gun fire. On the firing of the rockets at 7.20am the assaulting troops immediately advanced under splendid leadership. Two and a half minutes elapsed before the enemy fired his first rifle shot. There was no artillery fire at all. The enemy was completely taken by surprise, and was found mainly in dugouts. Not a single enemy machine gun was in action on the Battalion front. At 7.24am an SOS rocket, bursting into two red lights, was fired from well behind the enemy's lines. Meanwhile, mopping up parties had followed closely behind the front line of sections, but found the enemy to be in small strength. These were effectively dealt with, some being killed and some being taken prisoner. A few tried to run away but were heavily fired on.

At 7.30am our own protective barrage fell beyond the crater area, this being answered three minutes later by a poor counter-barrage directed chiefly on Gunners Siding. At 7.35am Companies had reached their objectives on the far lip of the craters, and telephone communication was established between them and Battalion Headquarters. At 7.43am consolidation was immediately proceeded with. Up to this time casualties were practically nil. Patrols were sent out to deal with Trench Mortar emplacements, and one was reported destroyed by mobile charge by the Left Company. Our own barrage, which was very heavy, seems to have dropped short, inflicting casualties, two men being killed and 8 wounded in the Left Company and approximately the same number in the Right Company.

Enemy retaliation dwindled down to very slight proportions between 8.30 and 10.30am. He did not appear to know on what points to fire. At 8.34am a message was received from the snipers that a party of nearly forty of the enemy were seen at the far end of Duck Bill extension. These were fired on and soon disappeared. Shortly afterwards news was received from the Australian Tunnellers to the effect that there were no mines in dugouts, and that all shelters were badly smashed, a pill box in Red Dragon Crater alone being untouched. Parties of the enemy in small numbers were seen running to the rear, and were dealt with by Lewis Gunners and Snipers, those escaping getting right into our barrage. At 9.20am consolidation was reported to be making good progress, while communication trenches were rapidly being dug by Pioneers, from Wolfe Road to Berkeley Street.

At 9.40am an SOS rocket was sent up from the area of the left Battalion. Enemy artillery was not firing at all at the time. Five minutes later the SOS was cancelled.

Shortly afterwards the enemy fired on the crater area for the first time, on Warlingham. Owing to our own artillery fire some patrols had difficulty in reaching Trench Mortar emplacements, and these were now sent out again. The Right Company reported reaching an emplacement, but found the mortar gone, though plenty of very heavy ammunition and a range finder were lying near. The Left Company reported the destruction of another emplacement.

Between 11 and 11.15am enemy artillery became much more active, blue cross shells falling on Givenchy, and the gas drifting over our area. This had cleared by 11.45am. From this time onwards, much heavier enemy barrages were put down on the crater area. Tea and sandwiches were got up to the front line troops about 12.30pm, and about half an hour later a hot meal. Considerable difficulty was experienced in getting rations over the broken ground to the crater area, and the work done by the Quarter-Master's Department was commendable. Perhaps a smile may be permitted here. This devoted personnel, its duty well and truly done, assembled for departure from the inhospitable region of the craters, which the Hun was now freely shelling. One member of the party was missing, and he the Company Quarter Master Sergeant. Impatience grew as the minutes passed, and when well-nigh insupportable, he appeared, to meet the indignant queries of his comrades, he silenced criticism with the explanation 'Well, I couldn't find t'dixie lid.'

Casualties to 1/4th KORL amounted to seven dead and twenty-three wounded. Over the next two days they consolidated the new positions and sent patrols forward to get in touch with the enemy. It was only on the second day that contact was made and the battalion snipers harassed their communication trenches, getting at least three hits. There was a fairly heavy German bombardment of the crater area for a few days, using high explosives and gas, but no serious counterattacks. On the 27th the 1/4th KORL were relieved by 5th King's Liverpools and went back to the camp at Drouvin.

During the last few days of August rumours began to circulate that the Germans were about to withdraw and 46th Division, to the north of 55th Division, made advances into the salient that had been formed during the April battle. Prisoners said that the German line was to be withdrawn behind Richebourg St Vaast – pretty much to where it had been on 9 April. On 1 September 55th Division received orders from I Corps to be prepared to follow up immediately any withdrawal using aggressive fighting patrols who were to make what ground they could and establish posts as far forward as they could. The divisional artillery was to be prepared to move forward to cover any advance and back roads were to be improved so that movement forwards could be speeded up.

Throughout September patrols pushed the outpost line back, especially north and east of Festubert. Posts were established 500 yards east of the craters, in the vicinity of Canteleux Farm, though there was still no sign of a planned German withdrawal and there were occasional counterattacks. Attempts to push forward by 16th Division immediately south of the canal met with fierce opposition, and their inability to clear the south bank delayed the advance along the north, especially in the Canteleux area, which was still enfiladed by German machine guns south of the canal. On 7 September 164th Brigade captured part of Canteleux Trench, but was driven back by a strong counterattack. 165th Brigade went into the line on the 8th, and when 1/5th KORL took over the front line itself on the 12th it was 3,000 yards further forward in the sector north of Givenchy, opposite Festubert, than it had been only a fortnight or so before. However, strong opposition on both sides of the canal itself still held up any serious advance in front of Givenchy. On the 14th 2/5th Lancashire Fusiliers mounted yet another attack on Canteleux Trench, which was met with fierce resistance. They did manage to advance some of their posts and drove off a counterattack with Lewis guns. On the 17th four companies of 1/5th King's Liverpools, in conjunction with an attack along the south bank by troops of 16th Division, captured the southern portion of Canteleux Trench at last and pushed their outposts along the canal. Further attacks to the north by 166th and 165th brigades resulted in the capture of Violaines and the front line pushed up close to the German defence line between La Bassée and Aubers.

The main defence line for Givenchy was now moved forward from the edge of the village itself to the far side of the crater zone, further east than it had been since October 1914. There was still the idea that a strong German counterattack might be being considered, and the forward posts were strengthened to break one up if it came. Givenchy itself was still vulnerable to shelling and 2/5th Royal Lancs Fusiliers suffered some nasty casualties after moving up to Windy Terrace to take over as brigade reserve battalion on 20 September. At 00.30 hours on the 21st a heavy barrage hit the battalion HQ, blowing in the orderly room and the runners' dugout. As both officer and men dug frantically to release the men trapped, a follow-up barrage, complete with gas, caught them in the open. Four officers, the CO Major J.H. Evans, the adjutant Captain A.H. Griggs, the signals officer Lieutenant B.E. Cridland and the medical officer, an attached American doctor, Lieutenant Goldman, were injured and twenty-six men were either wounded or gassed, four of whom subsequently died.

Throughout September the ground the Germans had captured during the April offensive had been regained. Mount Kemmel was evacuated on 31 August and Neuve Eglise recaptured on 1 September, followed by Richebourg St Vaast on the 3rd, Bailleul on the 6th and the pre-offensive line was more or less re-established by the middle of the month. 55th Division laid its plans for an advance when the time came – new roads were built by the divisional engineers, including one that went from Windy Corner and traversed the battlefield to Chapelle St Roch and then to Canteleux and close to the outskirts of La Bassée, which continued to be held by the enemy. Other roads were improved and tracks laid.

On 2 October a captured German officer revealed that a withdrawal had begun that morning from the defensive line, and 166th Infantry Brigade began to advance. 2/5th Lancashire Fusiliers pushed patrols into La Bassée itself, and a night patrol under Second Lieutenant Lush reached Salome, 3,000 yards eastwards. Their battalion HQ moved from Givenchy to Canteleux. Next day, despite some serious opposition, they reached Hantay, where they were relieved by 4th KORL, and on the 6th they returned to Givenchy for 'reorganisation and baths'; a clear sign that the village, or at least the site of it, was now outside the fighting zone.

As the battle moved away eastward peace fell upon the shattered battlefield. The previous inhabitants of Givenchy had not, for the most part, fled far, and soon began to return though there were no walls remaining that were higher than a few inches. Only the mound of rubble that had been the church stood out over the cratered landscape. German prisoners of war were set to clearing the ground of unexploded ordnance, filling in the trenches and shell holes and rebuilding the roads. It must be assumed that the tunnels, once the pumps were switched off, flooded rapidly – but, curiously, the current maire, Jacques Herbaut, recalls playing in some of them, presumably workings close to the surface, as a small boy in the 1950s.

The Italian government, and the government of the USA, through the Red Cross, offered to help provide for the village's orphans, and the Mairie, one of the first buildings to be rebuilt (albeit in wood), provided what information it could to help trace them. They were scattered far and wide – the two children of farmer Charlemagne Laignel, killed on 15 May 1915 at Flirey, fighting with the 68th Infantry Regiment, were both in Bethune; the three surviving Marechal children were at Mazingarbe; Gilbert Herbaut's two children were in Brittany; Lucien Sturzer's children were in Paris, their father having been killed in October 1914 fighting with 362nd Infantry Regiment at Hanmont. Two families had presumably been evacuated to the south to the Midi, where so many Belgian and northern French families had ended up in a series of refugee camps in 1914.

In June 1919 some British newspapers announced that the Givenchy battlefield was one of several chosen by a French government commission to be preserved in perpetuity as a memorial to the war. Other sites apparently chosen included the ruins of Bapaume and damaged buildings in Peronne, both of which were in fact reconstructed in their entirety, so we can only assume the scheme was halted.

In January 1920 Baroness Campbell undertook a motor tour of the old front and stopped briefly at Givenchy to look at 'the enormous craters'. She reported that there was a flagstaff standing on the enormous mound that was all that was left of the church. One of her party contrived to rip his breeches on barbed wire while collecting souvenirs; 'the whole place is full of them'. Though she was warned she would regret it, she left behind a German rifle and the handle of a French officer's sword.

Another visitor to Bethune in January 1920 reported on the good behaviour and discipline of the German prisoners of war engaged in the task of clearing the ground in the area, including in Givenchy itself. The repatriation of German PoWs began the same month, some by ship, but the vast majority by train. They had done good work, but in Givenchy much remained to be done.

The enormity of the work had not prevented the locals acquiring army surplus huts and erecting them on their old properties as a temporary measure; some are visible in photographs taken in 1920, including what appears to be the temporary Mairie. Work on rebuilding in brick and stone

Plinth erected on site for Memorial to the 55th Division at Givenchy.

Givenchy, probably taken in 1920, from the site of the 55th Divisional memorial. The temporary huts that composed the village are visible, as is the pile of rubble that was the church (under the arrow).

did not begin until the following year, and a visitor who was touring the old front line at that time noted that although Loos had been practically rebuilt, and the village of Cuinchy, just over the canal, was a trim village of raw new brick, in Givenchy itself:

> the broken walls of the church obtrude themselves on the road traveller, but the village yet remains mostly in the intermediate stage of temporary huts, and what was once its central 'square', and late was neutral ground and front line, lies now between parapets of grey earth festooned with mouldering dripping sandbags, facing each other and a shining white monument between them.

Some houses in the village still have the year 1922 proudly built into their brickwork, showing their year of completion. Most were built on exactly the same site and in exactly the same style as they had been in 1914, making navigation round the village in one's imagination so much easier.

On 28 September 1920 the Commune of Givenchy was awarded the Croix de Guerre for its part in the war.

Le Ministre de la Guerre cite:

A L'ORDRE DE L'ARMEE LA COMMUNE DE GIVENCHY LES LA BASSÉE QUI

'Bombardée jusqu'à la destruction totale, n'a cessé de faire montre de la plus belle attitude morale sous les obus et pendant l'occupation allemande.'

CES CITATIONS CONFORNENT L'ATTRIBUTION DE LA CROIX DE GUERRE 1914-1918 AVEC PALME

[Trans: The Minister of War mentions in army(-level) dispatches the Commune of Givenchy-lès-La-Bassée, which, bombarded to total destruction, never ceased to show the very finest spirit under shell-fire and during the German occupation.

This citation confirms the award of the Croix de Guerre 1914-1918 avec palme (bronze)].

In September 1919 a meeting of the 55th Division Comrades Association had passed a resolution 'That visible memorials to the 55th Division be erected at Liverpool and Givenchy and that the memorial at Givenchy should be of as simple a character as is consistent with the incidents which it is intended to commemorate'. It was suggested the sum of £10,000 should be sufficient for both memorials. Lieutenant Colonel Sidney Morter DSO, a Liverpool architect who had served in France with the West Lancs Royal Field Artillery, was commissioned to prepare a design and to procure land as close to the ruins of Givenchy church as possible. He wrote to the Battle Exploits Memorial Committee for their advice and they counselled that the land for the monument should be vested in a corporation to avoid the death duties that might be incurred if vested in an individual. They offered to procure the land and to have it vested in the Imperial War Graves

Commission. This was agreed but, due to shortage of funds, the 55th Division Comrades Association ignored the original plan and, with the assistance of the maire of Givenchy, negotiated directly with the landowner, Monsieur Willerval, and vested ownership with themselves. The monument itself was constructed of Belgian granite and was built by Monsieur Edouard Buisine, a recognised sculptor from Lille who personally supervised the erection. It was formally unveiled on 15 May 1921, by Marshal Joffre in front of an honour guard of 55th Division veterans in uniform, with General Jeudwine, General Topping, Lieutenant Colonel Shulte, Major Henry Milner and the Duchess of Sutherland, as well as the mayors of Liverpool, Givenchy and several other local French towns. The divisional band played the division's march *My Love is like a Red, Red Rose* and the national anthems of Britain and France. On his arrival Marshal Joffre inspected the guard of honour of British troops from 55th Division and shook hands with the British officers.

The unveiling of 55th Division's monument; Marshal Joffre (left) and General Jeudwine (right).

They lunched at the recently rebuilt mairie. In his speech at the unveiling General Jeudwine recalled Marshal Joffre's role in the war, thanked the inhabitants of the village for the warm welcome they had always given the British troops and expressed the wish that the ruins of the village would soon disappear and Givenchy would rise from the ashes more beautiful than before. Marshal Joffre went on to inaugurate Givenchy's own memorial to its war dead.

For the ceremony the mound, which was all that remained of the village church, was decorated with multi-coloured flags and a small bank was cut into the mound itself to house an improvised altar. In bright sunshine the village priest celebrated an open-air mass, surrounded by a crowd of men in

The 55th Division monument today.

Detail on the 55th Division monument – the divisional badge of the red rose.

dark suits, brightly dressed women, and children carrying Union flags and tricolours, while the choir sang in the background. A 55th Divisional flag was presented to the mayor, to be flown on 9 April to commemorate the battle. The whole event was judged a great success, but it was soon discovered that the monument had been built without the official permission of the French government. For six years the Imperial War Graves Commission patiently corresponded with 55th Division's Comrades Association, which seems to have spent most of the period ignoring them, before retrospective permission was finally obtained and the IWGC assumed responsibility for the monument and land surrounding it.

In the years immediately following the war there was a large and spontaneous movement in Britain for towns and cities to adopt part of the front line to forge powerful links in commemoration and reconstruction. In the Somme department Albert was adopted by Birmingham, Wolverhampton adopted Gommecourt, Canterbury adopted Lesboeufs and Morval and several other villages were adopted by other places. In the Givenchy area Bethune was adopted by Hastings, Neuve Chapelle by Blackpool and Festubert by Southport. A delegation from Preston passed through Festubert and Givenchy (their car getting stuck in the mud) in early 1920 en route to La Bassée, which they adopted. On 3 November 1921 a public meeting of Liverpool citizens decided to adopt Givenchy, subject to the approval of details. The lord mayor estimated that the sum of £10,000 would be required. At the meeting the French consul explained that although the French government was paying for the building of houses, money was needed for a water supply and the provision of such social services as dispensaries and maternity hospitals.

Regular exchange visits between Liverpool and Givenchy were begun and fundraising for specific projects was started. The 1924 visit from Liverpool was marked by the laying of a foundation stone for a new Memorial Hall, the funds for which had been raised by subscription in the city. The hall

The Memorial Hall in Givenchy today.

The Memorial Hall plaque.

was to contain facilities for orphans and elderly members of the commune, along with a recreation room and library. The mayor of Liverpool, Mr Rushton, made a speech declaring that the building would be a symbol of the friendship between the people of France and Great Britain and the maire of Givenchy thanked the city for its generosity on behalf of the people of the commune.

In September the Memorial Hall was opened in the presence of a formidable array of British and French officials. As well as the lord mayor of Liverpool, the British included Mr Stephen Walsh, minister of state for war, and Sir Robert Wigham, the adjutant general. The French were represented by General Nollet, the minister for war, and the Comte de Saint-Aulaire, the French ambassador in London. There were many visitors who were veterans of the fighting and *The Times* correspondent noted 'Now nearly all trace of war has vanished. The trenches have been filled in, the fields again cultivated, and, under the brilliant sunshine today Givenchy looked very new.'

The visitors were escorted through the village by French cavalry and a band with the local children looking on. A plaque on the newly completed hall read 'In Memoriam. The City of Liverpool to the Commune of Givenchy'. The lord mayor declared the building open and the maire replied with an eloquent speech of thanks. Two sycamore trees were planted in front of the hall, then the party walked down to the 55th Divisional Memorial and laid wreaths. Only two flags were flying at the memorial: the flag of the French republic and the flag of the King's Liverpool Regiment in honour of the British troops who had fought in the village in 1918.

The party then crossed the road to the French memorial, which was in the form of a cenotaph, and further wreaths were laid. *The Times* correspondent wrote:

> The French and British officers, in their uniforms, were at the base of the cenotaph and around them at a little distance were the civilian onlookers, most of whom, not so very long ago, had been in uniform themselves. Now they were nearly all in sombre black. In front, in the road, the French cavalry were drawn up at the salute and away in the distance the roofs of Cambrin, Annequin, Cuinchy and a multitude of other places with world-famous names.

These ceremonies ended the official celebrations and there was an informal lunch in the hall, at which Mr Walsh gave a short but eloquent speech on the theme 'Notre Alliée France'. The Memorial Hall was then thrown open to the public. A party of Liverpool schoolchildren presented a play about the city's adoption of the village, and presents were given to the French children. The schoolchildren of Liverpool had raised money to buy a piano for the hall.

For Stephen Walsh, whose son Captain Arthur Walsh had been killed in the fighting in the village in April 1918 serving with the South Lancs, the visit must have been particularly poignant. He spoke at the ceremony, says one newspaper report 'with considerable emotion'. After the ceremony, according to another newspaper report, he was taken to 'The English

Cemetery' to visit his son's grave. Arthur Walsh is commemorated on the Loos memorial to the missing, so his body is considered not to have been recovered. Enquiries to the Commonwealth War Graves Commission have failed to identify 'The English Cemetery' mentioned in the report, although the CWGC acknowledge that 'our record of memorial crosses is patchy, so it is possible there was once a memorial to him in one of our sites'.

There were constant reminders of the war. In August 1924 the bodies of fifteen British soldiers were uncovered during excavation work and removed to one of the nearby Imperial War Graves Commission's cemeteries, still in the course of consolidation and construction. Also in 1924 a former officer of the Royal West Kents (Hugh Nisbet) wrote that the authorities were still concerned about the location of an unexploded German mine, the exact whereabouts of which was unknown. The general area in which it was thought to lie remained undeveloped because of it.

A 1926 visit saw the Liverpool delegation participate in the unveiling of a memorial to the soldiers of Givenchy itself who had fallen in the war. After signing the distinguished visitors' book, they visited the 55th Division Memorial and then the site of the new memorial, where a mass was sung and sermons given by the village priest and the canon of Bethune. They then lunched with French officials at the Memorial Hall, and attended the official unveiling of the memorial. It was built on the ruins of the old church and consisted of a broken tablet and the effigy of France weeping over her dead. Behind it were the remains of one wall of the church. The lord mayor of Liverpool (Mr Bowring) laid a wreath of roses on behalf of the city and then walked to the 55th memorial and laid a wreath there. The iron gate and walls of the Memorial Hall were inaugurated, then Colonel Sir James Reynolds, representing 55th Division, presented a gramophone, and the former lord mayor, Frank Wilson, a wireless set, to the commune. Mr Bowring was presented with a gold medal by the maire of Givenchy and Sir Arnold Rushton gave tea to the village children.

In July 1929 the Liverpool delegation opened a hospice for the aged, which had been built at the expense of the city, and the mayor, Mr Miller, laid the foundation stone of the new church. On their way back the delegation had a meeting with the French president, Monsieur Doumerge, who presented the mayor with the Medaille d'Or de la Reconnaissance Française in recognition of Liverpool's assistance with the reconstruction. On all previous visits to Paris the Liverpool representatives had been met by Marshal Foch, but he had died earlier in the year so they laid a wreath on his tomb in the Invalides. Visits continued on an annual basis until the outbreak of the Second World War.

In 1930, after many years of services in temporary accommodation, a brand new church, in a more modern style and complete with an elegant tower, was built in the village on the site of the one demolished during the war. Three bells from the old church tower were recast and rededicated on 6 September 1931 when the church was formally opened.

Givenchy 1940

At the end of May 1940, during the retreat to Dunkirk, the village had one last brief, but destructive, experience of warfare. 5th Brigade of the 2nd Infantry Division was ordered to hold the line of the canal against German tanks moving up from the south. Brigade HQ was established north-east of Festubert. The canal line was already held by French troops of 131 Regiment and 7th Queen's Regiment, but the exhausted men of 5th Brigade (who had been retreating since 15 May and in action for much of the period) were ordered to relieve them on the night of the 25th. As had been noted during World War One, the north bank of the canal was usually overlooked from the slightly higher southern bank, and the Germans had observation along the whole of this front, giving rise to occasional sniping and shelling. 7th Worcesters took over billets in scattered farmhouses behind Givenchy and on the night of the 25th the battalion took over a frontage extending from Givenchy to the west edge of La Bassée (approximately 2.5 miles) along the northern bank of the canal. D Company, under Captain J.W. Tomkinson, were on the right around Givenchy, with A Company along the canal eastwards and C Company beyond them.

Next morning (the 26th), enemy activity increased and there was heavy shelling and intermittent mortar fire all day, directed by a reconnaissance aircraft, and the Worcesters took many casualties. Late in the afternoon or in the early evening some Germans managed to cross the canal in the centre of the battalion position. Early on the morning of the 27th a company of the 1st Camerons, supported by six French tanks, made a counterattack and Brigade HQ reported that they'd been driven back.

During the rest of the 27th all hell broke loose. The Bren carrier platoon moved up from rear HQ and were heavily bombed and shelled, suffering some casualties and losing two carriers on their way. They moved forward and made contact with German tanks that had broken through on A Company's front and, since no information had been received from them since the previous night, they were presumed to have been overrun. C Company, on the left, vanished without trace and must have suffered the same fate. The Camerons, further east, could see German tanks massing in what had been the Worcesters' positions and formed a defensive flank, but soon columns of tanks were observed advancing on La Bassée along the canal, striking north towards Violaines and circling north of La Bassée to cut the road to Estaires. After severe fighting most of the Camerons were overwhelmed in La Bassée itself.

With their left flank gone, D Company of the Worcesters, who were on the right, found themselves being encircled to the north by the Germans. They made Givenchy a strong point, holding the village with about seventy men until 3.30pm. The centre of the village was devastated in the fighting. The mairie was destroyed (along with more of the village records), the church, which had so recently been rebuilt, was demolished, and the Memorial Hall was badly damaged. Considerable casualties were inflicted on enemy infantry, but not without severe casualties to the company. Thirty-nine-year-old Lord Coventry, who was a lieutenant, was killed. At 4.30pm what was left of D Company withdrew to Festubert, along with 2nd Dorsets, who had themselves been fighting a German tank attack which crossed the canal further west. There they were surrounded and experienced an enemy tank attack. Overnight, the thirty or so men left from the company escaped across country with the remnants of 2nd Dorsets, led by their commanding officer, Colonel Stephenson. They reached Dunkirk a few days later. A dozen or so graves of men of the Worcesters, including Lord Coventry, lie in the communal cemetery near 55th Division's memorial.

The village was liberated in September 1944.

Givenchy today is a thriving community of over 1,000 inhabitants. Rather than let their villages die, the French encourage careful development and

The modern church.

The inside of the modern church. The Joseph statue is on the left-hand wall.

The new community centre built over the site of Mairie Keep.

The last vestiges of the wartime craters, filled with communal rubbish.

try to keep facilities open – the school has taken on a fifth teacher and a brand new multi-purpose municipal building has opened, housing a library of 8,000 books, catering facilities for the nearby school, meeting rooms and daycare facilities.

Of the dozen or so farms that were in the village in 1914, only three remain; many inhabitants commute to work in Bethune or in Lens (ten minutes away by train), where there are factories and shops. Most of the craters were filled in years ago, although it is possible, with a little imagination, to see the slight depression left by Red Dragon Crater and, to the north of the village, a small area of the crater field still exists, though it has been used as a dumping ground.

55th Division's memorial still stands proudly at the edge of the village, joined by a memorial to Sapper Hackett VC and the tunnellers. The Hill-Trevor memorial still stands opposite the reconstructed Orchard Farm. The church, having been destroyed twice, was replaced in the early 1960s by a

The 'iron harvest'.

Givenchy commune war memorial: note the reference to British troops at the base.

modern design, but still houses the statue of St Joseph removed by General Sir Edwin Alderson in 1915 and returned by his family. There is still an 'iron harvest' of shells, cartridge cases, trench mortar bombs, barbed wire and all the detritus of war after every ploughing.

The village war memorial, possibly uniquely, commemorates the village's dead and also pays public homage to the British and French troops who fell in the Givenchy sector.

Le Touret memorial to the missing, where so many men lost at Givenchy are commemorated.

Epilogue

The dead lie on Givenchy field
   As lie the sodden autumn leaves,
The dead lie on Givenchy field,
   The trailing mist a cerement weaves.

H. D'A B, 1917

Bibliography

The Official History of the War – Military Operations – France and Belgium, compiled for the Historical Section of the Committee of Imperial Defence by Brigadier General Sir James E. Edmonds and published in 1937. Though largely dealing with events at brigade level, it does contain some detail of battalion actions. Maps are in a separate volume.

The British Campaign in France and Flanders, Vol II, 1915, (Arthur Conan Doyle, Hodder and Stoughton, 1917) available online at http://freeread.com.au/@RGLibrary/ArthurConanDoyle/History/H242-TheGreatWar.html.

With the Indians in France General Sir James Willcocks, (Constable and Co. Ltd, 1920) also available online at https://archive.org/details/withindiansinfra00will.

Sepoys in the trenches – The Indian Corps on the Western Front 1914-15, Gordon Corrigan (Spellmount, 1999).

The Indian Corps in France Lieut Col J.W.B. Merewether, CIE and Lieut Col Sir Frederick Smith, Bart (John Murray, 1918).

The Indian Corps on the Western Front – A Handbook and Battlefield Guide Simon Doherty and Tom Donovan (Tom Donovan Editions Ltd, 2014).

The History of the Second Division 1914–1918, Everard Wyrall (Naval & Military Press reprint, 2000).

The Fifth Division in the Great War Brig General A.H. Hussey, CB, CMG and Major D.S. Inman (Naval & Military Press reprint, 2001) also available online at http://archive.org/stream/fifthdivisioning00huss/fifthdivisioning00huss_djvu.txt

The History of the Seventh Division 1914–1918, C.T. Atkinson (Naval & Military Press reprint, 2001).

Tunnellers, Captain W. Grant Grieve and Bernard Newman (Herbert Jenkins Ltd, 1936).

Underground Warfare 1914 – 1918, Simon Jones (Pen and Sword Military, 2010).

The Battle Beneath The Trenches – The Cornish Miners of 251 Tunnelling Company RE, Robert K. Johns (Pen and Sword, 2015).

The History of the 12th (Eastern) Division in the Great War 1914–1918, edited by Major General Sir Arthur B. Scott, KCB, DSO, compiled by P. Middleton Brumwell, MC, CF.

The 25th Division in France and Flanders, Lieutenant Colonel M. Kincaid-Smith (Naval & Military Press reprint).

The 42nd (East Lancashire) Division 1914–1918, Frederick P. Gibbon, Country Life, 1920.

Official History of the Canadian Army in the First World War – CANADIAN EXPEDITIONARY FORCE 1914-1919 Colonel G.W.L. Nicholson, C.D. Army Historical Section (available online at http://www.cmp-cpm.forces.gc.ca/dhh-dhp/his/docs/CEF_e.pdf).

With the First Canadian Contingent – Published on behalf of the Canadian Field Comforts Commission (Hodder and Stoughton Limited, 1915).

The Story of the 55th Division 1916–1919, The Rev. J.O. Coop, DSO, TD, MA, Senior Chaplain of the Division (Liverpool 'Daily Post' Printers, 1919). A relatively brief history of the division with maps, photographs and various appendixes.

They Win or Die who wear the Rose of Lancaster – Givenchy-Festubert April 9th–16th 1918, privately printed commemorative booklet produced by 55th Division.

The Irish Guards in the Great War, Rudyard Kipling, (Spellmount Ltd, 2007).

The 2nd Munsters in France, Lt Colonel H.S. Jervis, MC, (Gale & Polden, 1922).

The King's Own, 1/5th Battalion, TF Compiled by Albert Hodgkinson (published privately, printed by Lewes Printers, 1921). An excellent battalion history containing many personal reminiscences, maps and detailed lists of officers and casualties. Recently republished by the regimental museum.

The Fourth Battalion The King's Own (Royal Lancaster Regiment and The Great War, Lieut Colonel W.F.A. Wadham and Captain J. Crossley (privately published, 1920).

The Loyal North Lancashire Regiment Vol II 1914–1919, Colonel H.C. Wylly CB, Royal United Services Institution, London, 1933.

The Battle for Flanders – German defeat on the Lys 1918 Chris Baker (Pen and Sword Military, 2011). Chris Baker is also responsible for the excellent First World War website, The Long, Long Trail (http://www.longlongtrail.co.uk/), which is an invaluable resource on the British army and the war. I'd like to think I could have written this book without dipping into it regularly to check points of detail, but it wouldn't be true.

Deeds that Thrill the Empire, (Hutchinson & Co., London, undated).

VCs of the First World War–The Western Front 1915, Peter Batchelor and Christopher Mason, (The History Press, 1997).

Harry's War – the Great War Diary of Harry Drinkwater, edited by John Cooksey and David Griffiths, (Ebury Press, 2014).

The War the Infantry Knew, Captain J.C. Dunn, (Abacus, 2012).

1st Bedfordshires. Part one: Mons to the Somme, Steven Fuller, Fighting High Ltd, 2011.

The Gloucestershire Regiment in the Great War 1914–1918 Everard Wyrall, (Methuen and Co., 1931).

The Truce – The Day the War Stopped, Chris Baker, (Amberley Publishing, 2014).

Murderous Tommies, Julian Putkowsi and Mark Dunning, (Pen and Sword, 2012).

La Grande Guerre dans notre region, 1914 de la Guerre de movement a celle de Position, Jean-Claude Boulanger (privately published, 2005, by the author). M. Boulanger, who sadly died in 2013, has left the most splendid day-by-day account of the fighting in the Lens region, broken down into sectors, one of which is Givenchy.

The Battle of the Lys 1918 – Givenchy and the River Lawe, Phil Tomaselli, (Pen and
  Sword, 2011).
The Highland Light Infantry Chronicle 1913-14-15.
Givenchy l'hetcombe, Yves Buffetaut, *Tranchées* magazine, issue 19, 2014.

Other Sources

Unit War Diaries are now available to be downloaded from TNA website at http://
  www.nationalarchives.gov.uk/records/war-diaries-ww1.htm at a reasonable cost.
  They can be downloaded free if you actually visit TNA at Kew with a laptop. They
  have also become available on Ancestry but, at least in the experience of this author,
  are very difficult to find – but invaluable when you do.
A useful (sometimes) source of information on officers who fought at Givenchy are also
  at TNA in the WO 339 and WO 374 series. Cecil Humphries' file is, for example,
  in WO 339/4177. Contents of the files vary from just a few pages to several inches
  thick. They are not online.
Surviving service records for 'other ranks' are available on both Ancestry and Findmypast
  though the majority were destroyed during World War Two in a fire in the warehouse
  in which they were stored. Ancestry also has the individual Medal Index Cards for all
  soldiers who served abroad during the war (often all that remains of a man's service
  record) and citations for winners of the Conspicuous Gallantry Medal.
Local newspapers are a useful source of information, particularly for the early part of
  the war, before censorship of letters from soldiers began in earnest and they were
  examined in detail. Stories frequently made the local press, passed to them by their
  families. http://cymru1914.org/ The Welsh experience of the First World War
  has stories of Welsh soldiers who fought there and Findmypast is digitising British
  newspapers so there are stories from all over the country.
Both Ancestry and Findmypast have De Ruvigny's Roll of Honour 1914–1919, which
  often says where the person was killed, so can be searched for Givenchy casualties.
  Sometimes there are brief details of a soldier's final fight.
http://bedfordregiment.org.uk/index.html is a splendid website devoted to the
  Bedfordshire Regiment in World War One, which includes extracts from some of the
  war diaries covering Givenchy.
http://www.thewardrobe.org.uk/home is the website for the museum of the Berkshire
  and Wiltshire regiments, which also has searchable online war diaries. Battalions of
  both regiments served at Givenchy.
Morts pour la France de la Première Guerre mondiale at http://www.memoiredeshommes.
  sga.defense.gouv.fr/fr/article.php%3Flarub%3D24%26titre%3Dmorts-pour-la-
  france-de-la-premiere-guerre-mondiale is invaluable for tracing the fate of French
  soldiers and finding out a little about them.
The website of The Oldham Historical Society at http://www.pixnet.co.uk/Oldham-
  hrg/World-War1/territorials/a-menu.html proved invaluable in researching 1/10th
  Manchesters and Private Walter Mills.

Index